Lithics
Macroscopic Approaches to Analysis

This book is the first comprehensive manual on stone artifact analysis, with detailed examples of how to measure, record, and analyze stone tools and stone tool production debris. Logically ordered, clearly written, and well illustrated, it is designed for students and professional archaeologists. The first section provides the necessary background information, introducing the reader to lithic raw materials, and the classification of stone artifacts, basic terminology, and concepts. It goes on to discuss various methods and techniques of analysis. The final section presents detailed case studies of lithic analysis from different parts of the world, illustrating the application of the techniques and methods discussed earlier.

WILLIAM ANDREFSKY, JR. is Associate Professor of Anthropology at Washington State University.

CAMBRIDGE MANUALS IN ARCHAEOLOGY

Series editors

Don Brothwell, *University of York*
Graeme Barker, *University of Leicester*
Dena Dincauze, *University of Massachusetts, Amherst*
Priscilla Renouf, *Memorial University of Newfoundland*

Cambridge Manuals in Archaeology is a series of reference handbooks designed for an international audience of upper-level undergraduate and graduate students, and professional archaeologists and archaeological scientists in universities, museums, research laboratories, and field and field units. Each book includes a survey of current archaeological practice alongside essential reference material on contemporary techniques and methodology.

Already published:

J. D. Richards and N. S. Ryan, DATA PROCESSING IN ARCHAEOLOGY
   (0 521 25769 7)
Simon Hillson, TEETH (0 521 38671 3)
Alwyne Wheeler and Andrew K. G. Jones, FISHES (0 521 30407 5)
Lesley Adkins and Roy Adkins, ARCHAEOLOGICAL ILLUSTRATION (0 521 35478 1)
Marie-Agnes Courty, Paul Goldberg and Richard MacPhail, SOILS AND
   MICROMORPHOLOGY IN ARCHAEOLOGY (0 521 32419 X)
Clive Orton, Paul Tyers, and Alan Vince, POTTERY IN ARCHAEOLOGY
   (0 521 25715 8 hb; 0 521 44597 3 pb)
R. Lee Lyman, VERTEBRATE TAPHONOMY (0 521 45840 4)
Peter G. Dorrell, PHOTOGRAPHY IN ARCHAEOLOGY AND CONSERVATION
   (2ND ED) (0 521 45534 0 hb; 0 521 45554 5 pb)
A. G. Brown, ALLUVIAL GEOARCHAEOLOGY (0 521 56097 7 hb; 0521 56820 X
   pb)
Cheryl Claassen, SHELLS (0 521 57036 0 hb; 0521 57852 3 pb)

LITHICS

Macroscopic approaches to analysis

William Andrefsky, Jr.

CAMBRIDGE
UNIVERSITY PRESS

PUBLISHED BY THE PRESS SYNDICATE OF THE UNIVERSITY OF CAMBRIDGE
The Pitt Building, Trumpington Street, Cambridge, United Kingdom

CAMBRIDGE UNIVERSITY PRESS
The Edinburgh Building, Cambridge CB2 2RU, UK
40 West 20th Street, New York, NY 10011-4211, USA
477 Williamstown Road, Port Melbourne, VIC 3207, Australia
Ruiz de Alarćon 13, 28014 Madrid, Spain
Dock House, The Waterfront, Cape Town 8001, South Africa

http://www.cambridge.org

First published 1998
Fifth printing 2004

Printed in the United Kingdom at the University Press, Cambridge

Typeset in Times 11/13 pt [VN]

A catalogue record for this book is available from the British Library

Library of Congress Cataloguing in Publication data
Andrefsky, William, 1955 –
Lithics: macroscopic approaches to analysis / William Andrefsky Jr.
  p.   cm. – (Cambridge manuals in archaeology)
Includes bibliographical references and index.
ISBN 0 521 57084 0 (hc) - ISBN 0 521 57815 9 (pb)
1. Tools, prehistoric – analysis.   2. Tools, prehistoric – classification.
3. Stone implements – analysis.   4. Stone implements – classifiaction.
5. Flintknapping. I. Title. II. Series.
GN799.T6A54   1998
930.1'028 – dc21   97-35227 CIP

ISBN 0 521 57084 0 hardback
ISBN 0 521 57815 9 paperback

To Claire and Marilyn

CONTENTS

FIGURES

TABLES

xv

PREFACE

As a boy I remember my brother and I roaming the fields and woods along the creeks and rivers that empty into the Chesapeake Bay, and finding my first "arrowhead." Such treasures were interpreted by us as "missed shots" by prehistoric hunters, or the spot where a wounded warrior died in battle. However, most of the artifacts were discovered at a site where hundreds of stone artifacts could be found. I often wondered why perfectly good stone artifacts were left at such locations. On a good day sometimes dozens of "arrowheads" could be found at the same place. Did prehistoric people store these artifacts at the site and never return for them? Were stone age people so absent-minded that they would lose dozens of "arrowheads" around their camps? Perhaps the artifacts we found were rejects?

To this day, I still wonder why stone tools which appear to be perfectly functional and useful are left at sites. The more I look at them, the more I realize that many different factors influence their final disposition. Some lithic tools are rejects, others are lost, and still others may not be tools and instead are the by-products of tool production. Stone tools may have different values depending upon the amount of effort expended in their production or the availability of raw materials. The context within which a stone tool is made and used is important for determining how it will be discarded or preserved. All of these variable situational and social contexts are increasingly recognized as important influences in the understanding of stone tools. This book attempts to show how characteristics of stone tools and stone tool assemblages are affected by various contexts.

To achieve this goal I have had to review a great amount of literature related to stone tools and I have necessarily had to standardize several kinds of analysis. In this regard, the book reviews some very elementary concepts associated with stone tool analysis – terminology, classification, attribute definition. These concepts are used in later parts of the book to demonstrate analytical strategies and explain interpretations made from stone tool analysis.

This book was written for two audiences. First it was written for students interested in learning about lithic analysis. It has enough elementary material so that undergraduates who have experience with archaeology but not necessarily lithic analysis can use the book as a guide for understanding lithic assemblages. It also has more complex interpretive and analytical sections to help graduate students structure lithic analysis for their own research prob-

xvii

lems and regions. Secondly, the book was written for those who teach lithic analysis. The concepts introduced here are universal and applicable to all lithic assemblages. I provide specific examples of analytical studies and specific techniques for the measurement and recording of lithic artifacts, but those examples and techniques are easily adapted to chipped stone assemblages from any particular part of the world.

It is important to realize that this book is based upon many of my interests in lithic analysis. As such, it is worthwhile stating what it does not represent. It is not a "cook book" for lithic analysis. I have tried to emphasize the notion that artifact context is important for understanding how to conduct analysis and to make interpretations. I prefer to view the book as an example of various approaches to lithic analysis that have been used and could be used, given the kind of issues the researcher wishes to address. It is not a review of lithic analysis. Although a great amount of literature is covered, this is by no means exhaustive, nor is it intended to be. The materials reviewed are directly related to concepts and approaches presented. Finally, the book is not a culture historical review of lithic assemblages from around the world. Although examples of artifacts and techniques are taken from six continents, I do not emphasize lithic variability as culture historical markers or as temporal and spatial diagnostics. The emphasis of the book is upon lithic artifact analytical techniques and the interpretations that can be made from such techniques.

ACKNOWLEDGMENTS

In large part, this book is derived from a graduate seminar I first taught at the University of Alaska, Fairbanks in 1983. Since that time the class has evolved into a graduate lecture and laboratory course I have taught on four different occasions at Washington State University. The graduate students in those courses over the years helped me formulate some of the methods and techniques that appear within this book. I appreciate the insightful discussions and difficult questions that we dealt with, all of which make this a better study of lithic analysis.

I am responsible for designing the ninety-four figures. However, I was fortunate to have two talented artists draw technical illustrations of artifacts and create schematic illustrations to emphasize various points. I cannot thank Sarah Moore enough for her excellent artifact illustrations and schematics. Sarah did the artwork for the artifacts depicted in the book (Figures 2.1, 2.2, 2.4–2.7, 2.9–2.11, 4.1, 4.8–4.11, 5.1–5.3, 5.5, 5.7–5.13, 6.1–6.4, 7.1, 7.2, 7.8, 7.10, 7.14, 7.18, 7.20–7.24, 7.26, 7.27, 7.29, 8.1 and 8.2). She also did the schematic illustrations shown in Figures 2.15, 5.6, 7.3–7.7, 7.9, 7.11, and 7.19. Additionally, she redrew artifacts from sketches of photographs (Figures 2.3 and 2.16), and drew the artifacts in schematic diagrams that I subsequently altered (Figures 7.15–7.17, and 7.25). Jenny Fluter drew the schematic illustrations in Figures 2.8, 2.12–2.14, 2.17, 2.18, 5.4, 7.31, 7.32, 8.3 and 8.4). Jenny also drew the specimen b in Figure 7.19. I composed and drew the remaining twenty-eight figures with the help of my computer.

The two people who read and commented on the entire manuscript were Louise Barber and Marilyn Bender. They did an excellent job and I am grateful for their enormous efforts. Louise carefully performed a technical edit on the narrative portion of the book. In a short period of time her skills transformed my writing into English. Marilyn read the manuscript and performed the tedious job of ensuring my figures and tables actually related to the narrative. She also conducted the reference check and generally made sure I did not stretch the truth too far.

There are several people from whom I drew extensively either through their published works or through conversation over the years. These are not necessarily the same people I cite most heavily in the book, but their contributions were very important in shaping my opinions and ideas about specific topics. I thank the following people for their contribution, though they may not com-

xix

pletely agree with my position on various ideas and interpretations. Much of my basic belief about the way stone tools change throughout their uselife was influenced by the hunter-gatherer research of Richard Gould and Brian Hayden, and by my exposure to Errett Callahan's experimental archaeology field projects in the 1970s. The section on lithic fracturing properties benefited greatly from Brian Cotterell and Johan Kamminga's research. I could not have explained the genesis of chert without the excellent background provided by Barbara Luedtke. My understanding of artifact style and meaning was shaped by the ideas of Meg Conkey. Albert Ammerman and Vin Steponaitis helped me to understand the intricacies of classification. Without the insightful research of Paul Mellars I could not have begun to discuss the properties of Levallois technology. Finally, the section on artifact function was greatly influenced by the work of George Odell.

I also wish to acknowledge the help and support of the team from Cambridge University Press. In particular, Jessica Kuper guided the book through review, edit and production. Frances Brown did a marvellous job as copyeditor. The peer reviewers for Cambridge made this a better book. I especially wish to thank Randolph Donahue for his suggestions and insights.

This book would not have been possible without the encouragement and support of my wife Marilyn. This kind of project can take so much away from personal relationships. I am lucky to share my time with someone understanding enough to help me to complete such projects.

GLOSSARY

andesite A fine-grained igneous rock in the diorite family that is intermediate in color between the light end of the spectrum (rhyolite) and the dark end of the spectrum (basalt).

artifact An object or specimen produced by human agency. An artifact can usually be collected without being destroyed. This is in contrast to features, which are destroyed or dismantled after collection. All lithic debitage and lithic tools are considered artifacts.

backed blade A blade (or flake) that is intentionally dulled on a margin so it can be hand-held safely.

basalt The fine-grained member of the gabbro family of igneous rock. Its mineral composition gives it a dark or black color.

bending flake A detached piece produced by cracks initiated away from the point of applied force. These flakes usually have a pronounced lip, contracting lateral margins immediately below the striking platform, and no bulb of force.

beveled Usually referring to a tool edge that has been modified by the removal of a series of flakes to produce a desired edge angle.

biface A tool that has two surfaces (faces) that meet to form a single edge that circumscribes the tool. Both faces usually contain flake scars that travel at least half-way across the face.

bifacial thinning flake A flake that is removed during biface trimming and often contains a striking platform, that is rounded or ground, indicating preparation. It is usually thin relative to width, with a feathered termination.

billet A baton or club, of material other than rock, used to detach flakes from an objective piece by percussion. It is usually made of antler, wood, or bone.

bipolar flake A detached piece formed as a result of compression forces. Bipolar flakes often show signs of impact on opposing ends and have compression rings moving in two directions toward one another.

bipolar technology   A technique of resting the objective piece on an anvil and striking it with a hammer to spilt or remove a detached piece.

blade   A type of detached piece with parallel or subparallel lateral margins. It is usually at least twice as long as it is wide.

blank   A detached piece potentially modifiable into a specific tool form.

bulb of force   The bulbar location on the ventral surface of a flake that was formed as a result of the Hertzian cone turning toward the outside of the objective piece.

chalcedony   A cryptocrystalline fibrous quartz, usually light colored and translucent.

chert   A compact cryptocrystalline or microcrystalline variety of quartz originating from a sedimentary context.

clastic rock   A sedimentary rock composed of particles or fragments of smaller rock or of organic materials.

collateral flaking   The process of removing expanding flakes removed from the lateral margins of an objective piece at right angles to the longitudinal axis.

compression rings   Ripples or undulations on the smooth surface of rocks moving from the direction of the point of applied force.

conchoidal fracture   The production of smooth convexities or concavities, similar to those of a clamshell, when fractured.

conchoidal flake   A flake having the properties of conchoidal fracture. These flakes have a dorsal and ventral surface and often a bulb of force.

core   A nucleus or mass of rock that shows signs of detached piece removal. A core is often considered an objective piece that functions primarily as a source for detached pieces.

core tool   A core used for chopping, cutting, or some activity other than as a source of detached pieces.

cortex   Chemical or mechanical weathered surface on rocks.

cryptocrystalline   Refers to a rock of fine-grained aggregate crystals less than 3 um in diameter.

debitage   Detached pieces that are discarded during the reduction process.

debris   (see debitage)

detached piece   A portion of rock removed from an objective piece by percussion or pressure. These are often referred to as flakes, spalls, chips, and debitage.

diagonal parallel flaking   This is similar to parallel flaking except that the flakes are removed at an oblique angle to the objective piece edge.

distal end of flake	The location on a flake that shows the type of termination, opposite the striking platform.
dorsal ridge	A line or ridge formed on the dorsal surface by the previous removal of detached pieces from the objective piece. Also referred to as a dorsal arris.
dorsal surface of flake	The side of a flake or detached piece that shows evidence of previous flake removals or the original surface of the rock.
elasticity	The property of stone to return to its former state after being depressed by the application of force.
endscraper	A flake tool with retouch on the distal end. The retouched area has an edge angle that approaches 60° to 90°.
end shock	Transverse fracture due to the stone exceeding its elastic limits.
expedient tools	Stone tools made with little or no production effort. (see informal tools)
eraillure flake	A small chip detached from the bulb of force.
feathered termination	The distal end of a flake with a very sharp edge.
fissures	Radii usually originating at the margins of detached pieces on the ventral surface and directed toward the point of applied force.
flake	(see detached piece)
flake tool	A flake that has been subsequently modified by intentional retouch and/or by wear resulting from use.
flint	A form of chert usually found in accumulations of chalk.
flintknapper	One who forms stone implements by controlling the fracture of the objective piece.
force	The quantity of energy or power exerted by a moving body.
formal tools	Stone tools made as a result of extra effort in their production. These tools are in contrast to expediently made tools with little or no effort expended in their production.
hackle marks	(see fissures)
hammerstone	A rock used as a percussor to detach flakes from an objective piece. These usually show signs of impact damage such as crushed edges.
hard hammer	A hammerstone made of hard rock.
Hertzian cone	The cone formed as a result of conchoidal fracture in brittle solids.
hinge fracture	The scar left by a previously removed flake detached by hinge termination.
hinge termination	The distal end of a flake that is rounded or blunt.

igneous rock   Rock formed as a result of the hardening of lava or magma (molten rock). Examples of igneous rock are obsidian, basalt, and rhyolite.

informal tools   Stone tools made in a casual manner with only minor design constraints. These tools are often called expediently made tools or tools made for the needs of the moment.

jasper   A form of chert usually red, yellow, brown or gold in color.

lateral margins   Margins of detached pieces and objective pieces on either side of the longitudinal axis.

lava   Molten rock solidified on the Earth's surface.

lip   A projection found on the proximal ventral surface of a detached piece below the striking platform. Some researchers believe that a pronounced lip indicates the detached piece was removed with a soft hammer.

lithic   Derived from Greek word meaning stone or pertaining to stone.

load   Refers to the amount of force placed on the objective piece from either percussion or pressure. Load is generally increased when going from pressure flaking to percussion flaking and from soft hammer to hard hammer.

macrocrystalline   The texture of a rock with grains or crystals easily observed with the naked eye or over 0.75 mm in diameter.

mafic rock   Refers to igneous rock dark in color as a result of dark minerals such as olivine and pyroxene.

magma   Molten rock that cools and solidifies below the surface of the Earth.

metamorphic rock   Rock formed or changed either structurally or mineralogically by heat and pressure under ground.

metamorphosed   Usually refers to rocks that have been changed by heat and pressure.

metaquartzite   A quartzite of metamorphic origin as opposed to a sedimentary origin. The quartz grains in metaquartzite are usually deformed and fused from heat and pressure.

microblade   A bladelet or small blade. This term is usually associated with bladelets found in the Arctic areas of North America and northeastern Asia.

microcrystalline   Describes a rock in which the individual crystals can only be seen as such under microscope.

microlith   Very small blades usually geometric in form used in composite tools.

microwear   The traces of wear on stone tools that is not visible without magnification. Such wear may be in the form of a retouch or polish.

mudstone   General term used to describe a very fine-grained sedimentary rock. Mud-sized particles that have solidified under water or underground are often identified as mudstone.

objective piece   The rock or artifact being modified by the removal of detached pieces. Objective pieces may be cores that are used solely as sources of raw material or they may be tools such as bifaces or flake tools.

obsidian   A volcanic rock formed into natural glass. This rock is usually black but may be found in greenish and reddish colors or banded.

opal   An amorphous form of quartz unstable at temperatures and pressures found on the surface of the Earth.

orthoquartzite   A sandstone converted to quartzite with grains cemented only through infiltration and pressure. The cementing agent is usually quartz.

overshot termination   (see plunging termination)

parallel flaking   Flake scars are parallel to each other and leave a sharp edge on the objective piece. These flakes are removed in a serial fashion by following the ridge created by the previously removed flake.

percussion flaking   A method of striking with a percussor to detach flakes from an objective piece. Different methods of percussion flaking using different kinds of percussors tend to produce distinctive detached pieces.

petrography   A branch of the study of rocks in which they are examined in thin section and in hand specimen.

phenocrysts   The isolated large crystals in porphyry.

plunging termination   The distal end of a flake that turns toward the objective piece removing the lower end of the objective piece, creating a detached piece that has a large distal end relative to the proximal end.

point of applied force   The location on lithic artifacts where force has been applied to remove a flake from an objective piece. (see striking platform)

porphyry   An igneous rock consisting of coarse mineral grains scattered through a mixture of fine mineral grains.

pot lid fracture   A concave scar on the surface of rock usually caused by differential expansion and contraction of the rock, such as heating by fire.

pressure flaker   A tool used to press a detached flake from an objective piece. This tool is often pointed and made of antler or bone.

pressure flaking   The removal of a detached piece from an objective piece by pressing rather than by percussion.

projectile point   A biface that contains a haft area and is used as a projectile tip. These are often identified as arrow points, dart points and spear points.

provenience   The location or point of recovery of an artifact.

provenance   The geological origin of a rock.

proximal end of flake   The end of a flake or detached piece that contains the striking platform. On a conchoidal flake the proximal end will contain the bulb of force.

quartz   A mineral composed of the elements silicon and oxygen (silicon dioxide) that occurs in multiple forms.

quartz crystal   A hexagonal crystal of silicon dioxide.

quartzite   Generalized term for a sandstone that has been recrystallized or cemented. (see orthoquartzite and metaquartzite)

retouch   Intentional modification of a stone tool edge by either pressure or percussion flaking technique. Modification by use is considered usewear as opposed to retouch.

rhyolite   The fine-grained member of the granite family of igneous rocks. It is light in color and usually contains pink feldspar.

rock   Any naturally formed, firm and coherent aggregate or mass of mineral matter that constitutes part of the Earth's crust.

rock composition   Refers to the chemical elements and minerals from which rocks are created.

rock texture   Refers to the size, shape, and relationship of individual particles in a rock.

roll-out   (see hinge termination)

sandstone   A cemented or compacted detrital sediment composed predominantly of quartz grains the size of sand particles.

scraper   A generalized term used to describe a flake tool that has a retouched edge angle of approximately 60 to 90 degrees.

sedimentary rock   A rock composed of the by-products of other rocks that have been eroded or dissolved. Examples of sedimentary rocks are sandstone, mudstone, halite, and chert.

shale   A sedimentary rock formed by the cementation of very fine particles such as mud or silt.

sialic rocks   Refers to igneous rocks light in color because of light minerals such as quartz.

silica   A term used to describe silicon dioxide.

silicified   Refers to a rock hardened by silica.

siltstone   (see shale)

slate	A metamorphosed shale that breaks along flat planes.
soft hammer	This usually refers to a billet but may include hammerstones of very soft materials such as mudstone.
step fracture	The scar left on the objective piece after a previous flake has been detached with step termination.
step termination	The distal end of a flake that terminates abruptly in a right-angle break. This creates a "step-like" break, not to be confused with a hinge termination.
stone tool	An artifact that has been intentionally modified by retouch or unintentionally modified by usewear. Examples of stone tools are projectile points, unifaces, scrapers, and microliths. Debitage would not be considered tools, but would be considered artifacts.
striking platform	The surface area on an objective piece receiving the force to detach a piece of material. This surface is often removed with the detached piece so that the detached piece will contain the a striking platform at the point of applied force.
thin section	A thin rock slice prepared for microscopic study.
type	A class or group of item(s) characterized by similar attributes.
typology	A scheme to order multiple types in relational manner. A common typology orders types in an hierarchical manner.
uniface	A flake tool modified on either the dorsal or ventral side only.
usewear	Modification on lithic artifacts resulting from use as a tool.
ventral surface of flake	The smooth surface of a detached piece that contains no previous flake removals except sometimes an eraillure flake scar on the bulb of force.
weight	The force that gravity exerts on a body.

1

A BRIEF INTRODUCTION TO LITHIC ANALYSIS

On a global scale an argument can be made and easily defended that chipped stone tools and debitage represent the most abundant form of artifacts found on prehistoric sites. In many areas of the world they represent the only form of remains that have withstood the inroads of environmental and human perturbation, such as erosion, decay, and landscape development. Because of this, lithic artifacts represent one of the most important clues to understanding prehistoric lifeways. Yet many archaeologists and most laymen do not understand how stone tools can be analyzed to obtain information about prehistoric lifeways and behavior. Recently I was asked by a graduate student in anthropology what I had found at a site on which I had been working for the past several years. I briefly described a whole array of flake tools, production debitage, bifaces, and raw-material variability. The student was apparently from the school of thought that associates archaeology with the science of discovering buried cities and hidden treasures, because she responded, "how about the good stuff – did you find any good artifacts?" Believing these to be the good artifacts I described how various artifacts and their characteristics relate to time depth, prehistoric exchange, relative sedentism, function, and prehistoric economy. This exchange led me to think about the things lithics can bring to the broader field of archaeology and how the epistemology of lithic artifacts has changed over the past century since lithic studies were first given serious consideration in the archaeological literature. This chapter reviews some of the significant developments in the field of lithic analysis. Most of this review emphasizes topics that will not be covered in detail within this book.

The organization of the book

The goal of this book is to describe and explain how to conduct various kinds of macroscopic analysis of lithic artifacts, and to show how various types of analysis relate to prehistoric human behavior. There are three major sections. The first section comprises the first four chapters and provides the basic background information needed to begin lithic analysis. Chapters 5, 6, and 7, the second section, introduce the analysis of lithic debitage and tools and present technical material to show the reader how to measure, record, and

1

verify. The last section of the book is composed of lithic analysis case studies. Chapters 8 and 9 contain examples of lithic analytical techniques from various parts of the world and draw upon chapters in the first two sections as examples are discussed and explored. Concluding remarks are presented in chapter 10.

After a brief review of lithic studies in chapter 1, chapter 2 explains the principles of the mechanical production of stone tools. Within this context a basic terminology is introduced to the reader and this is gradually expanded and developed throughout the book. The basic concept developed in chapter 2 is that lithic artifacts are dynamic entities that changed shape and size as they were used in prehistoric cultural systems. This concept sets the foundation for many of the analytical techniques described and explained in later chapters.

To understand variability in lithic artifacts it is important to understand the nature of variability in lithic raw materials. Chapter 3 describes how lithic raw materials are classified. Rocks used for the production of chipped stone tools are given special emphasis. A primary focus of the discussion is upon rock genesis and how that genesis is closely linked to rock classification.

Chapter 4 discusses the identification and classification of lithic artifacts. It is not a review of numerical classification techniques, but instead covers the basic concepts of classification, and then introduces a generalized classification scheme useful for all chipped stone artifacts. Concepts such as attributes, attribute states, types, and typologies are reviewed. These are applied to various approaches to classification, such as monothetic and polythetic approaches, and divisive and agglomerative strategies. The generalized classification scheme introduced in this chapter is used as the framework for organizing different shapes of lithic artifacts and can also be used as a guide for a common vocabulary that is implemented in the subsequent chapters.

Debitage characteristics and the techniques used to identify and measure them are discussed in chapter 5. This chapter reviews some debitage studies and provides a basic guide to debitage measurement. Standardized techniques for measuring debitage size, cortex amount, striking platform types, dorsal flake removals, and curvature are illustrated and discussed.

Various approaches to debitage analysis are included in chapter 6, which is divided into two primary sections: debitage typological analysis and debitage aggregate analysis. Although both kinds of analysis overlap in the methods of their application typological approaches emphasize single artifact characteristics and aggregate approaches emphasize artifact populations.

Chapter 7 focuses upon various approaches to lithic tool analysis. Cores, flake tools, and bifaces are considered separately and different analyses are described for each. This chapter reviews some of the basic kinds of lithic tool attributes typically emphasized in the literature and demonstrates how to perform lithic tool analysis.

Several different lithic analysis studies are presented in chapters 8 and 9 in order to illustrate how lithic analysis relates to interpretation. All of the examples presented use various kinds of lithic artifacts and all revolve around a central theme. Chapter 8 emphasizes the relationship between artifact diversity and site function, and provides a review of artifact function as it relates to artifact form. Chapter 9 continues with additional case studies that use lithic artifacts as the medium for analysis. The central theme for this chapter concerns the manner in which lithic analysis can inform archaeologists about prehistoric sedentism. Within this context, lithic raw material analysis is introduced to illustrate how complicated lithic patterning can be and what potential problems researchers may encounter when making behavioral interpretations. Chapter 10 concludes with some observations on lithic analysis.

Early historical development

It can be said that the discovery of stone tools was instrumental in establishing the antiquity of humans. For example, in 1797 John Frere found stone tools in a brick-earth quarry near the English town of Hoxne. Those artifacts were located stratigraphically below the bones of extinct animals (Feder 1996:20). Most of the scientific community at the time believed that humans had been on Earth no longer than 6,000 years, the age of the universe created by God. Yet stone tools continued to be found in contexts which suggested that people had inhabited the Earth earlier than 6,000 years before the eighteenth century.

William Henry Holmes (1894) was one of the first archaeologists to attempt a systematic analysis of lithic artifacts. In his work Holmes described the goals and contributions of lithic analysis; these included using stone tools as chronological markers, understanding the evolution in form and function of stone tools, and understanding the processes of stone tool production and use. These are still goals for archaeologists interested in stone tool analysis today. From before the twentieth century through to the present, stone tool analysis has followed the lead of Holmes. Chronologies have been constructed using lithic tool styles as diagnostic traits in most parts of the world (Childe 1925; Clark 1932; Frison 1991; Griffin 1943; Kidder 1924; McKern 1939; Oakley 1949; Ritchie 1944). Archaeologists have also characterized the function of prehistoric sites based upon the inferred function of stone tools (Bordes 1961; Burkitt 1925; Clark 1958; Goodyear 1974; Harold 1993; Sieveking 1958).

One of the most significant developments in archaeology that had a major impact on lithic analysis was the replication of stone tool forms by craftsmen such as François Bordes and Don Crabtree in the 1950s and 1960s. Such replication studies stimulated interest in the investigation of lithic tool production techniques. Bordes and Crabtree were not the only archaeologists conducting replication experiments at this time (see Leakey 1954), and they were not pioneers (see Evans 1872); however they were instrumental in training a significant segment of the archaeological community to value such techniques.

The controlled replication of stone tool forms helped develop the related techniques of reduction sequence analysis and tool refitting analysis.

At about the same time that replication studies were being explored in archaeology the microscopic analysis of used stone tool edges was also being carried out. This work was first given serious scientific consideration in the 1930s by Russian scientist Sergei Semenov (Levitt 1979). Semenov's 1957 work was not introduced to western researchers until 1964 when *Prehistoric Technology* was translated into English (Semenov 1964). Significantly, his work suggested that overall stone tool morphology might not always coincide with stone tool function, and that it was possible to conduct direct functional analysis of stone tools by magnification of worked edges.

Another important discovery that affected the manner in which lithic tools are analyzed and perceived today centers upon the realization that stone tool shapes actually change throughout their limited uselife. Although many researchers probably realized this characteristic of stone tools, George Frison (1968) was among the first to make it explicit. If artifact morphology changed during uselife, then tool typologies must reflect such changes in order to be useful functional, temporal, or spatial indicators. The understanding that tools changed shape not only affected the utility of stone tool typologies as diagnostic indicators, it also inspired archaeologists to view stone tools as dynamic, ever changing elements of human material culture directly related to human organizational parameters such as mobility, scheduling, economy, and exchange.

Revelations about the character of lithic artifacts brought about by new methodological techniques and perceptual insights have not been easy for all archaeologists to accept. That a lithic typology may not reflect a prehistoric cultural assemblage or that a particular artifact shape may not be ascribed to a single function reaches deeply into the heritage of archaeology. For the reader who wishes to maintain the sanctity of that heritage, there is a great deal of evidence that suggests lithic types and typologies are firmly linked to function and cultural chronology in many regions of the world. The important thing to realize is that types and typologies can be interpreted differently in different places and in different contexts. More and more, lithic analysts are realizing that there are very few universals in stone tool analysis and that it is important to interpret lithic artifact assemblages within their unique individual contexts.

Much of the support or justification for various techniques of analysis introduced in this book comes from the experimental data generated from replication and microwear studies; however, the techniques of replication and microwear are not within the scope of this volume. Before introducing the formal treatment of macroscopic lithic analytical techniques it is worthwhile to summarize the historical development and contemporary status of lithic experimental studies.

A perspective on microwear

Microwear analysis attempts to determine the functions of stone tools by examining direct evidence in the form of usewear on the tool surfaces, particularly near the edges. Both high and low magnification microscopy are used in microwear analysis. As previously stated, microwear analysis in archaeology was stimulated by Semenov's (1964) microwear research in the 1930s. It is important to realize that before 1964 other researchers had attempted to determine lithic tool functions directly from tool surfaces without, but occasionally with, microscopy techniques. Observations on worn or battered stone tool edges had been noted as early as the second half of the nineteenth century (Evans 1872; Rau 1869; Spurrell 1892); researchers in the early twentieth century studied wear patterns in the form of sickle gloss or polish (Crawford 1935; Curwin 1930, 1935; Vayson de Pradenne 1920); and Witthoft (1955, 1967) and Sonnenfeld (1962) used microscopy to determine the function of lithic tools before Semenov was translated.

In the late 1960s and early 1970s a number of people experimented with microwear analysis and many articles appeared on the proper technique(s) and contributions of microwear analysis (Ahler 1971; Gould *et al.* 1971; Hayden and Kamminga 1973; Keeley 1974; MacDonald and Sanger 1968; Odell 1975; Tringham *et al.* 1974). In 1977 and 1978 three doctoral dissertations on microwear analysis appeared from different parts of the world. Lawrence Keeley's (1977) research on a British assemblage supported the position that microwear analysis was most effective when very high magnification (up to 500 ×) was used. Keeley also noted that microwear polishes were diagnostic for determining the type of material lithic tools were used upon. In other words, different worked materials produced variation in polish morphology and texture. According to Keeley's research, such polish variability could only be determined at high magnification levels. George Odell's (1977) research on a Dutch lithic assemblage was based on what has been referred to as low-powered magnification (under 100 ×). Odell's analysis is reported to determine the action of use (such as slicing, boring, and sawing) and the relative density of material being worked (soft or hard). In 1978 Johan Kamminga produced a third dissertation on microwear analysis in Australia. Unlike the Keeley and Odell studies that used experiments to verify microwear patterns on prehistoric lithic artifacts, Kamminga's study used microwear analysis to recognize functional differences on aboriginal stone tools with ethnographically verifiable functions.

Since 1978 the field of microwear analysis has grown steadily in one form or another. One of the most significant contributions to the field was the publication of papers from the first Conference on Lithic Use-Wear (Hayden 1979c). This edited volume covered a variety of topics that microwear analysis has come to address frequently in the archaeological literature, such as polish and abrasion of lithic tools, tool function, variability in raw materials, fracture of tools, and methodological and theoretical applications. Some of the recent studies of lithic microwear analysis have focused upon: (1) use of scanning electron microscopy (SEM) (Anderson 1980; Bienenfeld 1995; Knutsson 1988; Mansur-Franchomme 1983; Meeks *et al.* 1982); (2) tool hafting and prehension (Beyries 1988; Keeley 1982; Moss and Newcomer 1982; Odell 1980, 1994; Shea 1988); (3) prehistoric subsistence (Anderson-Gerfaud 1988; Juel Jensen 1989; Shea 1993; Sussman 1988; Unger-Hamilton 1985); and (4) specialization and ceremonial functions (Odell 1994; Pope 1994; Sievert 1992; Yerkes 1983).

Although the number and composition of microwear studies have increased rapidly, not all researchers believe that microwear analysis is as effective or as accurate as has been portrayed in the literature. Tests of low-powered micro-scopy have shown this to be an accurate technique of analysis (Odell and Odell-Vereecken 1980). However, this technique has never been precise enough to determine the kinds of materials on which stone tools were used. The approach has emphasized the action of the tool and the relative density of the material being worked. High-powered microscopy that examines the varia-bility in polishes, among other things, is reported to be successful in determin-ing the kind of material being worked by stone tools. However, even some of the original "blind tests" have shown high-powered microscopy to be problem-atic, particularly when the tool was used to cut or scrape more than one kind of material (Keeley 1980; Keeley and Newcomer 1977). Post-depositional alter-ation of the tool (Lévi-Sala 1986), raw-material color (Bamforth 1988), and replicability of polish signatures (Hurcombe 1988; Moss 1987) have been suggested as other factors that reduce effectiveness of functional identifications of tools undergoing microwear analysis. Some researchers strongly disagree that high-powered microscopy can discriminate tool function (Grace 1989; Grace *et al.* 1988; Newcomer *et al.* 1986; Unrath *et al.* 1986). Although criticisms of microwear analysis continue, as Yerkes and Kardulias point out (1993:104), most of the practitioners continue to use microwear analysis to determine lithic artifact functions.

The truth about replication

Lithic replication studies encompass a broad field of experimental approaches to stone tool analysis and attempt to understand the mechanisms of stone fracture and how these mechanisms produce lithic artifact assemblages. In replication analysis the debitage or by-products of stone tool production experiments are as important to understanding stone tool technology as the finished tools. Modern replication analysis emerged from the craft of flint-knapping – the use of primitive technology to make replicas of stone tools. Flintknapping or flintworking techniques used by primitive stone tool makers and users produced the lithic artifact assemblages excavated by archaeologists. To understand the place of replication analysis within the larger field of lithic analysis it is worthwhile to review briefly the history of flintknapping and the replication of stone tools.

Until recently there have been few modern-day flintknappers, and most were making gunflints and not replicas of aboriginal stone tools (Skertchly 1879). However, many of the same principles apply to both gunflint and primitive stone tool production. One of the first individuals to make replicas of primitive stone tools was the English craftsman Edward Simpson (Blacking 1953). During the 1850s he made replicas and sold them to antiquities collectors. By the late nineteenth and early twentieth centuries some researchers began to recognize the value of flintworking techniques in interpretations of the archaeological record and attempted controlled experiments to determine the mechanical principles of stone fracturing (Cushing 1895; Holmes 1891; Nelson 1916; Warren 1914). With the exception of a few studies in the early twentieth century (Ellis 1939; Pond 1930), flintknapping techniques were neither used nor accepted as viable research techniques by archaeologists interested in lithic analysis.

During the 1960s François Bordes and Don Crabtree brought flintknapping to the attention of lithic artifact researchers. Both were exceptional stone tool craftsmen who understood and could explain many of the principles of stone fracture that related to the craft of stone tool production. These two men were united with other professional and amateur archaeologists at the lithic technology conference in France that was instrumental in convincing the profession at large of the value of flintknapping in lithic analysis (Jelinek 1965). In the years following that conference several publications appeared that used results of flintknapping experiments to interpret lithic artifactual data (Bordes and Crabtree 1969; Crabtree 1966, 1967, 1968, 1970, 1972; Crabtree and Swanson 1968). In the 1960s and early 1970s the field of flintknapping was polarized between those interested in the benefits of flintknapping knowledge for lithic analysis and those interested in making high-quality replicas of primitive technology. Many flintknappers with ties to academic programs became interested in lithic analysis as a result of replicating stone tools as a craft. In addition to Bordes and Crabtree some of the other prominent flintknappers of the time were Errett Callahan, Jacques Tixier, J. B. Sollberger, and Bruce Bradley.

Throughout the 1970s and early 1980s replication studies relied more heavily upon the craft of flintknapping and less upon the science of stone tool production technology. Many archaeologists became flintknappers and a great deal of the literature on lithic tool replication focused upon the how-to or craft side of replication (Bradley 1974, 1978; Callahan 1974, 1976, 1979; Clark 1982, 1984; Flenniken 1978, 1981). However, this was a necessary step in the development of replication analysis because it was important to understand the range of production variability. Unfortunately, because much of that production variability was not systematically controlled in experiments, replication studies were criticized as nonscientific (Thomas 1986, 1989). However, the field of lithic replication studies was growing and moving in many directions. While some replication studies were criticized as nonscientific, others were criticized by flintknapping craftsmen as too scientific or laboratory sterile to be relevant for interpretations of prehistoric stone tools. The more controlled experiments shifted the emphasis of analysis away from the finished products of lithic tool production to the by-products of production (Andrefsky 1986a; Cotterell and Kamminga 1979, 1987, 1990; Speth 1972, 1974, 1975; 1981). As a result of this shift, lithic replication experiments gained new acceptance in the archaeological community as controlled scientific experiments that could provide important behavioral information to lithic analysis (Ahler 1989; Ammerman and Andrefsky 1982; Ammerman and Feldman 1978; Andrefsky 1983; Henry *et al.* 1976; Patterson 1979; Raab *et al.* 1979; Stahle and Dunn 1982). The use of more controlled experiments in replication analysis has grown to include not only debitage studies, but also the analysis of finished lithic tools (Flenniken and Raymond 1986; Frison 1989; Frison and Bradley 1980, 1981; Titmus 1985; Titmus and Woods 1986).

Critics of replication studies persist in charging that such studies demonstrate only how stone tools might have been made and used, but not how they actually were made or used. This is true. Yet such criticisms ignore the fact that controlled replication experiments produce a range of lithic artifact variability within differing parameters that can be controlled and understood. Such variability can also be compared with archaeological assemblages to gain insight into the parameters associated with the archaeological assemblage. Additionally, refitting or conjoining studies of excavated lithic assemblages have supported the findings of replication analysis associated with lithic tool reduction sequences (Cahen *et al.* 1979; Hofman 1981; Singer 1984; Villa 1982). Most of the powerful criticisms against lithic replication studies focus upon those that either lack precision on experimental controls or jump to interpretations about the archaeological record from experiments that are not well linked to archaeological assemblages. Since flintknapping is a part of lithic replication analysis and because most flintknappers are not scientifically trained archaeologists (Whittaker 1994:61), it is important to remember that interpretations derived from replication experiments do have varying scientific merit. *Flintknapping*, the recent book by John Whittaker (1994), emphasizes the relationship between debitage characteristics and tool production procedures, and takes flintknapping out of the arena solely of arts and crafts and shows its value in lithic replication analysis. The edited volume, *Experiments in Lithic Technology*, contains numerous examples of how replication experiments could be used to interpret archaeological stone tool data (Amick and Mauldin 1989a). Studies of this kind have gone a long way towards solidifying the role of replication studies in the larger field of scientific archaeology.

2

BASICS OF STONE TOOL PRODUCTION

Lithic artifacts include all culturally modified stone tool materials found on prehistoric sites. They include the finely worked shapes such as microliths and bifaces as well as the discarded pieces removed during the process of tool production and modification. Either in an archaeological laboratory filled with lithic artifacts or on a prehistoric site represented primarily by lithic artifacts, the great amount of variability in the shape of lithic specimens is inescapable. Some specimens will appear to be nothing more than broken fragments of stone and others will appear uniformly shaped into systematically pointed projectile tips. There may be large lithic tools over 20 cm in length and very small specimens less than 1 cm in length; usually the stone will vary in color and texture. For the person just beginning in lithic analysis, this assemblage variability can be unfathomable. Most will not be able to recognize the characteristics that discriminate lithic artifacts from natural stone. In fact, without proper context it may be impossible to determine the difference between lithic tool production debris and naturally fractured stone. What are the characteristics that allow archaeologists to recognize culturally modified materials? This may seem to some to be an insignificant question, but to those with very little exposure to the wide array of lithic artifact morphologies, the question is very important.

The best way to address this question is to understand how stone fractures, at least on the most rudimentary level, and how stone tools are changed and modified during the time they are made and used. Once basic principles of fracture mechanics are understood, and the concept of tool uselife is comprehended, it is much easier to make sense of the enormous variability of lithic artifact assemblages. However, before stone fracture mechanics and tool uselife are discussed, definitions are introduced that represent elemental terminology used in lithic analysis. These provide a common vocabulary for an understanding of fracture mechanics. A more detailed and comprehensive vocabulary follows when analytical techniques are described and explained in later sections of the book.

Basic terminology

Chipped stone artifacts can be conceptualized as being either objective pieces or detached pieces. Objective pieces are stone items that have been hit,

9

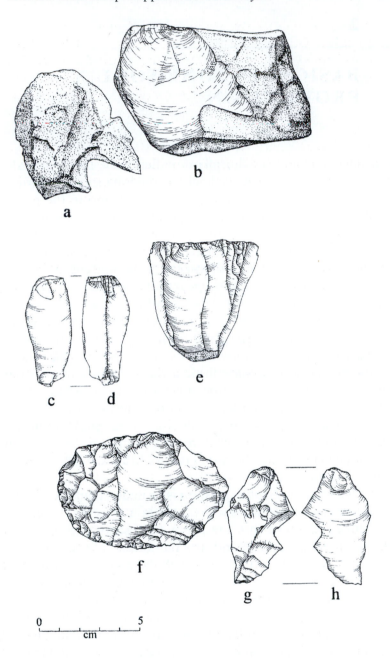

Figure 2.1   Examples of detached pieces and objective pieces: (a) detached piece, flake from nodule; (b) objective piece, river nodule; (c) detached piece, ventral view; (d) detached piece, dorsal view; (e) objective piece, unidirectional core; (f) objective piece, multidirectional core; (g) detached piece, dorsal view; (h) detached piece, ventral view.

cracked, flaked, or modified in some way, and may include nodules, cores, bifaces, or flakes. Detached pieces are stone items that have been removed from objective pieces during the modification process. Detached pieces may be flakes, chips, spalls, blades, shatter, or any piece that separates from the objective piece as it is being worked. Since stone tool technology is a dynamic phenomenon, it is possible that a detached piece may become an objective piece during the uselife of the artifact. For instance, a nodule of lithic material may be hit so that flakes are detached. The nodule is the objective piece and the flakes are the detached pieces. One of the flakes may be selected by the tool maker and modified by having pieces removed from its edges. That flake then becomes an objective piece because it is modified by removal of small detached pieces. The flake may be modified only slightly, as in the case of sharpening or straightening a cutting edge, or it may be entirely reworked into a projectile point or other tool. In either case the detached piece has become an objective piece. Figure 2.1 shows several examples of objective and detached pieces. Note that any detached piece may easily become an objective piece if it is selected for alteration.

Detached pieces are usually removed from the objective piece by either percussion flaking or pressure flaking. Percussion flaking is the removal of a flake or chip by striking the objective piece with a hammer or percussor. Usually the percussor is a cobble or pebble, also known as a hammerstone (Figure 2.2a, b). Percussors or hammers may also be made of bone, antler, or wood. Percussors not made of stone are usually called billets (Figure 2.2c). Sometimes a percussor is used in a manner so that contact is not made between the objective piece and the percussor, in which case the percussor is used to strike a punch that is placed on the surface of the objective piece. This technique is called indirect percussion. Pressure flaking is the removal of a flake or chip by applying pressure to the objective piece without striking. This is usually done by placing the tip of an antler tine or sharpened bone on the objective piece and pushing down and in on the point of applied force. The antler tine or bone is called a pressure flaker (Figure 2.2d).

One of the advantages of pressure flaking over percussion flaking is increased accuracy. During percussion flaking it is not uncommon to strike the objective piece at an unintended location, and cause the objective piece to shatter or crack. By placing the pressure flaker directly on the point of contact the possibility of missing the striking point is normally eliminated. The disadvantage of using a pressure flaker over a percussor is that much less force can be applied. In many circumstances a great amount of force is required to detach a flake, a force most people can only generate by percussion flaking. The processes of percussion and pressure flaking are called application of loads. Different amounts of force used to remove detached pieces are recognized as different load applications. Percussion flaking would have a greater load application than pressure flaking. Use of a heavy, hard percussor such as

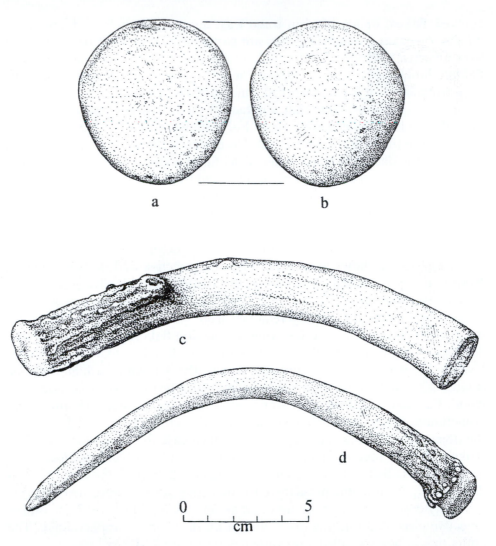

Figure 2.2   Flintworking tools: (a, b) hammerstone; (c) antler billet; (d) pressure flaking antler tine.

a quartzite hammerstone generally produces a greater load application than a lighter, softer percussor such as an antler billet.

   Probably the simplest type of objective piece is a core. A core is a mass of homogeneous lithic material that has had flakes removed from its surface. The primary purpose of a core is to supply flakes that can then be used for the production of various tools. As flakes are removed from the core it gets progressively smaller until it is finished or exhausted. Exhausted cores are found in the archaeological record in all parts of the world. Cores come in a variety of sizes and shapes and have a variety of names depending upon where

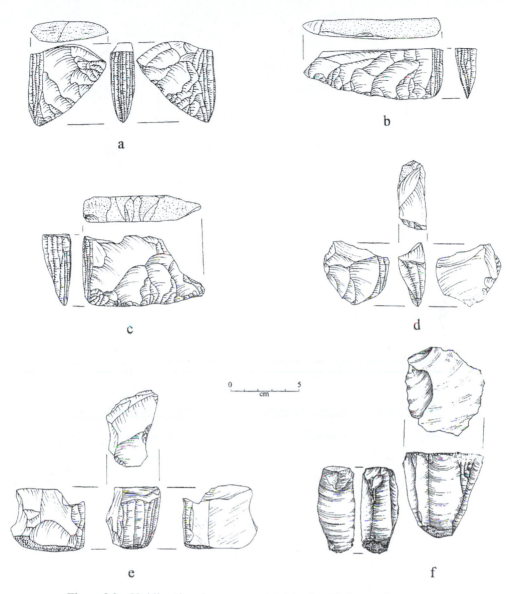

Figure 2.3   Unidirectional core examples: (a) microblade core from
Okedo-Azumi Site, adapted from Kobayashi (1970); (b, c) microblade cores from
Shirataki 30 Site, adapted from Kobayashi (1970); (d, e) microblade cores from
Campus Site, adapted from Mobley (1984); (f) polyhedral core from Andrefsky
collection at WSU.

they are found and how they are shaped. Unidirectional cores have flakes
removed from one direction, and usually have a single large flat surface that is
struck or hit to remove flakes. This surface is called a striking platform.
Different shapes and sizes of unidirectional cores have different names. The

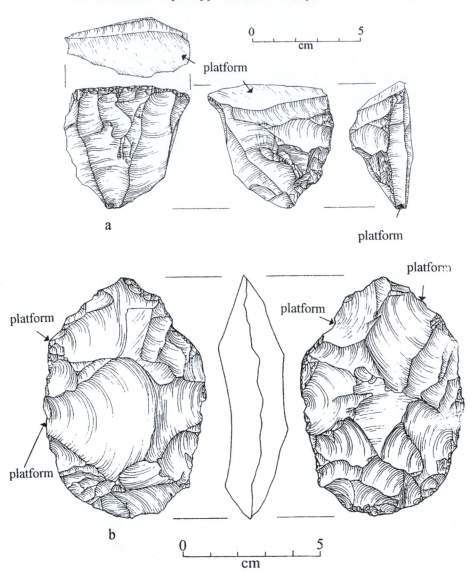

Figure 2.4   Multidirectional core examples: (a) rotated core with multiple platforms; (b) bifacial core with edges used as striking platforms.

Japanese call unidirectional blade cores Shirataki cores and Yubetsu cores (Figure 2.3a, b, c) (Andrefsky 1987; Kobayashi 1970). The North American Arctic term is microblade core (Figure 2.3d, e) (Aigner 1970; Anderson 1970; Morlan 1970) and the Mesoamerican core is polyhedral (Figure 2.3f) (Clark 1982, 1985; Crabtree 1968). Regardless of the name, all unidirectional cores have flakes removed from one direction and they have only a single striking platform.

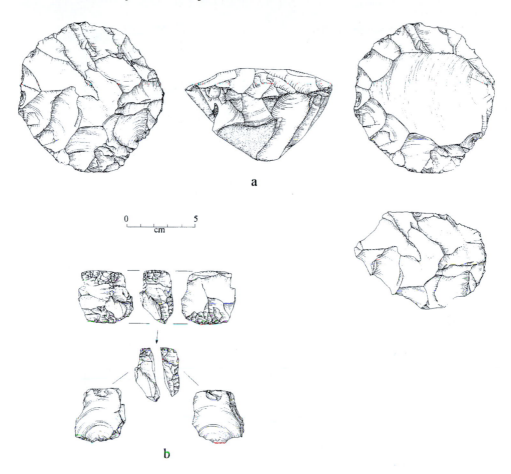

Figure 2.5 Multidirectional cores: (a) Levallois core showing detached Levallois flake; (b) bipolar core showing core before and after being split.

Multidirectional cores usually have several flat surfaces that are used as striking platforms (Figure 2.4). Flakes are removed from several different directions on these kinds of cores. Multidirectional cores must be turned or rotated to remove flakes from the different striking platforms and, as such, are sometimes called rotated cores. Some multidirectional cores have been shaped into a disc and the edges of the disc are used as the striking platforms. These disc-shaped cores with two faces that meet in an edge are often called bifacial cores (Figure 2.4b). Figure 2.4a illustrates several flat-surfaced platforms and Figure 2.4b shows bifacial edge platforms. Other multidirectional cores include the Levallois cores (Bordes 1961, 1968; Kuhn 1995; Van Peer 1992) and bipolar cores (Honea 1965; Johnson 1987:195) (Figure 2.5).

A detached piece is usually called a flake or blade. However, there are any number of terms for detached pieces depending upon the area of the world where they are found. In addition to the terms flake and blade, they may also

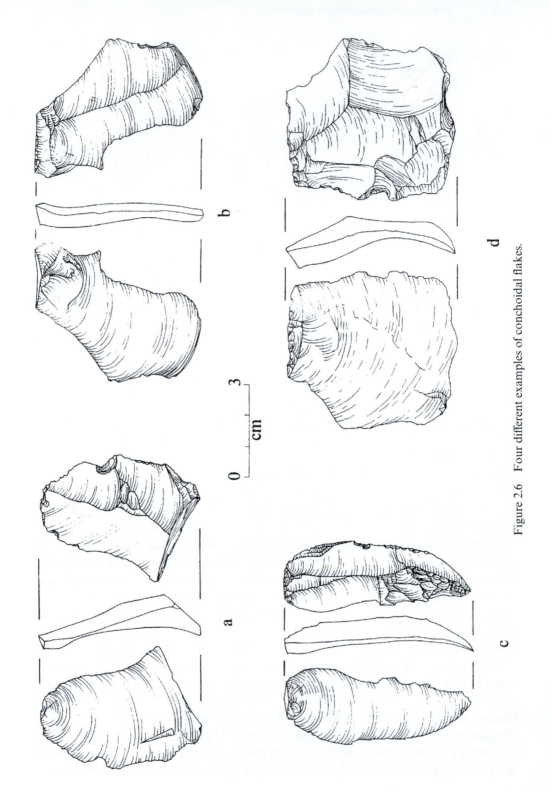

Figure 2.6   Four different examples of conchoidal flakes.

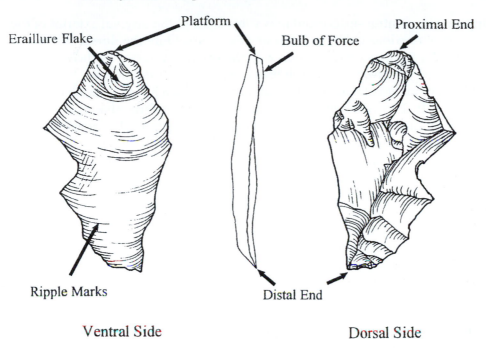

Eraillure Flake

Platform

Bulb of Force

Proximal End

Ripple Marks

Distal End

Ventral Side

Dorsal Side

Figure 2.7   Conchoidal flake showing common elements and terminology.

be referred to as chips, spalls, microblades, waste products, debitage, or refuse. When detached pieces or flakes are discarded without being used as tools or modified into tools, they are usually called debitage or debris. Debitage is considered to be the by-product of stone tool production or core reduction. Debitage or flakes may occur in almost any morphology. It is not uncommon for an objective piece to shatter during the shaping process and produce debitage in hundreds of different shapes and sizes. The morphology of pieces in a debitage pile may be analogous to that of a glass shatter pile made by dropping a crate of milk bottles. Although shattering of the objective piece can produce all sizes and shapes of debitage, controlled production of various kinds of stone tools can produce distinctive kinds of debitage. A skilled tool maker can detach almost any shape of flake needed to form a tool. All flakes removed in a controlled manner have morphological characteristics that provide clues to how and from what kind of objective piece they were detached.

Many flakes removed in a controlled manner have characteristics of conchoidal fracture. Conchoidal fracture of brittle materials like chippable stone produces smooth convexities or concavities. Flakes removed from an objective piece using this technique are called conchoidal flakes (Figure 2.6). Conchoidal flakes have a dorsal surface and a ventral surface. The ventral surface is the surface that has broken away from the objective piece and is usually smooth and shows no evidence of previous flake removals. The dorsal surface is opposite the ventral surface and may show signs of the original exterior of the rock or of previous flake removals or flake scars. Only the dorsal side of the conchoidal flake will have evidence of the original exterior of the rock. The ventral side will always be a fresh break relative to the dorsal side.

Conchoidal flakes that have not been shattered will have a striking platform (Figure 2.7). This is the location or point of applied force that removed the flake from the objective piece. Depending upon the physical characteristics of the original objective piece there are several different kinds of striking platforms. Some are flat, some have multiple facets, and others may be completely rounded from grinding. In some cases there will be a projection at the base of the striking platform on the ventral surface of the flake. This projection or rim is called a lip and some researchers believe it results from impact with soft-hammer percussion or pressure (Crabtree 1972:74). The end of the flake containing the striking platform is the proximal end.

Opposite the proximal end is the distal end. The distal end of the flake is where the force of the original point of impact terminates. This may be a smooth termination that gradually shears the flake from the objective piece, or it may be an abrupt termination that ends in a fracture. Smooth terminations are called feathered terminations or feathered distal ends. When flakes snap or break during removal, the termination is called a step fracture or step termination. Sometimes the force of the impact used to remove the flake turns or rolls away from the objective piece. This is called a hinge fracture or hinge termination. When the force of the impact rolls toward the objective piece the termination is known as a reverse hinge. Reverse hinge fractures are also called overshot or outrepassé terminations (Cotterell and Kamminga 1987:701) or plunging blades (Tixier 1974:16). Figure 2.8 is a schematic diagram showing the four kinds of terminations described above. A more detailed discussion of the mechanics of flake termination can be found in specialized studies (Cotterell et al. 1985; Faulkner 1972). The sides of the flake between the proximal and distal ends where the dorsal and ventral sides meet are called the lateral margins.

Directly below the striking platform on conchoidal flakes, there may be a raised hump on the ventral surface (Figure 2.7). This hump is called the bulb of force and may be very large and prominent or it may be diffuse and difficult to recognize. Some researchers believe that the size of the bulb of force gives some indication of the type of hammer that was used to remove the flake from the objective piece. Others believe the size of the bulb of force has more to do with the angle of applied force. The bulb of force is probably related to both of these characteristics. The bulb of force is always on the ventral surface of a flake, and never on the dorsal surface. Below the bulb of force and radiating away from the proximal end there may be ripple marks. Ripple marks show the direction of applied force as it traveled through the objective piece when the flake was detached (Figure 2.7). Another characteristic that is frequently found in associ-

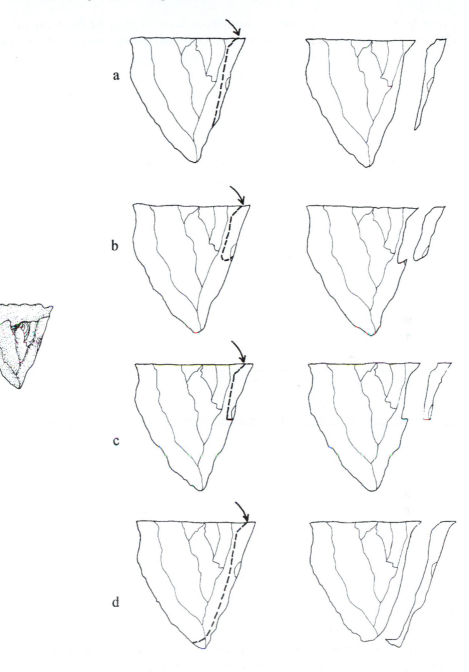

Figure 2.8   Schematic illustration of flake termination types based upon Cotterell and Kamminga (1987): (a) feathered termination; (b) hinge termination; (c) step termination; (d) plunging termination.

ation with the bulb of force is a scar from a small chip or flake on the bulb (Figure 2.7). This is called an eraillure flake scar and is produced during the original impact of the flake removal. When impact is first made on the objective piece in an attempt to remove a flake, sometimes more than one location is contacted on the striking platform. In fact, usually more than one point of contact is made during flake removal. These forces travel through the objective piece in a series of superimposed waves. Usually, one of the waves dominates and a conchoidal flake is removed. This domination usually occurs as the impact of the blow is producing the bulb of force. Sometimes one of the inferior waves contacts the dominant wave as the bulb of force is being created. This contact results in the removal of a chip from the bulb of force; this chip is the eraillure flake (Cotterell and Kamminga 1992:140–50; Faulkner 1972).

One of the things that should be apparent from the first few artifact illustrations in this chapter is the orientation of detached pieces. Throughout this book I use the "American" format for presentation of detached pieces, which is slightly different than the "European" format. The "European" format for illustration of detached pieces presents all specimens with the proximal end downward and the distal end up (Keeley 1980:17, 65, 71; Mellars 1996:100, 111, 117, 121; Van Peer 1992:45–8, 106). The "American" format presents detached pieces that have been modified (flake tools) with the proximal end down and the distal end up, similar to the "European" format. However, unmodified detached pieces (debitage) are illustrated with the proximal end up and the distal end down (Callahan 1979:55–62, 69; Cotterell and Kamminga 1992:131–3, 150; Crabtree 1972:44–6, 55, 69; Ritchie 1965:25, 27, 239; Whittaker 1994:32, 34, 35, 112, 230). This is a matter of preference on my part. There is no standard world-wide presentation style for detached pieces. Some European studies will use the "American" format and some American studies will use the "European" format. Other researchers will orient detached pieces in various ways depending upon what they are emphasizing (Bradley and Giria 1996:30, 32; Frison 1991:130, 131; West 1981:116–21; Whittaker 1994:124, 190, 191).

One of the most common types of objective pieces found on archaeological sites is the biface. Bifaces come in numerous sizes and shapes and have hundreds of specialized names that depend upon their shape and where they were found (Carlson 1996; Goodyear 1974:19–43; Hester 1993; Hiraguchi 1992; Mellars 1996:124–32; Sassaman 1994). All bifaces have two sides that meet to form a single edge that circumscribes the entire artifact. Both sides are called faces and both show evidence of previous flake removals (Andrefsky and Bender 1988:5.1–5.8; Collins and Andrefsky 1995:11–15). Bifaces are objective pieces that have been extensively modified by flake removal across the facial surfaces (Figure 2.9). Some were used primarily as cores or as sources for usable flakes (Goodyear 1979; Kelly 1988). Bifacial cores themselves may have been used as chopping or cutting tools (Ahler 1971; Andrefsky 1997b; Lewenstein 1987; Odell 1981). Other bifaces were modified for hafting or attachment

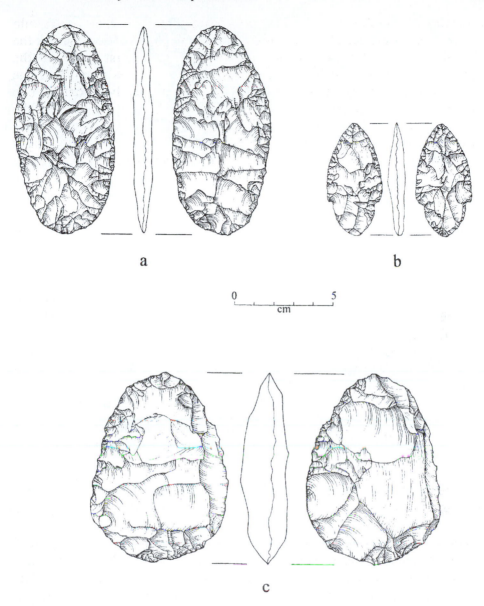

Figure 2.9   Example of biface variability: (a) biface knife; (b) hafted biface; (c) bifacial core.

to a handle or shaft. These hafted bifaces may have been used as projectile points for arrows or spears, or as tips for lances (Christenson 1986; Patterson 1985; Shott 1996). All hafted bifaces may also have been used as cutting or slicing tools (Greiser 1977; Lewenstein 1987).

Hafted bifaces have two primary elements – the haft and the blade (Andrefsky 1986b; Benfer and Benfer 1981; Gunn and Prewitt 1975). The haft

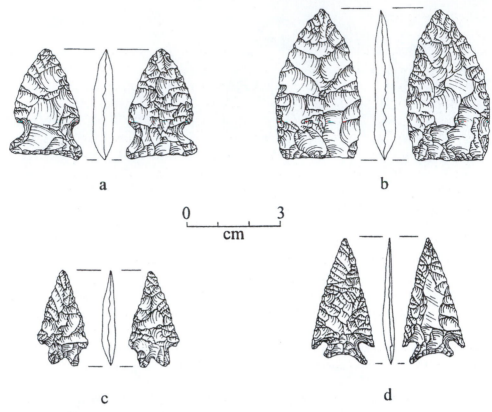

Figure 2.10   Variation found in hafted bifaces: (a) side-notched point; (b) lanceolate point; (c) basal-notched point; (d) corner-notched point.

element is the area of the biface that is attached to a handle or shaft. It is usually notched in some manner so that it can be more easily attached. Notching on hafted bifaces can be on the sides, corner, or base of the biface (Figure 2.10). Sometimes hafted bifaces do not have notches. In such cases, the haft area may be ground or dulled in some manner to prevent the biface from cutting the lashing used to attach it to a handle or shaft. Unnotched hafted bifaces usually show signs of resharpening that occurred after they were attached to a handle. The resharpened area of the biface usually determines the location of the haft and blade elements: the blade element on hafted bifaces is the area that is used for cutting, sawing, or piercing and will usually be resharpened (Andrefsky 1997b; Goodyear 1974; Truncer 1990). Some researchers believe that hafted bifaces with notches were used as projectiles and that hafted bifaces without notches were used as lances.

Fracture mechanics

Chipped stone artifacts are produced by tool makers who know how to crack off various sizes and shapes of rock from an objective piece – flintknapping or stoneknapping. The best kinds of stones for knapping are those that can be cracked in a reliable and predictable manner; such stones are brittle, homogeneous, and isotropic. In other words, the stones most suitable for flintknapping are those that are brittle and do not have direction dependent properties such as bedding planes, fissures, cracks, or inclusions. Natural glass or obsidian is probably the best example of this kind of material because it can be manipulated to crack in any manner the tool maker desires. Other kinds of stones that have the necessary properties include the cryptocrystalline silicates: these include cherts, flints, or chalcedonies with a high percentage of silica. Cryptocrystalline silicates (also known as quartz) are not as easy as natural glasses or obsidians to fracture predictably, but they can be very effective for stone tool production. Basalts, andesites, quartzites, and rhyolites are all used for chipped stone tool production but they have lesser degrees of homogeneity and are less brittle. As fracture mechanics are discussed below, it is important to remember that the concepts introduced and explained relate to perfectly homogeneous and isotropic masses from a controlled setting. Progressively less homogeneous materials may display progressively less predictable characteristics.

Many archaeologists have recognized the need to understand the mechanical properties of stone fracture (Faulkner 1972; Speth 1972, 1975; Tsirk 1979). Perhaps the most comprehensive research on stone fracture mechanics was conducted by Cotterell and Kamminga (1979, 1986, 1987, 1990), and it forms the foundation for the material presented below. Their greatest contribution to stone tool fracture mechanics is the description and explanation of the three flake types produced in flintknapping: conchoidal, bending, and compression or bipolar flakes (Figure 2.11). The difference between the three flake types can best be understood by examining how each flake type is produced.

According to Cotterell and Kamminga (1987:686), conchoidal flakes are initiated or started by the formation of a Hertzian cone at the point of applied force. Figure 2.12 illustrates a BB pellet making impact with a pane of glass. At the point of impact or the point of applied force, a series of concentric cracks develops. One of the cracks will dominate and travel through the brittle mass to form an approximately 136° cone. When making stone tools, the application of force is usually near the edge of an objective piece. This results in the formation of only a partial Hertzian cone (Crabtree 1972:54). Figure 2.13a illustrates Hertzian initiation at the edge of an objective piece, in this case a unidirectional core. A crack is initiated at the point of contact and travels into the objective piece to begin forming the cone. This increases outward pressure and causes the crack to curve away from the objective piece and this action

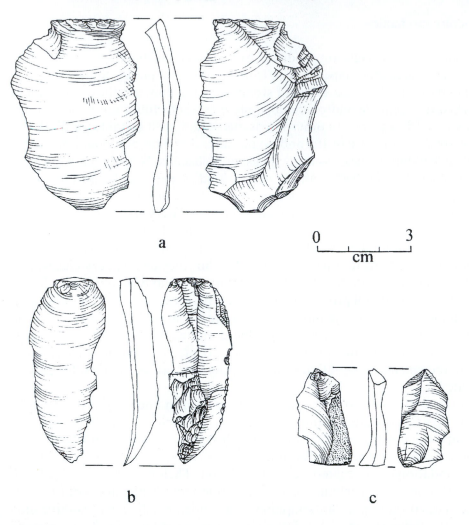

Figure 2.11   Three classic flake types: (a) bending flake; (b) conchoidal flake; (c) bipolar flake.

forms the bulb of force. Cotterell and Kamminga state that "the partial cone propagates initially into the body of the nucleus, and in doing so increases the outward bending on the developing flake. This increase in outward bending causes the crack to curve back toward the surface of the nucleus to complete the bulb of force" (1987:687). They also state that because conchoidal flakes require a great deal of pressure to initiate they are more easily produced with a hard hammer. Conchoidal flakes may be produced by antler and bone pressure flaking tools, but they are more commonly caused by hard-hammer percussion (1987:686).

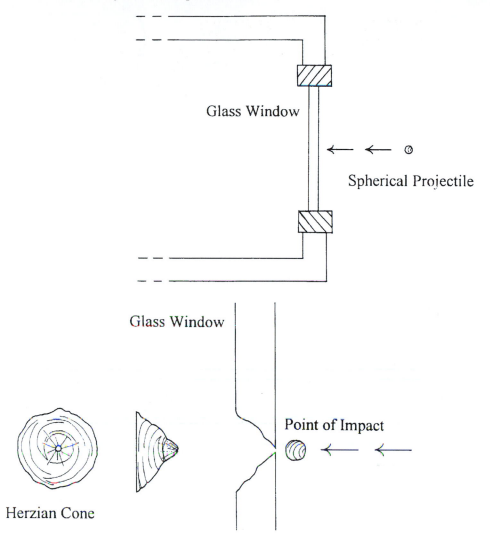

Figure 2.12   Schematic illustration of spherical projectile impacting a pane of glass at a 90° angle to produce a Hertzian cone.

The cracks that form compression or bipolar flakes are initiated and propagated in a different manner from conchoidal flakes. Compression or bipolar flakes are formed by wedging initiation during tool production or core reduction and this type of fracture initiation is caused by the impact of a sharp hammer. Upon impact concentric radii are produced much as they are during conchoidal fracture. However, with wedging initiation the force of the application load is concentrated in the center of the radii and a crack is formed at what would normally be the center of a Hertzian cone. This may also occur with blunt hammers when a great deal of force is applied. Figure 2.13c shows how

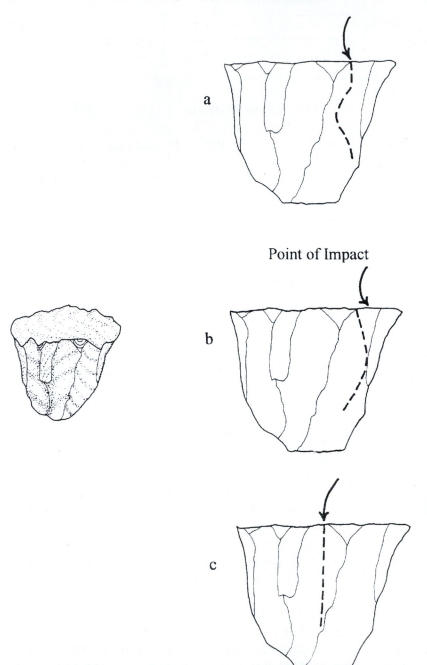

Figure 2.13   Schematic diagram of three types of flake initiation based upon Cotterell and Kamminga (1987): (a) Hertzian initiation; (b) bending initiation; (c) wedging initiation.

wedging initiation occurs. Wedging initiation may also occur when the point of applied force is away from the edge of the objective piece; hand-held cores or nodules can be split in this way. Wedging initiation can occur when detrital particles are wedged into an existing flaw on the surface of the objective piece (Cotterell and Kamminga 1987:688).

Bipolar reduction is a typical kind of flaking technology in which wedging is used as an initiation technique. No bulb of force is produced with bipolar technology or with wedging initiation (Crabtree 1972). In bipolar technology the objective piece is placed on an anvil or hard surface and struck from above with a hard hammer (Goodyear 1993), and the fracture is often initiated from the anvil end as well as the hammer end. As such, bipolar flakes may appear to have two points of applied force. Bipolar technology is often used when the objective piece is too small to be reduced by hand-held methods or when the tool maker is trying to maximize the use of a limited raw-material source (Andrefsky 1994b).

Bending flakes are those formed by cracks that originate away from the point of applied force. Stresses are imposed upon the objective piece that attempt to "bend" brittle material. Some of the most commonly occurring bending flakes are ones that are produced as a result of applying force on the acute edge of an objective piece. For instance, the sharp edge of a biface may snap or chip off in the formation of a bending flake when force is applied near the acute bifacial edge. The resulting bending flake will have a striking platform that is composed of a part of the original bifacial edge. Bending flakes are believed to originate as a result of soft hammers or pressure flakers (Cotterell and Kamminga 1990:142). Figure 2.13b illustrates the manner in which bending flakes are initiated.

Unlike conchoidal and compression flakes, bending flakes are not initiated at the point of applied force. The bending initiation may best be understood by considering the manner in which a fishing pole may snap under stress. Assume for example that a fishing line is snagged at the bottom of a lake and constant pressure is exerted upon the fishing pole held parallel to the lake surface; with enough force applied the pole will snap away from the point of applied force. In other words, the pole snaps somewhere in the middle, but not at the end where the force is applied. The bending of the fishing rod is similar to bending forces on the striking platform of an objective piece. When bending forces ultimately result in a bending flake, the flake is initiated away from the point of applied force. Since the initiation occurs away from the point of applied force, there are no concentric rings of stress associated with the point of initiation. As such, no Hertzian cone is formed and no bulb of force develops on the ventral surface of the flake. Instead, the initial crack travels into the objective piece at approximately a 90° angle then turns toward the outside of the objective piece (Cotterell and Kamminga 1987:690). This results in a flake that has few undulations on the ventral surface and very few secondary detachments or little flake shatter.

Each of the flake types is initiated by cracking in a different manner. Once the flake is initiated it propagates through the objective piece based upon the compression or stiffness of controlled forces (Cotterell et al. 1985). These forces act to guide the direction of the crack and ultimately the shape of the detached piece. The detached piece then terminates in one of several ways depending upon the direction of applied force and the amount of force applied. There are four kinds of terminations: feathered, step, hinged, and plunging (Figure 2.8). Feathered terminations are considered continuations of flake propagation; step terminations are produced as a result of discontinuous propagation, and hinge and plunging terminations are caused by increases in the bending forces that cause the force of impact to turn toward or away from the objective piece (Cotterell and Kamminga 1990:145).

The actual mechanics of chipping an objective piece into a preconceived form require the convergence of multiple interrelated variables. Among others, these variables include: size and shape of objective piece; density of objective piece; size, weight, shape, and density of hammer; type, angle, and location of load application; underlying support of objective piece; shape, size, and isolation of striking platform; and flaws in the objective piece. These variables are played against one another by the tool maker depending upon the particular presentation of the objective piece and desired shape of the detached piece. The interrelationships of the variables allow multiple strategies for detaching similar shapes of pieces. For instance, the application of an impact load perpendicular to a bifacial edge with a soft hammer may create a small, thick, bending flake. The application of the same load with the same hammer on the same bifacial edge, but at a 60° angle to the edge, may create a conchoidal flake much longer and thinner than the bending flake. The change in load application angle from 90° to 60° in this case may be achieved by altering the approach of the hammer. The same kind of conchoidal flake can be detached by keeping the approach of the hammer constant and pivoting the objective piece. Alternatively both the position of the objective piece and the approach of the hammer may be altered to achieve the 60° angle and the removal of a conchoidal flake. It should be remembered that other factors may also be adjusted to produce the same kind of conchoidal flake. The point of applied force or striking platform may be modified which then requires adjustments in the angle of hammer approach to produce the same detached piece. A change in the density, size, or shape of the hammer will also require adjustments in other factors to achieve the same detached piece.

The recognition of the three ideal flake types is extremely beneficial in conducting lithic analysis. Unfortunately these do not encompass the entire range of morphological variability in detached pieces found in the archaeological record. Lithic raw materials used in the production of archaeological tools may contain flaws or inconsistencies. Tool makers often do not make accurate contact with intended striking platforms, or pieces do not detach in the manner anticipated. These and other factors create detached pieces that may look nothing like the three ideal flake types. Much of the lithic analysis that follows explains how to obtain information from ideal flake types. However, the full morphological range of detached pieces produced during tool production and core reduction is also recognized, and techniques of lithic analysis are introduced for this debitage as well.

Stone tool morphological dynamics

Typologies based upon morphology allow specimens to be ordered into groups at a single point in time. In this sense, morphological typologies are static. This is true for all manner of items – whether birds, houses, or projectile points. However, one of the most fundamental characteristics of stone tools is that they are morphologically and functionally dynamic articles of human material culture. Stone tools undergo a process of production, a process of use, and a process of post-depositional change that cause this dynamic character. Each of these processes acts upon the lithic artifact and the population of artifacts to create different shapes and sizes of individual specimens. These dynamic processes cause the lithic tools to change and evolve, both individually and as an assemblage. When an archaeologist finds or collects a lithic tool, that tool is represented in its latest stage or final form. When the artifact is collected from a site context it is removed from its dynamic context and preserved in a static context. It is important to realize and understand that lithic tools physically change shape and that archaeologists collect lithic tools at static points in what may have been a process of change. This dynamic process associated with lithic tools has important implications for artifact typology and the assessment of artifact functions.

Obviously, all kinds of prehistoric technologies are affected by these same processes and all are dynamic. However, lithic technology, unlike other prehistoric technologies such as pottery production or house construction, is a subtractive process. In other words, houses and pottery are constructed by combining elements and pieces together; they are built or assembled. These kinds of technologies combine materials to increase size and composition. Lithic technology is just the opposite. Lithic technology begins with an objective piece that is modified by the systematic removal of different sized and shaped pieces. Lithic artifact production is always reductive. Stone is always removed to produce a tool and never added. Whether they are bifaces, burins, or scrapers, all are shaped by the systematic removal of flakes to produce a desired form. Cores are also systematically reduced to produce usable blades or flakes. The reductive character of lithic technology and the fact that lithic artifact functions may change as the artifact form is changed – the dynamics of stone tool morphology – are essential for lithic analysts to understand.

Lithic production processes

The amount of effort expended in stone tool production is critical for understanding tool production processes. Some stone tools can be produced with very little effort and others require a great deal of production effort. Some archaeologists have separated tools into types based upon this amount of production effort (Andrefsky 1994a; Binford 1979; Kelly 1988). Tools requiring little or no effort in their production are called expediently manufactured or informal tools. Those with a great amount of effort expended in their production are called formalized tools. An expediently made tool may be as simple as an unmodified flake or blade removed from a core. This detached piece can be used for any variety of tasks such as cutting, slicing, or scraping. Different shapes of detached pieces can be used for the same tasks or the same shapes of detached pieces can be used for different tasks. These expediently produced tools immediately introduce a great amount of variability into the lithic tool assemblage because their morphology is not constrained by design requirements.

Formalized stone tools, for instance bifacial projectile points, go through a sequence of production stages (Callahan 1979; Whittaker 1994) that gradually transforms the piece of stone into an armature capable of dispatching a large animal. Figure 2.14 illustrates various stages of biface production from acquisition of raw material to production of a hafted projectile point. Anywhere along this production continuum the projectile point can break and be discarded. Broken specimens are frequently found at production locations such as quarries (Reher and Frison 1991; Thacker 1996; Torrence 1984). Also it is possible that the tool maker may halt production of the bifacial projectile point at any stage of production for use at that stage in the production process or for transport to another location for further reduction.

Bifaces have been shown to be functionally variable stone tools (Andrefsky 1994a; Goodyear 1979; Kelly 1988:719–21). An early-stage biface is quite practical for use as a chopper or hand axe because of its relatively wide edge angle; its blade is ideal for chopping or hacking on hard materials such as wood with little danger of breaking. This same biface can be resharpened when the edges become dull or it can be thinned to perform better a cutting or slicing task. If flakes are needed to slice soft materials, the early- or middle-stage biface can act as a core or source of raw material for flake reduction. As usable flakes are removed from this bifacial core it can be simultaneously thinned to a yet later stage in the production process. If needed, the biface can be notched and hafted onto a handle or foreshaft for use as a projectile armature. However, the hafted biface does not need not be used exclusively as a projectile armature. It

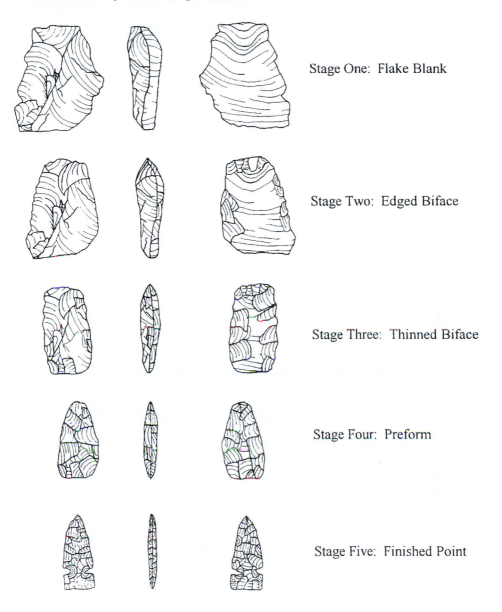

Stage One: Flake Blank

Stage Two: Edged Biface

Stage Three: Thinned Biface

Stage Four: Preform

Stage Five: Finished Point

Figure 2.14   Schematic illustration showing a bifacial reduction sequence with idealized stages of reduction from flake blank to finished hafted biface.

can be used as a hafted knife for sawing or cutting materials, and, when necessary, inserted into a spear or lance for use as a projectile armature.

The various stages of bifacial production yield specimens with different qualities suitable for various activities. It is conceivable that a biface ultimately attached to a haft and used as an armature or a lance was previously used as a

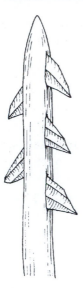

Figure 2.15   Schematic illustration of microliths inserted as barbs for a bone point.

chopping, scraping, or cutting tool. This production process not only changes the morphology of the biface, but may also change the function of the specimen. The production process may be responsible for a great range of morphological variability.

Even less formalized lithic tools undergo a sequence of manufacture in their production processes. For instance, if triangular microliths are needed for the production of arrow barbs (Figure 2.15), a core is prepared from which microliths can be detached. The suitable microliths are then fractured and retouched to their final triangular form. During this production process there is a good chance that some of the blades removed from a core will not be suitable for modification into triangular microlith segments. Those specimens and even the ones that may be suitable for microlith production can be drafted into service as slicing tools, drills, gravers, or some other function. Regardless of the tasks for which such artifacts may be used, it is important to understand that during the production process the artifact may be utilized differently. There is also the possibility that the microliths will not be adequately shaped into triangular segments during the production process owing to production failures. Similarly, the selection of individual microliths for use as barbs may vary depending upon other circumstances, such as the availability of lithic raw materials, the capabilities of the maker, and the amount of time available to prepare the tool. Clearly, the microlith production process has the potential to produce a great amount of individual morphological variability within the assemblage, and an individual artifact may undergo a production cycle that continually changes its form.

The production process is important in lithic technology because the range of variability of lithic artifacts has implications for immediate tool use as well as flexibility of tool design. The modern concept of tool design and tool use is fundamentally different from the design and use of prehistoric lithic tools. In most contemporary contexts we perceive tools as finished products. These include all manner of tools from simple hand tools such as hammers, knives, spoons, wrenches, pens, and pencils to more complicated tools such as blenders, coffee pots, table saws, and calculators. We perceive tool use in a context where these finished tools are drafted into service for a particular task or tasks. The process of making tools to perform an immediate or anticipated task is seldom incorporated into our contemporary tool use context. However, as described above, lithic tool design and use is more closely linked to production processes. As such, the dynamics associated with lithic tool production processes have implications for stone tool typology as it relates to tool design, function, and formal qualities.

Lithic use processes

Although chipped stone tools are relatively durable, they can become dull or break while they are used to slice, scrape, engrave, and/or puncture materials. When this happens, stone tools can be modified for additional use. The use process of lithic tools can change the morphology of the tool very quickly or gradually. For instance, during the uselife of a lithic tool, minor modifications such as sharpening or shaping an edge can be compounded to make great changes to the overall morphology of the specimen. However, this change occurs very gradually as the specimen is used and modified by small amounts. On the other hand, lithic tools may change shape almost immediately if they are broken and reworked into a usable tool. It is also possible that a tool may be dramatically reworked without being broken if no other alternatives are available for the prehistoric tool maker and user.

One of the classic studies of tool modification through use was conducted by Albert Goodyear on a Dalton assemblage from Missouri (1974). The Dalton assemblage was traditionally recognized as having several diagnostic tool forms such as knives, drills, and projectile points: these tool forms were recognized as characteristically Dalton by their notched haft element (Figure 2.16). Through a set of use and resharpening experiments, Goodyear demonstrated how the same specimen could change from one form to another through gradual use and resharpening. In effect, he showed that traditional types believed to have separate functions may in fact have been the same specimen types at different stages of their uselife.

Another example of the gradual reworking of tools through their use process is the modification of hafted scraper forms. Several researchers have remarked that the spurred endscraper is a diagnostic type of endscraper associated with Paleoindian assemblages from North America (Rogers 1986; Wilmsen 1968). It

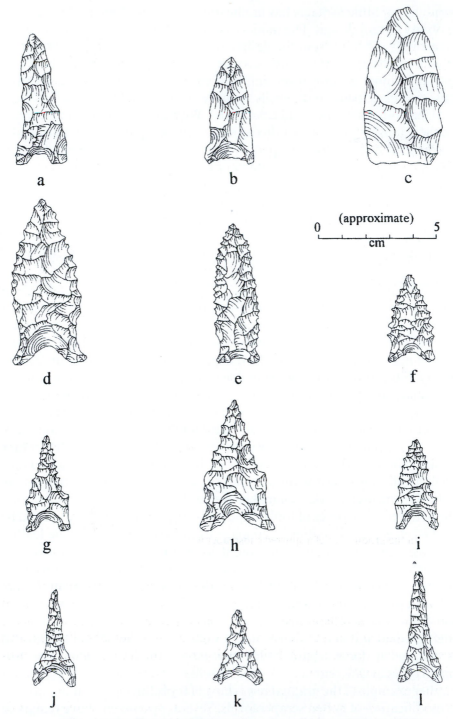

Figure 2.16   Sketches of Dalton bifaces from the Brand Site: (a–c) biface preforms; (d–f) Dalton points; (g–i) Dalton knives; (j–l) Dalton drills. All examples have been drawn from photographs in Goodyear (1974).

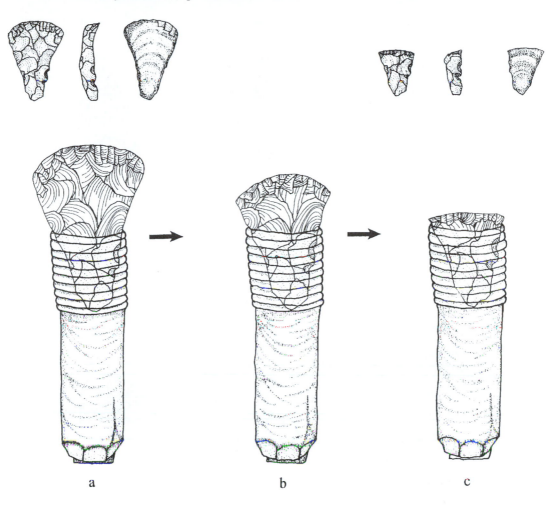

Figure 2.17 Schematic diagram of a hafted endscraper that is progressively resharpened from (a) to (c) while in the handle. The resharpening process results in the production of a spurred endscraper (c).

has been shown that spurred endscrapers represent only part of the endscraper assemblage from Paleoindian sites and that the spur may actually be an unintentional characteristic derived from resharpening the endscraper blade while it is mounted in a haft (Shott 1995). Figure 2.17 schematically diagrams the resharpening process for a hafted endscraper; the haft element has protected part of the endscraper blade from reduction and consequently a spur has been left when the haft was removed or decayed.

Figure 2.18 shows several examples of the Perkiomen endscrapers and drills from the Delaware River drainage (Kinsey 1972; Kraft 1970). These tools have haft elements identical to Perkiomen points. The only difference is that, instead

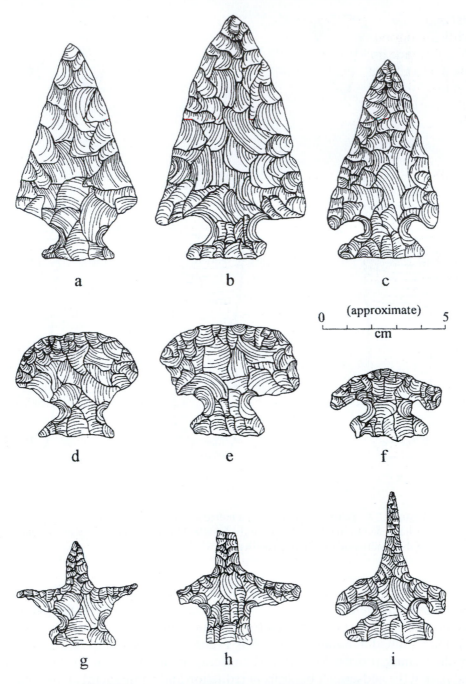

Figure 2.18   Examples of Perkiomen points (a–c), endscrapers (d–f), and winged drills (g–i) recovered from sites along the Delaware River. The examples are redrawn from photographs in Andrefsky (1984), Kinsey (1972), and Kraft (1970).

of having wide thin blades for slicing, they have classic endscraper blades or narrow, diamond cross-section drill blades. The endscraper specimens were probably made on broken Perkiomen points when the haft elements were still attached to a handle. The use process in the case of these endscrapers changed the morphology of the tool much more rapidly than in the case of Paleoindian spurred endscrapers that were modified gradually over a longer period of time. The Perkiomen drills were probably modified over a longer period of time as the biface was used and resharpened repeatedly. Note how the drills have protruding lateral margins or wings (Figure 2.18g–i). This characteristic probably developed as a result of the original blade being partially inset into the haft or handle during resharpening in a similar manner to the way that spurred endscrapers obtained their barbs. The diamond-shaped cross-section indicates that the blade was probably resharpened by retouching in one direction on each edge. Continued resharpening in this manner produced parallel beveling that resulted in a diamond-shaped cross-section.

Other investigators have suggested that the use process on hafted bifaces may actually be responsible for changing the haft element as well as the blade. In addition, Flenniken and his colleagues have used experiments to show how projectile points traditionally assumed to be temporally diagnostic indicators can be modified after being fractured into several different "types" of projectile points. Flenniken and Raymond (1986:609, 610) illustrate several examples of projectile points that have been reworked into different types after they have been broken from projectile impact. Stylistic features on broken and then reworked projectile points would indicate a different chronological period or cultural tradition based upon projectile point typology.

Summary

That individual lithic tools have a changing and dynamic morphology has been recognized in European archaeological literature for more than thirty years (Leroi-Gourhan 1964). For example, the concept of the *chaîne opératoire* in European lithic analysis is used to incorporate the processes of lithic production and lithic use into the classification and interpretation of stone tools (Sellet 1993; Van Peer 1992). The *chaîne opératoire* not only uses these processes to understand morphological variability but also acts to embed lithic technology into other aspects of human behavior and organization (Jelinek 1991). This concept also incorporates aspects of lithic raw material, such as abundance and availability, into stone tool morphology (Bar-Yosef 1991). The dynamic character of lithic stone tools has been recognized and accepted by researchers in some parts of the world, but American archaeologists have been less eager to do so, perhaps in part because of the historical development of typology in American anthropology and archaeology (Andrefsky 1997a). This perception is changing, however, as more and more studies have demonstrated that stone tool morphology is directly affected by tool production, use, and reuse (Amick et al. 1988; Andrefsky 1986a; Dibble 1988; Hayden et al. 1996; Kuhn 1992; Rondeau 1996; Tomka 1989; Towner and Warburton 1990).

Worldwide, stone tool analysts are becoming aware that stone tools and debitage excavated from prehistoric sites are the end result of a complex life history. The sequence from tool-stone procurement to stone tool discard is decided by cultural influences, situational constraints, and raw-material accessibility. These factors contribute to the dynamic character of stone tool types. Lithic tool morphology must be understood as it reflects short-term changes (the result of production and use), as well as long-term changes (the result of cultural and/or behavioral differences).

There are other contextual factors that influence the morphology of stone tools that need to be considered before structuring analysis and making interpretations. Ethnographic (Gould 1980:134; O'Connell 1977:280) and archaeological (Barut 1994; Dibble 1991; MacDonald 1991) studies have shown that different patterns of stone tool production will occur depending upon the relative abundance of lithic raw materials, and therefore the characteristics of tool morphologies are influenced by the relative availability of lithic raw materials. Similarly, the quality of lithic raw materials has been shown to be an important factor associated with the kind of tools produced (Goodyear 1979; Hayden 1982). In areas that contain high-quality, chippable raw materials in abundance, most artifacts will be made from those materials, regardless of the amount of effort expended in their production. Conversely, one of several different tool production patterns may occur when high-quality lithic raw materials are not readily available (Andrefsky 1994a:29–30). Studies have also shown that the shape and size of lithic raw materials are important for determining the kind of technology used. For instance, it has been demonstrated that bipolar technology is used instead of bifacial technology when lithic raw materials occur in sizes too small to be held by hand during reduction (Andrefsky 1994b:384; Goodyear 1993; Honea 1965). Additionally, whether a prehistoric group was sedentary or mobile affected the kind of tools the group made (Andrefsky 1991; Henry 1989; Jeske 1992; MacDonald and Allsworth-Jones 1994). Groups on the move tended to reduce the risk of being unprepared for a task by transporting tools with them; such tools were portable, multifunctional, and readily modifiable. Sedentary groups did not necessarily need to consolidate tools into a multifunctional, light-weight configuration. Other factors such as the kind of food sought or tasks performed also determined the morphological characteristics of stone tools.

Probably the most important thing to remember when conducting lithic analysis – and perhaps the most difficult to incorporate – is that stone tools are morphologically dynamic. This is difficult to incorporate into analysis because stone tools are observed, measured, and analyzed in a static condition; researchers deal with stone tools that are morphologically static. As such, we tend to think of stone tools in terms of static typologies. Before examining the materials from which stone tools are made and moving on to lithic analysis it is worth repeating: it is important to view individual stone tools as morphologically dynamic articles of a material culture system.

3

LITHIC RAW MATERIALS

Humans and human-like creatures were making and using stone tools before the discovery of fire. In this regard, it can be argued that stone or rock has been one of the most important kinds of raw material during most of human existence. The identification of rock types and the recognition of rock qualities for tool making and task production must have been second nature for humans for more than 90% or more of our existence. However, very few humans today appreciate rocks or recognize differences in their natural qualities because so little contemporary technology incorporates rock.

Archaeologists who study prehistoric technology are among the few people who handle different kinds of rock and must deal with rock classification and variability. Yet lithic raw-material identification by the archaeological community is poorly developed, owing partly to the lack of consistent lithic material definitions used by geologists and archaeologists, and partly due to the variations in local and regional use of terminology (Church 1994:13–15; Luedtke 1992:5). Beyond problems associated with consistent terminology, many archaeologists do not understand the characteristics that are important when determining lithic types. Should archaeologists be looking for variations in color, texture, composition, grain size, or all of these things? How is texture or composition determined? This chapter introduces and describes some rudimentary techniques to help determine lithic raw-material types. However, the variation in lithic raw-material types is enormous and only a fraction of that variation is directly associated with chipped stone tools. For this reason this chapter focuses upon those lithic raw materials that are frequently used for the production of chipped stone tools. These lithic raw materials have the qualities of very small or microscopic grain size and smooth texture, are very hard and brittle, and are uniform or homogeneous. Even though all kinds of rock are introduced below, the emphasis is upon those rocks used for chipped stone tool production.

Throughout the chapter the term "rock" is used synonymously with "stone" and "lithic." Rocks are defined as masses of solid minerals, and minerals are combinations of chemical elements. For instance, granite is a rock or lithic material; it is composed of several minerals including quartz and feldspar, and each mineral is composed of chemical elements. In the case of quartz the chemical elements are oxygen and silicon. One of the easiest ways to identify and classify rocks is to understand the genesis or the manner in which rocks are formed. An understanding of rock genesis lends credence to the range of variability found in rock characteristics.

In this chapter rock types and rock identification are considered, for the most part, from a macroscopic perspective. In other words, all stone identification techniques discussed incorporate observations made with the naked eye or with a hand lens of not more than $10 \times$. Archaeologists should realize that a geologist's field identification of a rock usually requires a freshly broken surface to reveal composition and texture. Because the opportunity to examine a fresh break seldom exists (most lithic specimens are in artifact form and there is usually an archaeological taboo against the destruction of artifacts) the archaeologist may find himself/herself in a difficult position with regard to the identification of lithic material. Fortunately, there are several characteristics useful for rock identification that can be observed on the surface of chipped stone artifacts, and others can be inferred from the patinated surface of chipped stone artifacts.

The material below draws heavily on several excellent studies and summaries of lithic raw materials. The section on geochemical techniques relies greatly upon a review of such techniques by Kempe and Templeman (1983) and Parkes (1986). Much of the general background material on the genesis of rock and its classification comes from the laboratory manual on physical geology by Hamblin and Howard (1971). The section on the genesis of chert is significantly influenced by the excellent work of Luedtke (1992).

One of the primary purposes of lithic raw-material identification is to determine the provenance or source location of the stone used for the production of stone artifacts. Although macroscopic techniques can be helpful for provenance studies, their precision is subject to greater degrees of error than geochemical techniques. However, since many of the rock types used for chipped stone tools have as much variation within a source location as between source locations, even geochemical techniques are subject to error. This is particularly true for raw materials such as chert that tends to form over long periods of time and undergo several episodes of diagenesis. Because the emphasis here is on macroscopic rock identification and classification, geochemical techniques of identification are not explained in detail. However, before proceeding to macroscopic techniques, a brief review of geochemical techniques is necessary; a more detailed summary and discussion of geochemical techniques is found in Kempe and Templeman (1983) Meschel (1978) Parkes (1986) and Reeves and Brooks (1978).

A brief review of geochemical techniques

Geochemical techniques of stone analysis are used to determine the elemental composition of lithic artifacts. These techniques give the proportion of different elements found in the sample being studied. By matching the elemental composition of artifacts to raw material from various source areas the provenance of raw material used to make artifacts can be determined. There are several different techniques of geochemical analysis and they each provide different kinds of information and may require different kinds of samples. Some techniques examine only the outer surface of artifacts and others evaluate the entire specimen; some techniques are destructive and others are harmless to the artifact. Some techniques are more suited than others to gather information about certain elements.

Stone is composed of elements classified into one of three groups: (1) major elements (those that make up 2% or more of the sample); (2) minor elements (from 2% to 0.1% of the sample); and (3) trace elements (those in concentrations less than 0.1%). Geochemical techniques frequently focus on trace elements to determine provenance. Geochemical analysis usually determines the relative percentages of elements. This means that neither chemical compounds nor minerals are identified. Neither can other aspects of rock, such as texture, crystal inclusions, or fossils be determined from geochemical analytical techniques. The best way to determine the mineral content of rocks is to conduct petrographic analysis using thin section microscopy. This entails cutting a section of the rock or artifact with a rock saw, attaching it to a glass slide, and grinding the sample to approximately 1 mm in thickness. The sample is then scanned using a polarized microscope to determine mineral content and rock texture. All geochemical techniques measure the radiation emitted or absorbed by atoms when the nucleons or electrons move between various energy levels. By studying the radiation levels it is possible to determine the type and number of atoms involved and hence to determine the elements present in the sample (Parkes 1986:145).

X-ray fluorescence spectrometry (XRF)

X-ray fluorescence spectrometry penetrates the rock sample only to about 200 microns and therefore primarily evaluates the surface of the specimen. Small objects such as complete flakes can be irradiated with little or no damage using this technique. Sometimes samples are crushed to powder to obtain elemental data from more than just the surface area, which is, needless to say, destructive. XRF is typically used to determine the composition of obsidian and to a lesser extent chert (Church 1994; Latham *et al.* 1992; Warashina 1992).

According to Parkes (1986) the sample is irradiated with a beam of X-rays that excite electrons into higher energy levels. The electrons then settle back and emit secondary or fluorescent X-rays. The fluorescent X-rays have wavelengths characteristic of the element from which they were emitted. By measuring the intensity of the X-rays at different wavelengths it is possible to determine the concentrations of different elements in the sample. However, differences in surface characteristics and contours can cause problems with measuring the intensity of different wavelengths (Bouey 1991), and this is particularly true for complete specimens such as chipped stone tools. This can be overcome by cutting a uniform sample from the specimens or crushing the specimens to uniform units of analysis.

Particle induced X-ray emission analysis (PIXIE)

Another technique involving X-rays is particle or proton induced X-ray emission analysis. This technique is very similar to XRF and produces the same kind of electron excitement and emission. The one major difference is that the particle beam can be focused on a small area of the sample, in contrast to XRF that analyzes the entire surface of the specimen. PIXIE allows for different areas of the sample to be evaluated (Annegarn and Bauman 1990). One disadvantage of PIXIE when compared to XRF is cost, the latter being relatively inexpensive. Additionally, the surface of the specimen must be highly polished for PIXIE to be effective and the resulting damage created by polishing may far outweigh its advantage over complete sample XRF (Parkes 1986).

Electron microprobe analysis (EMPA)

According to Kempe and Templeman (1983:45) electron microprobe analysis has become the most popular method of elemental analysis. Its main advantage lies in its ability to provide quantitative analysis of single crystals without destroying their relationship to the texture of the rock. Whole artifacts or a section of the sample can be used in the analysis. The sample is scanned with a focused electron beam that causes the mineral to emit secondary X-rays; these can be separated and measured in the same way as XRF. This technique is best used on chemically and mineralogically homogeneous rocks such as chert and obsidian (Kempe and Templeman 1983).

Instrumental neutron activation analysis (INAA)

This technique requires irradiation of a sample in a nuclear reactor by a prolonged neutron bombardment. Under these conditions some elements will undergo nuclear reactions to produce radioactive isotopes (Widemann 1980). The amount of gamma photons produced when isotopes decay is proportional to their concentration. The technique requires a small sample size and the entire artifact can be irradiated; it is therefore a nondestructive technique. Approximately fifty elements can be identified using INAA (Church 1994), and Kempe and Templeman (1983) claim INAA is very accurate and precise. It has been found to be effective for identification of rocks between and within formations. Provenance studies of chert, steatite, and quartzite have used INAA (Church 1994).

Inductively coupled plasma emission spectroscopy (ICP)

In this technique a solution of the sample is heated until it becomes a plasma flame at a temperature of 6,000° C. This is done by injecting the solution into a stream of argon and heating with a radio frequency coil. The emission spectrum is analyzed to reveal the elements present and their relative concentrations (Parkes 1986). ICP has been found to be more effective than XRF for determining the provenance of silicates (Jarvis 1988; Thompson *et al.* 1986). Since the technique only requires a sample of approximately 0.03 g (Kempe and Templeman 1983), it is effective for identifying most major, minor, and trace elements.

Atomic absorption spectroscopy (AAS)

Atomic absorption spectroscopy is another flame photometry technique (McLaughlin 1977). In AAS the sample (approximately 1 g) is crushed and put into a solution. The sample solution is then sprayed into a flame, causing the compounds in the sample to dissociate into their constituent atoms. Light of the characteristic wavelength for the element being investigated is shone through the flame. The atoms of the element absorb the light, and the total amount of light absorbed is calculated to determine concentrations of each element. Each element studied requires a specific lamp of the appropriate wavelength.

The elemental composition of rocks is best determined by various geochemical techniques. Archaeologists are often more interested in gross mineral composition. To better understand mineral composition it is important to understand the manner and conditions under which rocks form, or the genesis of rocks.

Rock genesis

It is important to understand the genesis of rocks in order to understand how rocks are classified. The classification is based primarily upon composition and texture. Composition refers to the chemical elements from which rocks are created. These are usually determined by the identification of the minerals found in a rock. Texture refers to the size, shape, and relationship of individual particles in a rock. Both the composition and texture of rock are directly affected by its genesis or formational processes.

There are three broad families of rocks based upon genesis: igneous, sedi-

Table 3.1   *Rock families and conversion processes*

Parent rock	Conversion process	Product rock
Igncous	Weathering	Sedimentary
Sedimentary	Heat and pressure	Metamorphic
Metamorphic	Melting	Igneous

mentary, and metamorphic. Igneous rock is formed from cooled molten rock, that can solidify deep beneath or on the surface of the Earth. Molten rock solidified on the Earth's surface is called lava; magma is molten rock that cools and solidifies below the surface. Sedimentary rocks form by the cementation of sediments at ordinary temperature at or near the surface. Sediments can be as fine as clay particles or as large as boulders. Metamorphic rocks are those which form from either igneous or sedimentary rocks within the crust of the Earth by high temperature and pressures, and are transformed while in a solid state. It is important to realize that the three rock families represent ideal types which transform from one to another over long periods of time. Table 3.1 shows the relationship between the various rock families and conversion processes. Any rock type can be transformed into another rock type given time and the right conditions. For instance, an igneous rock such as granite can form as cooling magma, then be uplifted as a mountain range, and gradually eroded along talus slopes and ultimately carried off on drainage systems. The tumbling of broken granite in high-altitude streams crushes the sharp edges of the rock and forms rounded cobbles and tiny sand grains. The sand grains may be carried far downstream and deposited along river point bars or on river deltas along seas or oceans. Ocean waves may sort the sand grains into different sizes. These beds of sand may be buried below subsequent deposits and over time form into the sedimentary rock called sandstone. Sandstone may be uplifted to form parts of mountain ranges or plateaus. It may also be buried deep within the Earth's crust under more and more layers of sediment. The sandstone may be transformed in a solid state by pressure and heat as more and more weight is loaded on by the sediments above, and may be deformed to become quartzite, a metamorphic rock. The quartzite may be melted to form a magma or lava and solidified to form an igneous rock, or it may be exposed to surface weathering and break into fragments that are deposited to form sedimentary rock. This process is continuous and rocks can be observed at all points along this continuum.

Rocks are composed of chemical elements, and chemical elements are combined under certain limitations to form minerals, each of which has specific physical properties such as hardness, cleavage, color, luster, tenacity, and crystal form. Hamblin and Howard (1971) provide good definitions and laboratory techniques to investigate each of these physical properties. For the purposes of lithic analysis it is important to understand that minerals can be identified by the variability in these properties. As molten rock cools, different minerals are formed owing to the rate of cooling and the chemical elements contained within the molten solution. In the classification of rocks it is appropriate to start with a description of igneous rocks, or those rocks that form as a result of lava or magma solidification.

Igneous rocks

Approximately 99% of all igneous rocks are composed of eight elements – oxygen, silicon, aluminum, iron, calcium, sodium, potassium, and magnesium. These eight elements generally form six distinct minerals. Ninety-five percent of all igneous rocks are composed of one or several of these minerals – feldspar, olivine, pyroxene, amphibole, quartz, and mica. The color of igneous rocks can be used to help infer mineral composition. Mafic rocks are those rich in magnesium, iron and calcium and are frequently composed of the minerals olivine, pyroxene, amphibole, and calcium plagioclase. They are dark colored because of their dark mineral constituents. Rocks rich in silica and aluminum are called sialic rocks and tend to include the minerals quartz, potassium feldspar, and sodium plagioclase; they are generally light colored. According to Hamblin and Howard (1971:19) there are three criteria used to identify mineral components in igneous rocks: (1) the presence of quartz, (2) the composition of feldspars, and (3) the types and proportions of ferromagnesian minerals. These rocks all form as a result of differential cooling of molten rock.

The size, shape, and relationship among adjacent minerals in a rock are referred to as texture. Rocks such as magma that cool slowly allow time for crystals to grow. Slow-cooling rocks tend to have larger crystals than do fast-cooling rocks such as lavas. Individual crystals, since they are larger, can be easily identified in slowly cooled rock. Fast-cooling rocks do not often have crystals that can be seen with the naked eye and appear structureless. An example of an extremely fast-cooling rock is obsidian. Obsidian cools so quickly that crystals have no time to grow and the rock texture is literally as smooth as glass; obsidian is, in fact, naturally formed glass.

There are generally six kinds of textures found in igneous rocks: phaneritic, porphyritic-phaneritic, aphanitic, porphyritic-aphanitic, glassy, and fragmental. Phaneritic textures, as can be seen in granite, have large individual crystals; aphanitic textures, as in basalt, have crystals so small they cannot be seen without a microscope; aphanitic rocks appear as a homogeneous mass of rock without structure. Porphyritic means that phenocrysts appear within the matrix of the igneous rock whether the matrix is aphanitic or phaneritic. Rhyolite is often a porphyritic rock which has an aphanitic texture with phenocrysts or large crystals scattered within the rock matrix. Glassy textures do not have crystals even under high magnification. Fragmental textures consist of angular fragments of material ranging in size from fine dust, such as tephra, to cobbles, such as pumice, that are often ejected from volcanoes. Igneous rocks of glassy and aphanitic textures are the most common rocks used to make chipped stone tools, and include, but are not limited to, obsidian, rhyolite, andesite, and basalt.

Igneous classification

Igneous rocks can be classified on the basis of characteristics of texture and composition. Figure 3.1 illustrates the relationship between texture and composition in most igneous rocks. There are three primary families of igneous rocks, each named after the phaneritic member of the family – granite, diorite, and gabbro. The coarse-grained member of the granite family is granite and the fine-grained member is rhyolite. Gabbro and basalt are the coarse- and fine-grained members of the gabbro family respectively, and diorite and andesite are the coarse- and fine-grained rocks of the diorite family. Members of the same family are composed of the same relative frequencies of minerals. In other words, rhyolite and granite have the same chemical composition but differ only in texture. The same is true for gabbro and basalt, andesite and diorite.

The mineral composition of phaneritic rocks is relatively easy to establish because the crystals are large enough to identify. Determining the relative percentage of feldspar will help determine the rock family. The granite family has a relatively high percentage of potassium feldspar. Pink feldspar is almost always potassium feldspar. White or gray feldspar is either plagioclase or potassium feldspar. If the feldspar has striations it is most certainly plagioclase. A high percentage of plagioclase feldspar is typical of the diorite family. Another indicator of the granite rock family is the relative percentage of quartz. The granite family contains 10% to 40% quartz, and the diorite family contains quartz, but usually less than 10%. The gabbro family usually does not contain quartz. Although the relative percentages of various minerals may be easy to estimate in the phaneritic rocks, aphanitic rocks possess microcrystalline structure and crystals cannot be seen without a microscope. Thus, the best way to determine the relative composition of these rocks is by color and the type of phenocrysts if any are present. The relative percentage of dark minerals determines if the rock is mafic ($>70\%$), sialic ($<10\%$), or intermediate (approximately 50%). Generally, as stated above, mafic rocks will be black or dark in color, sialic rocks will be lighter in color, and intermediate rocks will be grey in color. The type of phenocrysts helps determine the type of aphanitic rock. Phenocrysts of potassium feldspar or quartz indicate the rock is rhyolite. Andesite contains phenocrysts of amphibole and basalt contains phenocrysts of pyroxene or olivine. Although aphanitic igneous rocks are the most difficult

ROCK TYPES

			Light	Intermediate	Dark
Texture	Aphanitic	➡	RHYOLITE	ANDESITE	BASALT
	Phaneritic	➡	GRANITE	DIORITE	GABBRO
Color			Light	Intermediate	Dark
Mineral	Potassium Feldspar	➡	15%-80%	<15%	none
Composition	Plagioclase Feldspar	➡	<15%	15%-80%	15%-50%
	Quartz	➡	10%-40%	<10%	none
	Biotite	➡	<10%	<10%	none
	Amphibole	➡	<10%	10%-20%	0%-10%
	Pyroxene	➡	none	0%-25%	20%-60%
	Olivine	➡	none	none	0%-60%

Figure 3.1   Igneous rock identification chart presented as based upon
information presented in Hamblin and Howard (1971).

igneous rocks to identify owing to their fine-grained homogeneous particle
size, the fine-grained texture is the reason they were selected by prehistoric
people for production of chipped stone tools.

There are a few common igneous rocks used for chipped stone tools that do
not fit into the chart on Figure 3.1; these include obsidian and quartz. The
natural glass, obsidian, is an excellent raw material for stone tool production.
It is usually black in color but may also be greenish and have red or clear
streaks or patches. Obsidian occurs as a volcanic pyroclastic or as a lava flow.
Sometimes minerals have enough time to grow into crystals as molten rock
cools to form an igneous mass. Quartz crystals may grow in cooling rock. They
are clear, six-sided minerals that can be used for chipped stone tool production. Sometimes quartz does not have enough time to grow into crystals and
forms, within cracks or veins in the cooling rock, into a microcrystalline rock
that can also be used as a chipped stone raw material. The following section on
sedimentary rocks discusses quartz genesis in more detail since quartz also
occurs in a sedimentary context.

Sedimentary rocks

Sedimentary rocks are composed of the by-products of other rocks that have been eroded or dissolved. By-products such as rubble on talus slopes, sand, and dissolved mineral components such as calcium and silicon are redeposited or precipitated to form sedimentary rocks. The processes involved with the genesis of sedimentary rock include: (1) the physical and chemical weathering of the parent rock; (2) the transportation of the weathered by-products by ice, wind, gravity, or running water; (3) the deposition of the by-products; and (4) the compaction and solidification of the sediment into a solid mass (Hamblin and Howard 1971:31). The by-products of weathered rock may occur in a wide range of sizes and shapes. Large rounded river cobbles may be compacted to form a conglomerate; angular broken rock may form a breccia and very fine silt or clay particles may solidify to form a shale. Usually these by-products become sorted by size as a result of transport. Large rock fragments may travel only a short distance while small rock fragments like sand may be carried farther before being deposited. The differential transport, sorting, and deposition of sediments by size results in sedimentary rocks of different textures and compositions. In addition to particle size differentiation, chemicals may also dissolve from parent rock and be redeposited to form sedimentary rock.

Sedimentary rocks can be identified by recognizing the sedimentary structures found in the rock. The most obvious sedimentary structure is stratification or the layering of sediments. As sediments accumulate from a weathering context the various-sized particles are deposited in episodes. For instance, seasonal flooding may deposit silts on a flood plain once a year, or over the long term a river terrace may be flooded by deposits once every 100 or 1,000 years. The variation in depositional history produces sediments that are laid down in distinct strata, that when solidified form the sedimentary structures observable as horizontal layers within the rock. A sedimentary layer may be as thin as a millimeter or as thick as a meter depending upon the context in which it was deposited. Other kinds of sedimentary structures also relate to the deposition of rock by-products. For instance, sand deposited on a beach is often molded by wave action to form ripple marks which may become preserved in the sand when it is compacted and consolidated into stone. Rain drop marks in mud or mud cracks may also be preserved in sedimentary rocks. Frequently animals or plants trapped within or between layers of sediment are preserved in some manner. All of these consequences of depositional history may be considered sedimentary structures.

There are three primary types of sedimentary rocks: (1) clastic rocks are formed as a result of solid rock by-products being deposited and solidified; (2) chemical precipitates are formed from dissolved chemicals (such as calcium carbonate or silicon dioxide) that have been precipitated into a location and solidified into rock; and (3) organic rocks are formed when plant or animal

Table 3.2   *Common clastic sedimentary rocks*

Rock name	Texture	Composition
Conglomerate	Coarse (>2 mm)	Rounded fragments of any rock type
Breccia	Coarse (>2 mm)	Angular fragments of any rock type
Quartz sandstone	Medium (2–1/16 mm)	Quartz with other minor minerals
Arkose	Medium (2–1/16 mm)	Quartz with >25% feldspar
Graywacke	Medium (2–1/16 mm)	Quartz with high clay content
Siltstone	Fine (1/16–1/256 mm)	Quartz and clay minerals
Shale	Very Fine <1/256 mm)	Quartz and clay minerals

remains are deposited and compacted in much the same way as clastic rocks. For the purposes of chipped stone analysis the two most important types of sedimentary rocks are clastic and chemical precipitates. Organic rocks formed from mollusk shells that have solidified into rock layers to form coquina or fossiliferous limestone, for instance, are seldom used for chipped stone tool production, and will not be discussed below.

Clastic sedimentary rocks

Clastic rocks are primarily classified by particle size and composition. Table 3.2 lists the common names for clastic rocks along with particle size and composition. Only the clastic rocks that are fine to very fine grained are useful for chipped stone tool production. Of the fine-grained clastic rocks, only those that are very hard and brittle can be used for flintknapping. In other words, a conglomerate, breccia, sandstone, arkose, or graywacke is unsuitable for flint-knapping because the grain size is too large to allow control of the removal of flakes. Additionally, these rocks tend to fracture around the particles and do not break conchoidally. Siltstones and shales are composed of fine to very fine particles and are generally more suitable for production of chipped stone tools. However, unless the siltstone or shale is very hard, it tends to crumble around its grain particles upon impact, similarly to other kinds of clastic rocks previously mentioned. Therefore, only those very hard and brittle clastic rocks with a fine texture are good for chipped stone tool production. The strata within such clastic rocks must also possess uniform hardness and composition; if layers within a fine-grained clastic rock are of differing hardness, the rock tends to break along bedding planes, a condition obviously detrimental to knapping.

   Of all the different clastic sedimentary rocks only a very limited range are useful for the production of chipped stone tools. These are the rocks usually cemented with silicon dioxide or quartz – one of the hardest minerals found on Earth once it solidifies from a solution. While in solution, quartz can travel between particles of clastic sedimentary rocks and harden as a cementing agent; this process is known as silicification. Clastic sedimentary rocks that have not been silicified tend to break around their constituent particles, and crumble when struck with a hammer. Silicified shales or siltstones tend to fracture across particles and permit conchoidal fracturing. In addition to siltstones and shales, sandstones may also be indurated by silica and formed into silicified sandstone that also breaks conchoidally. Silicified sandstones are known as orthoquartzites, or quartzites that have not been metamorphosed. The differences between sedimentary quartzites and metamorphic quartzites are discussed below.

The process of silicification makes clastic rocks fracture conchoidally so they can be used to produce chipped stone artifacts. The greater the amount of silica that migrates into the parent rock, the harder and more brittle the rock becomes. However, as the relative proportion of silica increases it becomes difficult to distinguish silicified clastic rocks from silicious chemical precipitate rock forms. This is particularly true for chemical precipitates which form in beds or layers within a sedimentary context.

Chemical precipitate sedimentary rocks

During the weathering process of most rocks various chemical elements, such as silicon, and oxygen are dissolved. These elements may combine to form minerals that are precipitated into cavities to form rocks or they may grow as crystals. Common forms of chemical precipitate rocks include halite or rock salt, gypsum, calcite or limestone, and chalcedony. Most chemical precipitates are relatively soft or dissolve easily in water and are not good raw materials for making chipped stone tools. However, one of the hardest minerals that forms as a chemical precipitate is silicon dioxide or silica – the same material that makes fine-grained clastic rocks effective for flintworking. To understand how to recognize this chemical precipitate it is important to understand how it originates.

Silicon dioxide (also known as quartz) is composed of silicon and oxygen, the two most common elements on the planet. Quartz occurs in hard mineral forms as well as in amorphous forms (known as opals). Opals (both opal-A and opal-CT) are unstable at temperatures and pressures found on the surface of the Earth (Luedtke 1992:7). For this reason the forms of quartz used for artifact production are of the hard mineral variety. Generally there are two forms of hard mineral quartz – macrocrystalline and microcrystalline. Macrocrystalline quartz occurs as a large free-standing six-sided crystal. Although more rare, these have been used as raw material for production of chipped stone tools (Reher and Frison 1991). Microcrystalline quartz, sometimes called crypto-crystalline quartz, is probably the most frequently used raw material for the production of chipped stone tools. This material is often referred to by locally or regionally designated names in the archaeological literature; it has been called chalcedony, flint, chert, jasper, agate, and a variety of other names. Luedtke (1992:5) provides a good discussion on the names of microcrystalline quartz, and refers to all microcrystalline quartz as chert, the term used in this book. The only exception to this standardized terminology is the fibrous form of quartz called chalcedony, in which the quartz crystals form as long thin fibers that may twist and wrap around each other. Regardless of the form of crystalline quartz, whether it grows as a six-sided crystal, as chalcedony, or as a microcrystalline chert, it is all chemically identical.

Depending upon the specific formation and context of genesis, cherts will occur in a range of colors and textures, and with various inclusions. Different trace elements and impurities within chert give it different colors and textures. The entire range of textures are all very smooth in relation to clastic rocks. Chert is homogeneous and individual particles or crystals are not visible without the aid of a microscope; it breaks with a conchoidal fracture.

Theories of chert formation processes are controversial and have changed rather drastically as new data have been gathered. Generally, it is now believed that most chert is formed in a deep-sea environment. Crystalline chert is precipitated from amorphous, soluble kinds of silica under the right pH and temperature conditions. More specifically, chert is formed through a sequence of silica transformation from opal-A to opal-CT to quartz (Williams and Crerar 1985). Approximately 80% of the silica found as opal-A is produced by silica-secreting organisms, specifically diatoms (Luedtke 1992:23). Diatoms remove silica from ocean waters and deposit it in the form of opal-A. As diatoms die and sink to the ocean floor their skeletons (made of opal-A) dissolve. Most ocean floors have high levels of dissolved silica, that is believed to originate almost entirely from diatoms (Siever *et al.* 1965). Ocean sediments are saturated with opal-A, which dissolves and precipitates as opal-CT. It is believed that opal-CT again dissolves and precipitates or recrystallizes into quartz under the right conditions (Luedtke 1992; Murata *et al.* 1977). Figure 3.2 illustrates this process of the three types of quartz genesis.

Chert often occurs as nodules or bubbles in a parent rock such as limestone. It is believed that nodular chert is precipitated under conditions of low pH, where carbonate materials tend to dissolve. Limestone and dolomite formations are typical places where chert nodules tend to be found. Cherts are also found in massive beds or layers. Bedded chert formations are typically associated with sedimentary rock strata such as shale and also with volcanic deposits. Some researchers believe bedded cherts obtain silica from volcanic sediments and not from diatoms (Calvert 1983). It is possible that chert can also form as a result of precipitation directly within a sedimentary ooze or marl at the bottom of oceans, particularly if the sediments have a basic pH. Precipitation in this context (when the suspended sediments are very fine grained, such as clays) may produce cherts that are very similar to silicified shales or

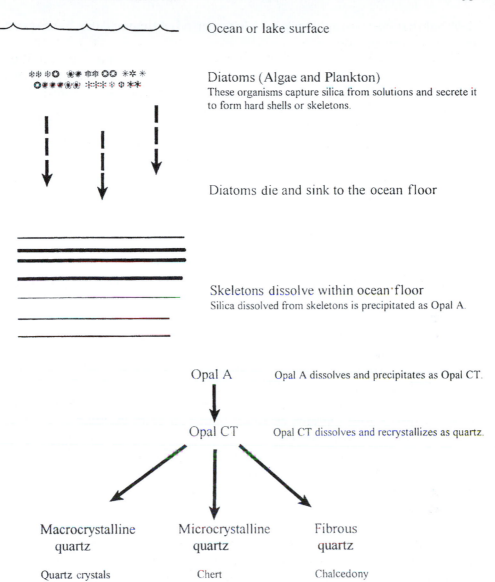

Ocean or lake surface

Diatoms (Algae and Plankton)
These organisms capture silica from solutions and secrete it to form hard shells or skeletons.

Diatoms die and sink to the ocean floor

Skeletons dissolve within ocean floor
Silica dissolved from skeletons is precipitated as Opal A.

Opal A   Opal A dissolves and precipitates as Opal CT.

Opal CT   Opal CT dissolves and recrystallizes as quartz.

Macrocrystalline   Microcrystalline   Fibrous
quartz   quartz   quartz

Quartz crystals   Chert   Chalcedony

Figure 3.2   Schematic diagram of quartz genesis showing silica transformation from diatoms to Opal-A to Opal-CT to crystalline quartz.

siltstones. It can be argued that silicified siltstones and cherts formed in this manner grade into one another depending upon the amount of quartz precipitated. Luedtke (1992) discusses the formation of several different chert sources. Her examples reveal a wide variety of conditions and contexts for the genesis of chert. Chert forms not only in a deep-sea environment, but in shallow waters, and may also form as an indirect result of volcanic activity. In most cases, it is believed that chert forms over a very long period of time and can have several episodes of crystallization.

Metamorphic rocks

Metamorphic rocks are formed from existing rock that has been deformed or metamorphosed by heat and pressure. Metamorphism may alter existing rocks in a variety of ways. Heat and pressure may cause the chemicals within rocks to recombine and grow new minerals, a process that may occur with or without the addition of new elements from circulating fluids and gases (Hamblin and Howard 1971:44). In the presence of heat and pressure mineral grains in existing rock may be stretched or deformed by metamorphism. Under certain conditions minerals may also be recrystallized to form larger grain sizes.

Since metamorphic rocks form as a result of the alteration of existing rock, it is difficult to classify metamorphic rocks on the basis of composition. Initially, they are usually classified by their structure as either foliated or nonfoliated rock. Foliated metamorphic rocks have a planar structure or a parallel arrangement of platy minerals. Foliation results in an appearance that is similar to stratification of layers found in sedimentary rocks. However, foliation is the result of heat and pressure that have realigned minerals; sometimes foliated rocks have minerals aligned so uniformly that the rock breaks along parallel lines or beds to form parallel cleavage. Slate is a good example of a foliated metamorphic rock with parallel cleavage. Other examples of foliated metamorphic rocks include phyllite, schist, and gneiss. Because of parallel minerals most foliated rocks are not adequate raw materials for the production of chipped stone tools as they may fracture along planes.

Nonfoliated rocks are typically massive and structureless, and tend to be composed of only one mineral. The only structure that might appear in nonfoliated metamorphic rocks consists of elongated or deformed grains. Quartzites, marbles, and metaconglomerates are typical kinds of nonfoliated metamorphosed rocks. Of the three, only quartzites are frequently used as chipped stone artifactual material; metaconglomerates tend to be too coarse grained and marbles, although fine grained, tend to be too soft.

Quartzites

Quartzites formed as a result of metamorphism are called metaquartzites. These rocks are very hard because they tend to be made primarily from quartz. Typically metaquartzites result from deformed sandstones. As discussed previously, sandstone is a sedimentary rock composed of cemented beds of river or ocean sand. The sand grains tend to be particles of quartz. Sandstone, like

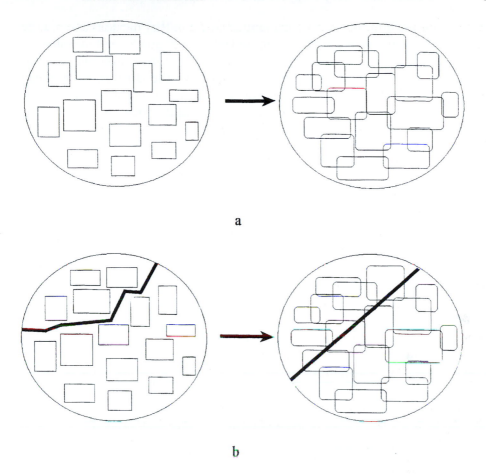

Figure 3.3   Schematic diagram of quartz particle deformation and fracture: (a) sandstone particles metamorphosed to quartzite; (b) fracture line breaking around quartz particles in sandstone and fracture line breaking across quartz particles in quartzite.

most clastic sedimentary rocks, does not break with conchoidal fracture but instead tends to crumble around constituent sand grains. When sandstone is metamorphosed, however, the sand grains tend to interlock as a result of deformation (Figure 3.3a). When the hard quartz sand grains are interlocked, breaks tend to travel across the individual grains resulting in conchoidal fractures (Figure 3.3b). Sand grains are sorted into a range of different sizes and, as a result, some quartzites have extremely small quartz particles and others have particles that can be clearly seen with the naked eye. Finer-grained quartzites tend to fracture with more control than the larger-grained quartzites and are more suitable for flintknapping.

Metaquartzites differ from orthoquartzites because the latter have not been metamorphosed. Orthoquartzites also originate from sandstone, but the individual grains are interlocked by a cementing solution that hardens around the grains. This solution is frequently composed entirely of quartz, but may also be composed of carbonate minerals (Pettijohn 1975:295). Orthoquartzites may be characterized as silicified sandstones. Recognizing the differences between orthoquartzites and metaquartzites is not easy, however. Metaquartzites tend to have deformed interlocking quartz grains and orthoquartzites have cemented, but not deformed, quartz grains. Recognition of individual quartz grains is difficult when the sand grains are extremely small.

Argillites and hornfels

As I discussed above, aphanitic clastic sedimentary rocks are potentially good raw material for chipped stone tool production. However, such fine-grained rocks usually must be hardened by an intrusion of quartz, the process known as silicification. Silicified shales and siltstones are commonly used for chipped stone technology. Yet another process can alter very fine-grained clastic rocks to make them effective for flintworking; this process transforms aphanitic sedimentary rocks such as shale into argillite. Argillites are metamorphosed aphanitic shales or siltstones that are hard, brittle, and homogeneous (Andrefsky 1984:172). They tend to be dull and not have a glassy luster or sheen. One of the primary differences between argillites and silicified shales is that argillites do not have quartz as a usual cementing agent.

Argillites form from low-grade metamorphism, or metamorphism at low temperatures and pressures (Didier 1975:97). Shales and siltstones are formed from sediments compressed near the surface of the Earth under low pressures. Heat may also fuse the sediments in a manner similar to clay being baked into a ceramic. Like ceramics, argillites fracture conchoidally, particularly if they are fresh or have not been exposed to weathering processes. Partially because argillites have little or no quartz they are not as hard as silicified shales or chemical precipitates such as cherts. As a result, argillite patinates relatively quickly. Prehistoric chipped stone tools made of argillite may be almost completely weathered to a soft chalky material that shows little sign of flake scars (Kinsey 1972; Kraft 1975).

Some shales and argillites undergo alteration at high temperatures and pressures. This kind of metamorphism usually recrystallizes minerals within the parent material to produce a crystalline sheen on a dense, brittle rock called hornfel (Didier 1975). Hornfels may be characterized as highly metamorphosed aphanitic sedimentary rocks, are nonfoliated, and are characterized by extremely small particle size.

Summary

The classification of rocks used for chipped stone tool production is important particularly if provenance studies are undertaken. Provenance studies of lithic raw materials are best completed by geochemical techniques. Identification of rock types from macroscopic observations is done by evaluating the rock for composition, texture, and structures. The discussion above emphasizes the genesis of rock forms as it relates to composition, texture, and rock structures. Two things obvious from this discussion related to stone tool technology are: (1) the range of rock variability is limited, and (2) compositional similarity of rock types exists.

What I mean by a limited range of rock variability is that almost all rocks used for chipped stone tool production have very small or invisible grains, are all very hard and brittle, and fracture conchoidally. Rocks used for chipped stone tool production must have all these characteristics. Not all very fine-grained rocks can be used for chipped stone technology nor can all very hard rocks be used. When all of the rocks in the world are considered, only a very limited set of rocks, both numerically and characteristically, can be used for making chipped stone tools.

The other characteristic of rocks used for chipped stone tools that is apparent from the discussion above relates to their classification. Many archaeologists are obsessed with identification of the correct name of a given raw material of an artifact. For instance, it is important for some archaeologists to differentiate between andesite and basalt, or silicious shale and chert. Such differences are important if particular names of raw materials are linked to particular raw-material locations, or to particular technologies or chronologies. Without such connections the names of raw materials can be misleading as they relate to assemblage diversity and content. It is important for archaeologists to realize that one type of raw material can grade into another, and that the line that separates one from another can be arbitrary. Silica may intrude into a mudstone to produce silicified shale, or it may precipitate into an extremely fine-grained marl to form bedded chert; compositionally there may be no difference between the two forms. Observationally there may be no difference between the two raw material types. The only difference may be the genesis of each form, and that may also be quite similar. Silicified shale may have a granular texture due to a parent material that is composed of clastic sediments. However, the texture will be relatively smooth if quartz has fused the rock. Quartzite may have the same kind of granular texture and be composed of approximately the same kinds of minerals, and the difference between the two rock types may be negligible. Extremely fine-grained sandstone that has been metamorphosed into quartzite may be chemically identical to and have the same texture as chert, but differ only in genesis. These examples reveal how similar, both chemically and by texture, various rock types may be, even though they may have different names.

The names of lithic raw materials may not be as important as their properties and characteristics. If a microcrystalline silica can be related to a particular formation or outcrop because of a particular color or because of fossil inclusions, what difference does it make if one researcher calls it a fine-grained ferruginous metaquartzite and another researcher calls it highly silicious siltstone with a high iron content? They both may be correct. Geologists frequently agree to disagree about the names and genesis of particular raw materials. This is partially due to their exposure to the multiple and varied conditions and contexts under which rocks form. Archaeologists interested in lithic raw-material classification could benefit from a better understanding of rock genesis.

4

GETTING STARTED IN LITHIC ANALYSIS: IDENTIFICATION AND CLASSIFICATION

In 1967 it was written that approximately 80% to 90% of an archaeologist's time and energy is spent in classifying materials (Chang 1967:71). It can be argued that classification is still the "cornerstone of archaeological methodology" (Odell 1981:321). One of the principal purposes of classification for use in lithic artifact analysis is as an aid to the summarization of data for descriptive purposes. It is the same reason that classification is used in all fields of human enquiry. Classification reduces variability into manageable units to facilitate communication. Classifying items is ubiquitous for all cultures in all parts of the world (Ellen 1979:6–8). It is impossible to hold a conversation with someone without using a classification system of some kind. Like all phenomena, chipped stone artifacts have an infinite range of morphological variability. Because of this variability, chipped stone artifacts require some kind of ordering before they can be adequately discussed. It is much easier for others to understand the composition of an archaeological site if the reporter lists the number of artifacts found in each class of tool at the site as opposed to describing each tool individually: to say that a site is composed of 95 broken bifaces, 12 whole bifaces, and 589 blades is much more concise than describing the morphology of 696 individual artifacts found at the site. The reduction of variability into classes aids in the understanding of phenomena being investigated or discussed.

The second primary purpose of classification is its role as an heuristic device. Classification of lithic artifacts facilitates comparison and is a way of generating questions about the data. If different lithic artifact assemblages are classified in the same manner (using the same types or classes), the different assemblages can be compared to one another and inferences can be made regarding the similarities or differences between them. For instance, if one site has a high relative percentage of cortical flakes compared to noncortical flakes, and a high relative percentage of larger flakes to smaller flakes, and this site is compared to a second site with no cortical flakes and only relatively small flakes, it may be assumed that different kinds of production activities have taken place at each site. It may also be assumed that the former site was positioned more closely to a source of lithic raw material for stone tool production than the latter, or that earlier stages of tool reduction occurred at the former site than at the latter. These testable assumptions are generated as a result of the classification of artifacts (flakes) into types based upon size and cortex composition.

In lithic analysis, classification of stone tools has traditionally been used for two basic purposes: (1) to identify the diagnostic markers or fossil indicators of prehistoric cultures, and (2) to identify functional or behavioral indicators of those cultures. When used as a cultural marker, stone tool types are frequently identified as traits of a prehistoric people and are usually given temporal or chronological connotation. The inferred function of a prehistoric tool type is used to describe the activity supposed to have taken place at a site. If scrapers are found at a site, for instance, it may be interpreted as a place where animal skins, hides, or wood was worked. If numerous projectile points are found, the site may be interpreted as a hunting camp. The use of stone tool typologies as either culture historical markers or behavioral-functional indices is among the earliest uses of classification in archaeology and continues to be among the most important today.

Lithic artifact analysis begins with the identification and classification of specimens. Before any other kind of analysis can be conducted, some form of identification and/or classification is undertaken. There are numerous articles (Andrefsky 1986b; Benfer and Benfer 1981; Christenson and Read 1977; Gunn and Prewitt 1975; Read 1974; Spaulding 1953) and books (Clarke 1978; Dunnell 1971; Whallon and Brown 1982) on the classification of stone artifacts. This literature explains and argues the positive and negative aspects of various techniques, and discusses the roles, reasons, and values of classification in archaeology as well (Adams and Adams 1991; Cowgill 1982; Ford 1954; Spaulding 1953). I will not dwell upon the various techniques of artifact classification. These can be found in any elementary quantitative methods book. There are also quantitative methods texts written explicitly for archaeologists and anthropologists (Doran and Hodson 1975; Sneath and Sokal 1973; Thomas 1976). This chapter explains the theoretical and methodological principles of stone artifact classification, and introduces a universal classification scheme that is used throughout the later chapters of this book.

Attributes and attribute states

In this book, types are synonymous with classes. A type or a class is a group of similar specimens found in a population. An entire population may be composed of one or more types. A systematic arrangement of types in a population is called a typology. Similarly, the systematic arrangement of classes in a population is called a classification scheme.

Phenomena are classified into types based upon criteria that give each of the types the most internal cohesion and the most external isolation (Cormack

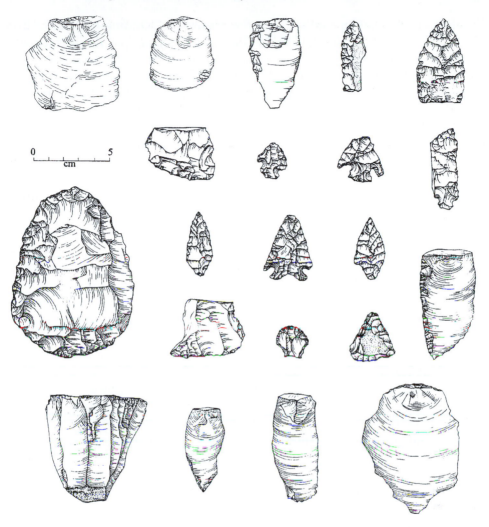

0   5
cm

Figure 4.1   Gross variability found in chipped stone artifacts.

1971:329). This means that most similar items are grouped together into a type and items least similar are separated into different types. Classification schemes attempt to produce types with a great amount of within-group similarity and a great amount of between-group difference. There is much discussion in the quantitative literature on classification regarding how types should be separated and the number of types that should be made from a population of items. For our purposes, it should be realized that there can be as many types in a population of specimens as there are number of specimens in the population, and that there may be as few as one type found in an entire population regardless of the total number of specimens. This means that the number of types is dependent upon the reason for building a classification scheme and the criteria used to make the types. For example, if the specimens shown in Figure 4.1 were to be classified into types, any individual researcher could probably do an adequate job of classification. However, if ten different researchers classified the specimens, there could easily be ten different typologies. Some typologies might have only two types represented and other typologies might have ten. Even if two typologies had the same number of types, there would be a good chance that individual specimens would be grouped differently in the different typologies.

In lithic artifact analysis, classification of specimens may be as dynamic as the life histories of the stone artifacts themselves. In some contexts artifacts may be classified into types based upon morphological similarity. In other contexts those same artifacts may be classified into types based upon lithic raw-material characteristics or upon the function of the artifact. Those same artifacts may be classified entirely by size if size is important for answering a particular question about the prehistoric population being studied. Alternatively, the artifacts may be classified on the basis of many characteristics simultaneously. This leads to an important characteristic necessary for all classification schemes – replicability. For a classification scheme to be useful, it must be replicable so that people can communicate about phenomena in a reasonable and systematic manner.

All replicable typologies recognize a set of criteria or characteristics that constitutes the basis on which specimens are included in various types. All replicable typologies also use a set of rules to administer those criteria. If the criteria and the rules for administering the criteria are known, then the typology can be replicated. In the classification literature, these criteria or characteristics of specimens are known as attributes of specimens. Attributes of specimens may have assorted states depending upon the specimen. For instance, a simple attribute of an object is color. The various states of this attribute may be red, green, blue, pink, or any of an infinite range of hues. Common attributes used in lithic analysis are length, thickness, weight, wear, completeness, and size. It is important to remember that there are an infinite number of attributes that can be measured on any phenomenon. Fortunately, human culture allows us to recognize certain characteristics that are important for understanding various typologies: if we see an organism with fins swimming in the water, we probably recognize it as a fish. However, the attributes that the researcher keys in upon when classifying lithic artifacts are determined by the needs of that researcher.

Attribute scale

Even though there is an infinite number of attributes of any phenomenon, all can be identified as belonging to one of four types on the basis of the potential state of each attribute. These states are recognized by four different kinds of scales: nominal, ordinal, interval, and ratio. In nominal scales all states of the attribute are mutually exclusive and exhaustive. No state of the attribute is greater or better than any other state in nominal scales. Examples of nominal scale attributes would be raw material (obsidian, chert, quartzite), color (brown, white, green), and artifact type (projectile point, burin, core). Many nominal attributes are coded in a binomial manner such as yes/no, present/absent, $+/-$. Attributes on lithic artifacts such as wear or cortex are often recorded in nominal scales. Wear can be either present or absent, just as cortex can be either present or absent.

Ordinal attributes are sometimes referred to as ranked attributes. Ordinal scale attributes involve a relative ordering of attribute states. The ordering of attribute states is along a continuum but the distance between each state is unknown. Ordinal attributes have all the properties of nominal attributes but include the property of rank. Ordinal ranking allows us to interpret the relative value of all states of the attribute. For instance, if $A > B$ and $B > C$, then it follows that $A > C$. Ordinal attributes are commonly used in lithic analysis. The attribute size is often ordinally ranked as small, medium, and large. Platforms on debitage are sometimes ranked on the basis of the amount of preparation found upon them. Ordinally ranked striking platform preparation states may include none, minor, major, and extensive.

Interval scale attributes possess all the characteristics of ordinal scale attributes but also have the property of equal distance between states. Calendar years are a good example of interval scales. For instance, we know that there are exactly five years between AD 1402 and AD 1407, and we also know that the amount of time between AD 1402 and AD 1407 is the same amount of time as between AD 1991 and AD 1996. Each calendar year has an equal interval between itself and the preceding and next calendar year. Another characteristic of interval scale attributes is that the zero point is arbitrary; in other words, there is no true zero on an interval scale. Since zero is arbitrarily assigned, the ratio of two interval states cannot be meaningfully compared. Consider the Fahrenheit temperature scale. This scale has an arbitrary zero point with equal intervals between states. It makes no logical sense to say that 20° F is twice as hot as 10° F. Nor does it make sense to say that someone born in AD 400 is twice as old as someone born in AD 800. Only when zero points are determined by the character of the phenomena themselves can ratio comparisons be correctly made.

Ratio scale attributes have all the properties of interval scale attributes, with the addition of a fixed zero point. The zero point on ratio scale attributes is not arbitrary. Attributes such as length, weight, thickness, and diameter can be measured using a ratio scale. For instance, a microlith that is 60 mm long is exactly twice as long as a microlith that is 30 mm long. An assemblage of debitage that has a mean weight of 10 g per specimen contains specimens half

Table 4.1   *Attribute scale and arithmetic operations*

Scale Operation	Nominal	Ordinal	Interval	Ratio
equal, does not equal	yes	yes	yes	yes
less than, greater than	no	yes	yes	yes
add, subtract	no	no	yes	yes
multiply, divide	no	no	no	yes

Source: Table adapted from Thomas (1976:28).

the mean weight of an assemblage that has a mean weight of 20 g per specimen. Ratio scale variables can be derived from other ratio scale variables. For instance, artifact density can be derived for a site by dividing the number of artifacts by the site unit area. Table 4.1 lists the arithmetic operations permissible for each scale of attribute.

Types and typologies

The attributes selected to characterize types will determine the typology. It would not be uncommon for the same population of artifacts to be classified differently given different attributes used to determine the types. However, it is also possible that different typologies can be generated from the same data when the same attributes are used, but when different rules are administered. The rules administered to the data determine, for instance, the scale of attributes, the sequence of attribute evaluation, and the weight of attributes. Ratio scale data can be converted to interval scale, that can be converted to ordinal scale, that can be converted to nominal scale data. In many cases the investigator has a choice as to which scale he or she wishes to use to view the data. Sometimes typologies give greater weight to certain characteristics than to others. In other words, certain characteristics or attributes are given greater value than others in some typologies, and when that happens, different typologies may result. In the classification of vertebrates into class and order for instance, the manner in which young are born (nominal attribute) may be more important than the length of the spinal column (ratio attribute). However, if these attributes are given the same weight, or if spinal length is given more importance than birth method, the class and order of vertebrates may result in something different from what we are familiar with.

Consciously or subconsciously classification schemes use a set of criteria and a set of rules to construct classes. If, for instance, the artifacts shown in Figure 4.1 are classified, the classification protocol may start by separating the entire population into two groups. Each of these two groups might be separated into another two groups, and each of these four groups may be divided into another pair of groups. Alternatively, specimens that look most alike might be placed together. A second pair could next be put together and then a third pair. One or more of the pairs may be enlarged by adding a specimen or two. This procedure might be followed until all the specimens are assigned to a group. Another strategy might be to select three or four specimens that appear to be most different. Then all other specimens can be grouped with one of the original selections. After all the specimens are put into types, some individuals may be moved from one group to another to make more suitable types. Each of these strategies represents a different kind of classification scheme with a different set of rules governing the formation of types.

Monothetic and polythetic approaches

It is important to understand some of the basic differences in typologies, and this can be done without going into mathematical detail. Doran and Hodson (1975) and Steel and Torrie (1960) provide good reviews of the detailed mathematics. Typologies can be conceived of as either monothetic or polythetic approaches. Monothetic approaches to classification are those based upon the identification of a single attribute at any one time, in contrast to polythetic approaches where no single attribute is the most important at any one time. If you were classifying birds into different types, a monothetic approach would perhaps look at the shape of the beak first and divide the population into birds with pointed beaks, flat beaks, and hooked beaks. The monothetic strategy might next examine size. Each of the groups defined by beak shape could be stratified into groups based upon ordinal size classes or ratio size classes. The monothetic strategy systematically characterizes the population by examining one attribute at a time. A polythetic strategy on the same bird population would classify individuals into groups based upon the overall similarity of individuals without giving preference to any one characteristic. For instance, small birds with flat beaks and webbed feet might be grouped together. Another group might be composed of small birds with hooked beaks and talons. The combination of attributes is more important than any single attribute in the polythetic approach.

Agglomerative and divisive approaches

Another difference in typologies is that of divisive and agglomerative strategies. Agglomerative strategies begin by recognizing each individual as belonging to a type by itself. These individuals are then gradually combined with similar objects to form larger and larger groups. A divisive strategy begins by recognizing the entire population as a single group and gradually divides the population into progressively smaller groups. Both of these strategies can be

Total population

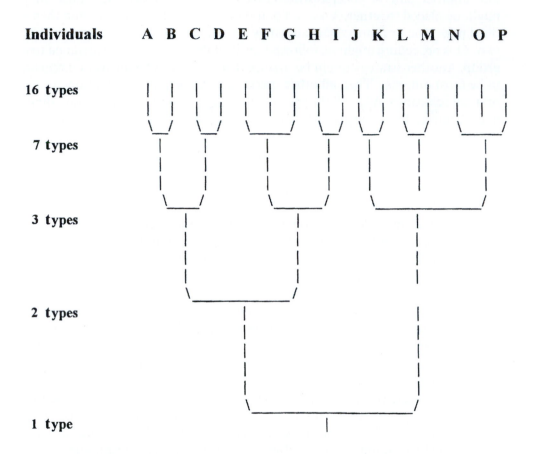

Figure 4.2   Dendrogram showing sixteen individuals in a population separated into as many as sixteen types and as few as one type.

illustrated as a dendrogram (Figure 4.2). One end of the dendrogram encompasses the entire population into a single type and the opposite end of the dendrogram categorizes each individual as a separate type.

Dissection and modal approaches

Probably the grossest form of classification is known as dissection. This is where a population is divided into classes based upon artificial deviation on a variable. Table 4.2 lists weights of individual bifaces. If we were to use a dissection strategy to classify these bifaces, we might group together bifaces based upon a systematic range of weights. Type D1 would include specimens that weighed 1–10 g, Type D2 would include specimens of 11–20 g and so on.

Table 4.2   *Biface weights and typological groups*

Biface no.	Weight (g)	Dissection type	Modal type
01	7	D1	M1
02	8	D1	M1
03	9	D1	M1
04	10	D1	M1
05	11	D2	M1
06	12	D2	M1
07	13	D2	M1
08	13	D2	M1
09	14	D2	M1
10	25	D3	M2
11	26	D3	M2
12	26	D3	M2
13	26	D3	M2
14	27	D3	M2
15	27	D3	M2
16	28	D3	M2
17	28	D3	M2
18	28	D3	M2
19	28	D3	M2
20	28	D3	M2
21	29	D3	M2
22	29	D3	M2
23	29	D3	M2
24	29	D3	M2
25	29	D3	M2
26	48	D5	M3
27	49	D5	M3
28	49	D5	M3
29	50	D6	M3
30	51	D6	M3
31	51	D6	M3
32	51	D6	M3
33	52	D6	M3
34	52	D6	M3
35	52	D6	M3
36	53	D6	M3
37	54	D6	M3
38	54	D6	M3
39	54	D6	M3
40	55	D6	M3

In this particular case there would be six types of bifaces, with Type D3 (20–29 g) having the greatest number of specimens (n = 16), and Type D4 (30–39 g) with no specimens. However, some researchers prefer modal analysis; a modal analysis considers the frequency of occurrences as a criterion for classification

Table 4.3   *Blade length and width values*

Blade no.	Length (cm)	Width (cm)
01	5	2
02	10	1
03	5	2
04	5	2
05	6	2
06	6	2
07	6	2
08	6	3
09	9	2
10	7	4
11	8	4
12	8	5
13	8	5
14	10	2
15	7	3
16	10	1
17	9	1
18	9	1
19	9	1
20	7	3
21	8	4
22	8	1
23	7	3
24	7	3
25	7	3
26	7	4
27	5	2
28	6	2
29	6	2
30	6	1
31	6	2
32	6	3
33	6	2

of individuals to groups. The data in Table 4.2 show a trimodal distribution based upon biface weight. Most bifaces fall within one of three places in the weight range. In this case Type M1 includes bifaces weighing from 7 to 14 g, Type M2 includes bifaces from 25 to 29 g and Type M3 includes bifaces from 48 to 55 g.

Typologies using single attributes may not be the most effective because variability in the population may be hidden when one looks only at a single attribute. For example, if we were interested in developing blade types using a modal approach we might measure length of each blade and stratify the population into types based upon the number of modes. Similarly, we might measure the width of each blade to do the same thing. Consider the length and width values for thirty-three blades in Table 4.3. When the values are plotted by count for length, a single mode appears in the frequency distribution (Figure 4.3a). Width values also reveal a single mode in the distribution (Figure 4.3b). This distribution suggests that the blade population has only a single type based upon examination of one attribute at a time. However, when the same data are plotted with two attributes simultaneously, two modes emerge from the population (Figure 4.4). A bimodal distribution suggests that more than one type of blade might be found in the population. The distribution of blades shows two cluster groups. The longer blades tend to be narrower than the shorter blades.

Association and disassociation

The difference between association and disassociation is an important concept in classification. One way to understand the difference between these two terms in classification is to ask the question, "are types defined as a result of significant association of attributes or are types made by the lack of significant association?" Classification schemes based upon association typically use a test of statistical significance to determine types. A good example would be the use of a chi-square test to determine association and ultimately types. Figure 4.5 shows two 2×2 contingency tables with attribute data for bifaces. Figure 4.5a shows that twenty of the bifaces have haft elements and twenty do not. Of the twenty which have haft elements ten have been resharpened and ten have not be resharpened. Ten of the bifaces with no haft elements were also resharpened. If a chi-square test were performed on these data, no significant association would be found for these attributes. Since there is no association, no types would be defined. Conversely, if the biface data were structured as shown in Figure 4.5b, types would be based upon the association of attributes. A chi-square test would indicate significant association. In this example, bifaces without haft elements tend to be resharpened and some archaeologists might believe that such artifacts were used as knives. As the edges get dull from cutting, they get resharpened. Bifaces with haft elements tend not to be resharpened and might be considered projectiles of some sort. Such bifaces may have been hafted onto a shaft or foreshaft of an arrow or spear.

Other researchers believe that association of attributes is not the best way to define types, and that types are better defined by disassociation or discontinuities in attributes. Researchers who believe that disassociation is more important than association for typologies also believe that differences between items are more important than similarities between items when defining types (Hodson 1982). Figure 4.5a shows no association between variables, and a classification scheme based upon association would indicate no types. However, if the

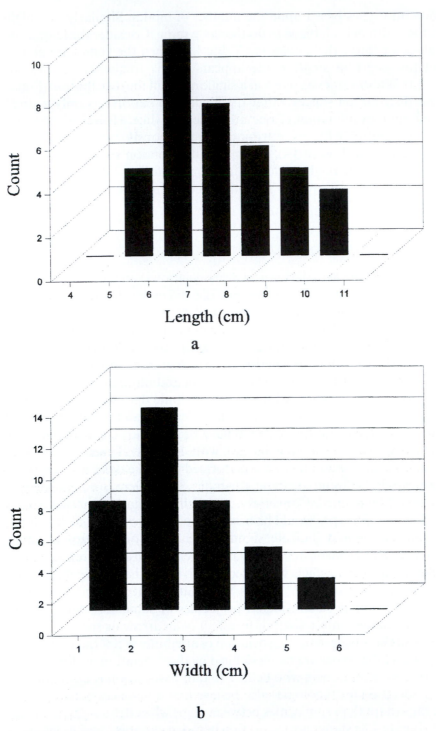

Figure 4.3   Unimodal distribution of blade characteristics: (a) frequency by blade length; (b) frequency by blade width.

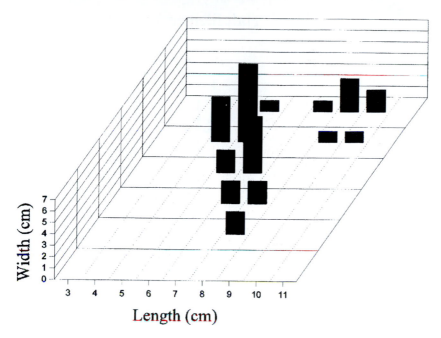

Figure 4.4   Two-dimensional plot of frequency data from Figure 4.3. A bimodal distribution becomes apparent when blade characteristics are viewed simultaneously.

dichotomous variables in this example were something more familiar, we might have a better understanding of types within the population. Figure 4.6 presents the same distribution of data as shown in Figure 4.5a, but the attributes are now gender and age. A test of association such as chi-square would show no significant association, and no types if we were using a typology based upon association. However, it is apparent that four legitimate types of organisms are shown in the contingency table; mature males, mature females, immature males, and immature females. This example suggests that significant association between variables may not be required to form types, and that unassociated variables may be used for classification.

A basic chipped stone typology

From the previous discussion it is apparent that there can be any number of typologies for chipped stone artifacts. Typologies are universal and fundamental in the broad field of archaeology and within chipped stone artifact analysis in particular. One of the primary purposes of chipped stone typologies is to develop diagnostic types or assemblages that can be keyed to a chronology

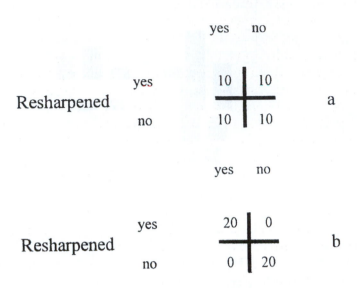

Figure 4.5   Contingency tables for biface characteristics of resharpening and haft elements: (a) frequency shows no significant association between characteristics; (b) frequency shows significant association between biface characteristics.

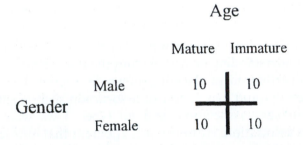

Figure 4.6   Example of gender and age characteristics with no significant association, yet where four viable types are recognized: mature males, mature females, immature males, and immature females. Example taken from Hodson (1982).

(Frison 1991:38–116; MacDonald and Allsworth-Jones 1994; Ritchie 1965; Straus and Clark 1986:367–82; West 1981). Different temporal periods or cultural traditions are then recognized at sites or in collections by diagnostic artifact types. There are literally thousands of typologies found in the literature for different temporal spans in different regions of the world. Specific typologies are even developed for very small geographic areas. An example is provided by the state of Oregon (in the Pacific Northwest United States); it is divided into five geographic areas and each contains a specific diagnostic typology of chipped stone artifacts (Aikens 1993).

Beyond chronological typologies, there are functional typologies that group artifacts together on the basis of their apparent or perceived function. These kinds of typologies usually equate the form of an artifact with its function. Chipped stone artifacts with a steep edge produced by removal of small flakes are usually called scrapers for instance. If the modified edge is found on the distal end of the original detached piece it is usually called an endscraper. Scrapers are found all over the world and in many different temporal periods, and are usually interpreted as hide working tools (Hayden 1979a; Kamminga 1982). The function of endscrapers as tools used to remove hair or flesh from hides has been challenged by some (Odell 1981; Siegel 1984), but many archaeologists still equate the form of this tool with a hide scraping function. The same can be said about any number of tool forms. Terms used to identify various shapes of tools, such as dart points, gravers, drills, strike-a-lights, knives, and netsinkers also connote certain functions in many circumstances. Dart points are used as projectiles on Atlatl spears (Winters 1969), gravers are used to incise bone (Oakley 1957), and strike-a-lights are used to start fires (Werner 1972). In many cases these functional interpretations may be correct. However, in other cases it has been shown that the form of an artifact does not necessarily match its assumed function (Lewenstein 1987; Odell 1981).

It is not within the scope of this book to describe chipped stone artifact typologies from all over the world, or to review the most common typologies; it is also not intended to be a forum to explore the function of various chipped stone artifact types. However, to communicate about various methods and techniques of lithic analysis in later sections of the book, a universal lithic artifact typology is introduced that, although very basic, is intended to facilitate communication about chipped stone artifact shapes. The typology is based upon the morphology of chipped stone artifacts and is not intended to reflect function or chronology of artifacts. The typology described below is designed only to discriminate the shapes of chipped stone artifacts, yet it is broad enough to include all chipped stone artifact shapes from across the world, and specific enough to identify mutually exclusive unambiguous types. It is further limited to chipped stone artifacts, and includes both tools and debitage. Even though terms such as projectile point and flake drill are used to describe various types, these type names do not assume a function – they assume only a morphology. This kind of basic typology can be modified, collapsed, or expanded to address specific questions put forward by specific researchers. For example, the category of hafted biface may be expanded to develop a typology of hafted bifaces for any specific region. The flake category may be modified so that a typology of flakes is developed that accounts for attributes related to their technology such as striking platform type, thickness, width, bulb of force, etc. The basic chipped stone typology presented below is

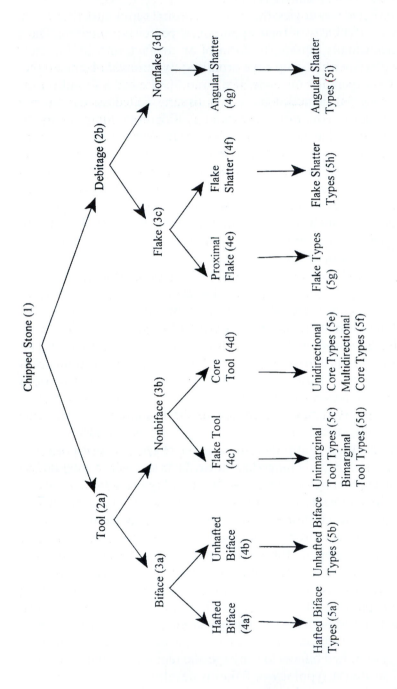

Figure 4.7 Generalized morphological typology for all chipped stone tools expressed as a nominal variable flow chart. Based upon Andrefsky and Bender (1988:Figure V.1) and subsequently modified by Andrefsky *et al.* (1994a:101).

(1) Human Modification (yes = tools, no = debitage).
(2a) Bifacial Flaking (yes = bifaces, no = nonbifaces).
(2b) On Flake (yes = flake debitage, no = nonflake debitage).
(3a) Contains Haft Element (yes = hafted biface, no = unhafted biface).
(3b) On Flake (yes = flake tool, no = core tool).
(3c) Contains Platform (yes = proximal flake, no = flake shatter).
(3d) Angular or Blocky Shatter.

intended to be modified to suit the needs of the researcher, and is presented in order that a common terminology is understood by all readers of this volume. This basic typology for chipped stone artifacts is referred to in the narrative below as the morphological typology – underscoring its reference to artifact shape only.

This terminology covers chipped stone artifacts that were defined in chapter 2 as those objective pieces and detached pieces produced as a result of percussion or pressure flaking technology. In both kinds of technology the size and shape of detached pieces are usually anticipated and intentionally removed. In most cases, the lithic raw materials used to make chipped stone artifacts are homogeneous, very fine grained, and cryptocrystalline, as described in chapter 3. Artifacts produced from grinding and pecking are not included within the chipped stone group. Furthermore, the morphological typology is monothetic, divisive, and recognizes nominal scale attributes.

Tools and nontool artifacts

Figure 4.7 illustrates the morphological typology, and the discussion in the remainder of this chapter refers to items listed on this morphological flow chart. All stone implements produced as a result of chipped stone technology are considered chipped stone artifacts. The first dichotomy made in the morphological typology is between artifacts that are tools and artifacts that are not tools. All chipped stone tools (Figure 4.7, 2a) located on the left side of the chart are objective pieces that have been intentionally modified or modified by use to produce a product that has less weight than before it was modified. Materials that are removed from objective pieces during the shaping process constitute debitage (Figure 4.7, 2b).

Since this book deals only with macroscopic approaches to lithic analysis some kinds of wear found on artifacts may not be observable. For instance, microscopic striations and polishes may not be visible to the unaided eye and the artifacts involved are therefore treated as nontool artifacts. This is a drawback to using only macroscopic analysis on lithic artifacts. However, lithic artifacts that have been used as tools often do show signs of modification visible to the unaided eye. Also, those artifacts that reveal only microscopic traces of wear may not necessarily be tools. Such slight traces of wear have been found to be caused by nonhuman, post-depositional agencies such as sheet wash, freeze and thaw, and trampling (Coffey 1994; Knudson 1979; Prentiss and Romanski 1989; Shackley 1974; Tringham *et al.* 1974).

Biface tools

Tools are initially stratified by the presence of bifacial flaking. To review, bifaces are objective pieces that have been extensively modified, and have two

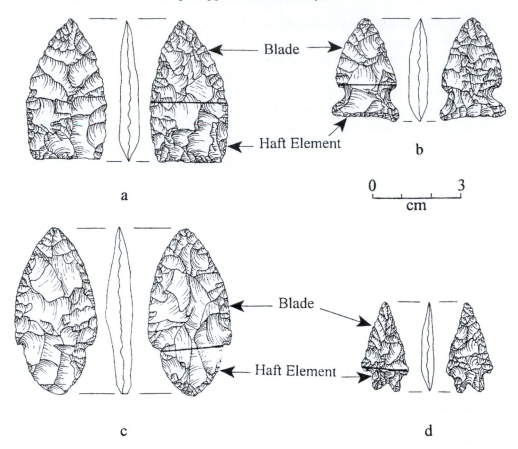

Figure 4.8   Location of blade elements and haft elements on selected biface forms: (a) lanceolate biface; (b) side-notched biface; (c) contracting-stemmed biface; (d) basal-notched biface.

sides or faces that meet to form a single edge that circumscribes the entire artifact; both faces show evidence of previous flake removals (Figure 2.9). If the tool has bifacial flaking it is identified as a biface (Figure 4.7, 3a), and if not, it is included within the nonbifacial group (Figure 4.7, 3b). The classification scheme for bifaces next examines whether a haft element is present or absent on the biface. A haft element is the location on a biface that articulates with a handle or shaft. This is the place where the biface is attached to another element of a composite tool (Figure 2.10). Some hafted bifaces were attached directly to an arrow shaft. Other bifaces were attached directly to a handle or a foreshaft that could be inserted into a spear or used to hold the tool in the hand as a cutting or sawing implement. Figure 4.8 illustrates the location of the haft element and blade on variously shaped specimens. Note that the haft element can be recognized on bifaces by the presence of notches or shoulders, or by the presence of wear along the edges of the biface. That portion of the biface used as a haft element often has ground or dulled edges so the materials used to lash the biface to the handle are not cut. The ground edges on the haft element may also be produced as a result of wear from the biface being inserted into a socket. Hafted bifaces such as the lanceolate form shown in Figure 4.8a have evidence of a haft element not only by wear present on the haft area, but also by the slightly asymmetrical shape of the biface. In many cases hafted bifaces are used as knives and are resharpened when the knife becomes dull from use (Goodyear 1974). These bifaces are usually resharpened while still being attached to the handle, with the result that the blade portion of the biface becomes progressively smaller and the haft portion of the biface retains its original shape and size. In the morphological typology, bifaces with haft elements are called hafted bifaces (Figure 4.7, 4a), and those without haft elements are called other bifaces (Figure 4.7, 4b). The hafted biface category includes all those items traditionally recognized as arrow points, spear points, hafted knives, and hafted drills. The other biface category includes all those bifaces that simply do not have haft elements, and are known as preforms, point tips, and bifacial knives, etc. Again, the morphological typology does not infer function for any of these artifacts. Chapter 7 provides a more detailed discussion of bifaces and biface analysis.

Flake tools

The nonbiface category of tools (Figure 4.7, 3b) is also stratified into two groups based upon the presence or absence of flake characteristics. If the nonbifacial tool is made on a flake it belongs in the flake tool category (Figure 4.7, 4c); if it is not made on a flake it belongs in the nonflake tool category (Figure 4.7, 4d). Flake characteristics are discussed in chapter 2 and again in more detail in chapter 5 and include such things as a dorsal and ventral surface, a striking platform, proximal and distal ends, and others features. To review, flake tools are objective pieces that have been produced from a flake blank that has been modified to some extent, and may no longer possess the original flake characteristics. When this is the case, it can be difficult to determine the difference between flake tools (Figure 4.7, 4c) and nonflake tools (Figure 4.7, 4d). In the morphological typology flake tools are defined as those tools that have the remains of an objective piece with a recognizable ventral and dorsal surface. If the nonbifacial tool does not have a recognizable dorsal and ventral surface it is considered a nonflake tool. It must be remembered that flakes and flake tools only have a single ventral and single dorsal surface. Nonbifacial tools are considered nonflake tools if they have more than two surfaces or have two surfaces but neither can be identified as either a dorsal or ventral surface.

The flake tool category (Figure 4.7, 4c) is divided into three types: unimarginal flake tools (Figure 4.7, 5a), bimarginal flake tools (Figure 4.7, 5b), and combination flake tools (Figure 4.7, 5c). By definition all flake tools have been

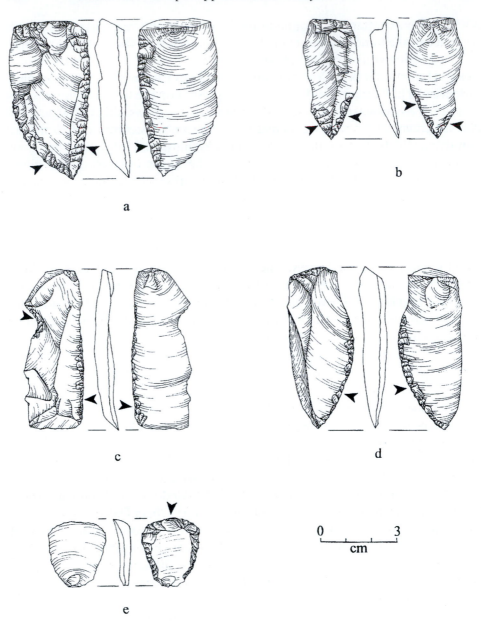

Figure 4.9   Flake tool examples: (a) combination flake tool with bimarginal and unimarginal retouched edges; (b) bimarginal flake tool with two edges worked bimarginally; (c) combination flake tool with one bimarginally worked edge and one unimarginally worked edge; (d) bimarginal flake tool with one worked edge; (e) unimarginal flake tool with continuous retouch around approximately 80% of the tool edge.

modified by humans in some manner. Human modification is a result of intentional retouching or chipping of the flake to form a certain kind of edge, surface, or shape. On the other hand, human modification can also be the result of tool use. In the latter case, an unmodified flake may have been used as a cutting or scraping tool, and as a result of being used, the tool becomes modified with wear. In situations where unmodified flakes have been drafted into service as tools, the wear produced on the tool varies depending upon the manner in which the tool has been used and the material being worked. For our purposes, all recognizable human modification on flakes will qualify the artifact as a flake tool. In some cases both intentional retouch and usewear are found on the tool. The flake is included as one of the three flake tool types if the modification is recognizable, regardless of how the human modification was produced on it.

The difference between the flake tool types has to do with the location of the wear or retouch. If a flake tool has been modified only on either the ventral or the dorsal surface it is considered a unimarginal flake tool (Figure 4.7, 5a). Some unimarginal flake tools will have been modified on both the dorsal and ventral surfaces but at different locations on each surface. Bimarginal flake tools (Figure 4.7, 5b) have been modified on both the ventral and dorsal surfaces at the same location on the flake. In such circumstances the modified edge is very similar to a bifacial edge, the difference being the extent of the modification. Bifaces have flakes removed across the entire surface of the tool. Bimarginal flake tools have flakes removed only from the edge or margin of the tool. Figure 4.9 illustrates several examples of unimarginal and bimarginal flake tools. Different places on flake tools are frequently used as cutting or scraping edges. It is not uncommon to find several different places on a tool that have been modified (Keeley 1982). In this regard, a flake tool may have a unimarginal edge at one location and another unimarginal edge at a different location. In such a case the tool is still classified as a unimarginal flake tool in the morphological typology. Similarly bimarginal modification may occur at more than one location on the artifact and it will still be classified as a bimarginal flake tool (Figure 4.9b). There may also be cases with unimarginal modification at one location and bimarginal modification at another location on an artifact; this artifact is classified as a combination flake tool (Figures 4.7, 5c; 4.9a, c).

Classic flake tool forms such as endscrapers and backed blades can easily be fitted into the morphological typology. For instance, endscrapers are usually modified by retouch on the dorsal surface only, and usually at the distal end of the original flake. Such a tool will be classified as a unimarginal flake tool. If the endscraper has a lateral margin also modified on both the dorsal and ventral surfaces, it will be classified as a combination tool. Microliths with various degrees of modification may also be classified using this morphological typology. Remember, the morphological typology presented here is purposely broad to encompass all variations in tool form. The typology is intended to be expanded if it is necessary to subdivide flake tools into more types for analytical purposes. It can also incorporate established regional names for various shapes, such as microblades, backed blades, drills, and microliths.

Core tools

Core tools are the final major category of nonbifacial tools, that are also nonflake tools (Figure 4.7, 4d). By definition these artifacts must contain some kind of modification such as retouch or wear, and they must not have characteristics that classify them as flake or bifacial tools. These tools are called core tools in the morphological typology, and for the most part they fall within the traditional category of cores. A core is an objective piece that has had flakes removed from its surface. Some archaeologists believe that the primary purpose of a core is to supply flakes that can then be used for the production of various flake tools. As discussed previously in chapter 2 cores may also be used as cutting or chopping tools and the purpose of a core can vary depending upon the context of its use. Some archaeologists believe that cores should be included in the nontool category of chipped stone artifacts since they may only have been used as sources of raw material and may have no other utilitarian function (Shott 1993). However, in the morphological typology cores are included with tools and not with debitage because of the presence or absence of human modification. Cores, like all other tools are objective pieces and debitage consists of detached pieces. Core tools (Figure 4.7, 4d) do not necessarily include only traditionally recognized cores, but also all chipped stone tools that are nonbifacial and not produced on a flake. For instance, a block of stone such as obsidian may possess an edge that has small flakes removed to form a serrated cutting tool. Such an artifact would not be classified as a biface, even if the edge were bimarginally retouched. Nor would the artifact be classified as a flake tool since there is no single recognizable dorsal and ventral surface; it would be classified as a core tool. Another example would be a river nodule that has had several flakes removed to form a cutting edge. Such a tool may have had the flakes detached so that each of the flakes could be used as a cutting tool. In such a case the nodule would fit well within the traditional definition of a core. On the other hand, the flakes may have simply been discarded, in which case the primary purpose of flake detachment would have been to shape the objective piece. In either case, however, the morphology of the objective piece would be the same. A third possibility is that both the objective piece and the detached pieces were sought as tools and tool blanks. In each circumstance, the modified river nodule would be considered a core tool (Figure 4.7, 4d).

A core in this typology is best understood as a modified nucleus or mass of chippable stone rather than a tool with some particular kind of function. The nucleus is not a recognizable flake nor is it a biface. There are two general types of core tools: unidirectional (Figure 4.7, 5d) and multidirectional (Figure 4.7, 5e). The difference between the two core tool types is the number of directions in which detached pieces have been removed. These detached pieces may include large flakes that are removed from an entire surface or the detached pieces may have tiny retouch along a single edge. If detached pieces are removed from a single direction it is classified as a unidirectional core tool, and if detached pieces are removed in more than one direction it is classified as a multidirectional core tool (Figures 2.3, 2.4, 2.5).

Debitage

The right side of the morphological typology includes all the nontool chipped stone artifacts or debitage (Figure 4.7, 2b). Debitage represents the discarded and unused detached pieces of lithic material produced from the reduction of an objective piece. Debitage is initially stratified into artifacts that have flake characteristics (Figure 4.7, 3c) and artifacts that do not have flake characteristics (Figure 4.7, 3d). The flake characteristics that are important for this typology are recognizable dorsal and ventral surfaces. If an artifact contains a single recognizable dorsal and single recognizable ventral surface it is considered flake debitage (Figure 4.7, 3c). If single dorsal and ventral surfaces are not recognizable the artifact is classified as nonflake debitage (Figure 4.7, 3d).

Flake debitage is divided into one of two types: flakes (Figure 4.7, 4e) and flake shatter (Figure 4.7, 4f). Flakes include all flake debitage with a discernable point-of-applied-force or striking platform (Figure 4.10). Flake shatter includes all flake debitage with no recognizable striking platform. One of the reasons flake debitage is stratified in this manner is because of unambiguous morphological differences between flakes and flake shatter. Another reason is that flake debitage may break into numerous pieces at any time in the reduction and depositional history of the artifact, and researchers who rely upon flake counts in analysis can adjust for breakage by segregating flakes and flake shatter. For example, skilled flintknappers can remove the size and shape of the detached piece they want from an objective piece by using a single impact. The detached piece may be removed as a single item. Less skilled flintknappers may remove a flake that breaks into two or more fragments upon impact. If there are only a few fragments they may be refitted to reveal the complete size and shape of the flake. In such situations, only one of the flake fragments contains the point-of-applied-force. A flake may also break after it has been deposited onto the site by trampling and other post-depositional processes. In either case, only one of the flake fragments contains the point-of-applied-force. Reduction of an objective piece usually produces only a single specimen that contains a point-of-applied-force for each impact, and this applies to pressure flaking as well as percussion flaking. As such, comparisons of flake debitage

Proximal End   Proximal End

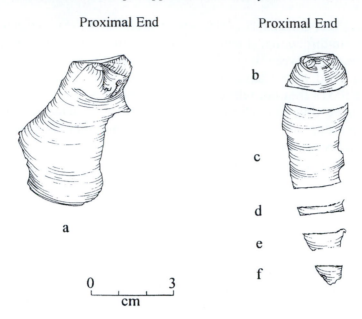

Figure 4.10   Flake debitage specimens: (a) complete flake with intact point of
applied force; (b) proximal end of broken flake with step fracture termination;
(c–f) flake shatter with no evidence of a striking platform.

counts from one assemblage to another to determine density or composition
may be extremely misleading. However, separating flake debitage into flakes
(Figure 4.7, 4e) and flake shatter (Figure 4.7, 4f) might permit the investigator
to obtain more accurate comparative data. An assemblage that contains a
single unbroken flake is not necessarily ten times smaller than an assemblage
that contains a single flake that has shattered into ten pieces. If such assemblages were divided into flakes and flake shatter, both would contain one
specimen with its characteristic point-of-applied-force. Note that one of the
specimens in Figure 4.10 is composed of five individual fragments. All of the
five fragments contain evidence of a dorsal and a ventral surface, but only one
of the five contains evidence of a striking platform. Chapter 5 introduces flake
debitage analysis and describes flake debitage characteristics associated with
broken specimens in more detail.

All detached pieces do not necessarily break into shapes with recognizable
dorsal and ventral surfaces. In the morphological typology, such pieces are
called nonflake debitage (Figure 4.7, 3d). Nonflake debitage may include large
blocky chunks of lithic material removed from a relatively large objective
piece, or it may include very tiny pieces of lithic material produced when a
detached piece shatters on impact. Nonflake debitage is primarily recognized
by the lack of a recognizable single dorsal and single ventral surface. In the
morphological typology all nonflake debitage is called angular shatter (Figure

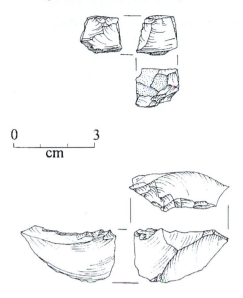

Figure 4.11   Examples of nonflake angular shatter debitage.

4.7, 4g). Figure 4.11 illustrates various examples of nonflake debitage. Non-flake debitage or angular shatter may have surfaces that resemble, or may have been, dorsal or ventral surfaces at one time; however, on angular shatter it is not possible to determine these surfaces given the shape of the specimen. Angular shatter frequently has more than two flat surfaces.

Summary

In some regions of the world, chipped stone typologies used by some or most researchers are composed of a combination of morphological, functional, and contextual characteristics. For instance, a tool might be called a chopper by one researcher because the edge may appear battered, presumably from a chopping function. That same tool might be called a core by another because of its overall shape. Others may call it a core chopper or a core tool depending upon the context of the site from which it was recovered. I must emphasize that the morphological typology presented here is a very broad scheme to sort chipped stone artifacts by shape and is not meant to take the place of any existing regional typologies, that are, in fact, encouraged. However, the mor-phological typology presented here is general enough to encompass most regional typologies. Each of the nine types described may be expanded into a separate more detailed typology or specialized analysis can be conducted on attributes and variables found on each of the types. For instance, under the morphological type, flake tools (Figure 4.7, 4c), a more detailed classification scheme could be recognized that includes different sizes such as tools made on blades, bladelets, and microliths. Any of these could be further divided into types based upon shape of various microliths, such as rods, triangles, and rhomboids. Such designations are encouraged, particularly if researchers in the area of study have previously recognized various shapes and sizes of chipped stone tools.

A major reason for this morphological typology is to standardize a set of artifact shapes with a standardized artifact terminology. As descriptions of analysis are presented in subsequent chapters, standardized terminology will expedite communication about various artifact shapes.

In addition to being a general or universal typology based upon variability in tool shape, the morphological typology is easy to use with mutually exclusive types recognized by standardized attributes and rules for administering attributes. In this sense the morphological typology is replicable. For those researchers who may not be familiar with chipped stone tool analysis, the morphological typology can be a good way to begin the analysis of a chipped stone assemblage.

5

FLAKE DEBITAGE ATTRIBUTES

In the morphological typology presented above, flake debitage includes all stone artifact types shown in Figure 4.7, 3c. When researchers evaluate or read debitage analysis studies they often become frustrated because of the lack of consistent terminology (Sullivan and Rozen 1985). A study may talk about flake thickness or number of dorsal ridges, but not explain how either is measured. Flakes almost always vary in thickness from the proximal to the distal end. It is important to explain how thickness was measured for any particular study. The same can be true for counting dorsal ridges. What is the definition of a dorsal ridge? Most flakes have several prominent ridges on the dorsal surface but if examined very closely, flakes may have hundreds of dorsal ridges. Which ridges are counted, and what are the factors that determine if a dorsal ridge is counted or discounted? There are two chapters in this book that introduce flake debitage analysis, this chapter and the one that follows. This chapter is purely descriptive and presents standardized techniques to recognize and record attributes on flake debitage. In a sense, this chapter emphasizes "how" flake debitage attributes are recorded and not "why" they are recorded. Chapter 6 provides more detailed discussions and review on "why" the various flake debitage attributes are recorded and also describes various techniques of debitage analysis. The analysis of flake debitage attributes are separated in this manner for two reasons. The first is that many debitage studies emphasize why flake attributes are important for understanding technological behavior but never show how to record such attributes in a consistent and reliable manner (Flenniken 1978; Magne 1989; Magne and Pokotylo 1981; Patterson and Sollberger 1978; Tomka 1989). Replicability in flake debitage recording and measurement is not only crucial for later analysis and interpretation, it is also very difficult to do consistently. The second reason I separated the "how" from the "why" in this manner is that I feel it is important first to identify precisely how the flake debitage attributes are defined and recognized before discussing the various merits and problems with using various debitage attributes in analysis.

Debitage condition and termination

Flake termination is the condition or character of the distal end of detached pieces. Four types of flake terminations were introduced in chapter 2 (Figure

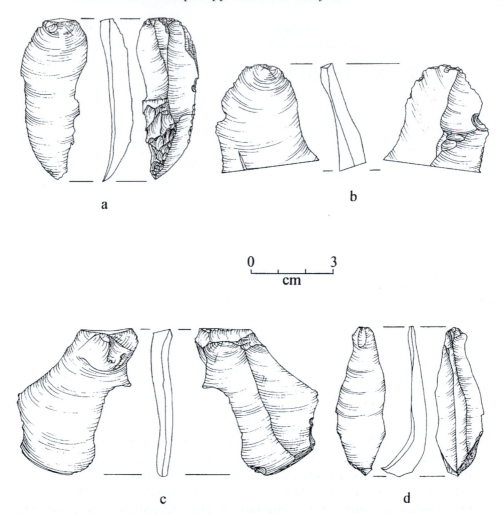

Figure 5.1   Flake termination examples: (a) feathered termination; (b) stepped termination; (c) hinged termination; (d) plunging or overshot termination.

2.8). Smooth terminations that gradually shear the flake from the objective piece are called feathered terminations (Figure 5.1a). Flakes which snap or shatter during removal to form an almost 90° angle with the ventral surface are called step fractures or terminations (Figure 5.1b). When the distal end of the detached piece is rounded or sloped it is usually called a hinge fracture (Figure 5.1c). Hinge fractures occur when the force of the impact used to detach the piece turns or rolls away from the objective piece. When the force of the impact rolls toward the objective piece it is called an overshot or plunging termina-tion. Overshot terminations usually remove a large portion of the objective piece that is attached to the flake at the distal end (Figure 5.1d). Flake terminations not only reveal information about the kinds of forces used to

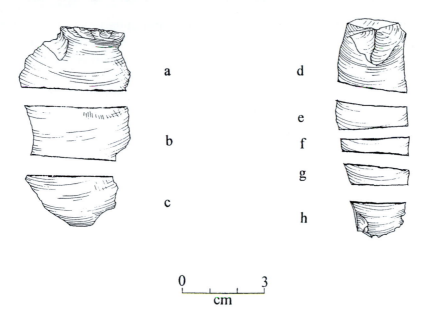

Figure 5.2   Shattered flake fragments observed from the ventral side: (a, d) proximal ends with attached point of applied force; (b, e–g) medial fragments; (c, h) distal ends with feathered terminations.

detach the piece, but also are very important for interpreting other flake characteristic data. For instance, if flake length and width are measured for all detached specimens, it would be important to know which flakes had feathered, hinged, and overshot terminations (complete specimens) and which flakes had step terminations (broken specimens).

As with flake termination, the condition of a flake may tell a great deal about how the flake was removed and how other flake attributes should be interpreted. A flake that shatters into five fragments each weighing 2 g may mean something very different from five whole flakes each weighing 2 g. Some researchers have recorded debitage condition as simply broken or unbroken (Mierendorf and Bobalik 1983; Odell 1989:166; Sullivan and Rozen 1985). Others have identified broken flakes as distal, medial, and proximal ends depending upon the attributes found on the specimen (Crabtree 1972:22; Lyons 1994:23). Figure 5.2 illustrates examples of flakes that have been broken in one or more places. Proximal fragments are noted by the letters a and d. Distal fragments are marked as c and h, and medial fragments are noted as b, e, f, and g.

Proximal fragments include all those specimens that contain a striking platform. These specimens are included as type 4e on the morphological typology chart in chapter 4 (Figure 4.7). Proximal fragments may be whole flakes or broken flakes. In all cases proximal ends have an intact point of applied force or striking platform. Flakes that contain the proximal end are probably the most important of the three flake conditions because they represent the minimal number of impacts in a production process. If a detached piece breaks into five different fragments upon impact there is a high probability that only one of those fragments will contain the striking platform. In this sense, all proximal flakes, whether they are broken or intact can provide uniform production information regarding the number of impacts required for tool production or core reduction.

Medial flake fragments include all those broken flake specimens that have no proximal end and a stepped distal end. Medial fragments may have been produced during detachment or they may have been produced intentionally by the tool maker. It is not uncommon to find detached pieces, such as blades, that have been snapped into several fragments for insertion into a composite bone harpoon. Microliths from Mesolithic sites are frequently interpreted as intentionally broken or snapped to fit hafting contexts (Myers 1989). Intentionally snapped pieces or pieces broken upon detachment may exhibit step or hinge fractures.

When a detached piece snaps into two fragments, one fragment will contain the striking platform (proximal end). The other fragment will have the distal end and is called the distal flake fragment. A proximal flake that step fractures during detachment will not have a feathered termination. If that flake were subsequently to be broken into two pieces, one fragment would contain the striking platform (proximal flake fragment), and the second piece would contain the step termination. In this case, the second piece would be classified as a medial fragment. Otherwise, there would be no way to discern the difference between medial fragments with step fractures and distal fragments with step terminations. By this definition, all distal flake fragments have no striking platform and have intact distal ends with feathered, hinged, or plunging terminations.

Debitage striking platforms

Striking platforms on debitage has been examined and measured in many different ways. Variability in striking platforms has been used to determine type of hammer used (Cotterell and Kamminga 1987; Frison 1968; Hayden and Hutchings 1989), type of objective piece being modified (Magne and Pokotylo 1981), and stage of biface production (Dibble and Whittaker 1981; Johnson 1989; Katz 1976). In experiments where obsidian cobbles were reduced to bifaces, Gilreath (1984) monitored striking platform type and striking platform preparation. She found that as the stage of production increased from the original nodule to a finished biface the amount of striking platform preparation increased. Similarly, striking platform types changed from stage to stage. Magne and Pokotylo (1981:36) have found that biface production from a flake blank produces a greater range of striking platform scar count on debitage than does core reduction. This is similar to Tomka's results with striking platform facet counts that show greater frequencies of multifaceted striking platforms on biface and dart production debitage than on core reduction debitage (1989:147). Striking platform scar counts or facets have also been used to determine stage of biface production (Morrow 1984:21). Generally, the greater the number of facets found on debitage striking platforms, the later the stage of biface production. Magne and Pokotylo (1981) have also found that striking platforms on debitage produced during bifacial manufacture can be discriminated from striking platforms associated with core reduction, and more grinding has been found associated with biface and point production than with core reduction (Tomka 1989:147).

Striking platform width can be useful in determining stage of reduction (Pokotylo 1978). It has been shown that striking platform width correlates with the size of debitage that also varies with reduction stages or sequences (Magne and Pokotylo 1981). Odell has shown that striking platform width and striking platform thickness are good overall discriminators of reduction trajectories (1989:185). Other characteristics of the striking platform are also useful for discriminating various stages of reduction and for identification of the objective piece. For instance, striking platform angle on biface debitage has been shown to have an inverse relationship to degree of reduction (Dibble and Whittaker 1981). As such, it has been used to determine reduction stages or sequences in bifaces (Raab *et al.* 1979). Striking platform type or class has been used to identify core reduction debitage from biface production debitage (Andrefsky *et al.* 1994a, 1994b; Lyons 1994; Shott 1994:80).

Experimental research clearly recognizes striking platform attributes as discriminators of reduction stages and the tool types produced. Unfortunately, I have found that striking platform characteristics are among the most difficult to measure consistently with accuracy. Discussed below are several common striking platform attributes used in lithic analysis, some of which I feel are useful while others are too problematic to be used.

Striking platform angle and facet count

Probably the most difficult striking platform characteristic to measure is striking platform angle. Striking platforms are usually small, and sometimes it is difficult even to determine if they are present or absent. They are also found in many different shapes and sizes. Some striking platforms are rounded, others are flat, and others may have two, three, four, or more sides or facets. The specimens shown in Figure 5.3 illustrate some of the morphological range of striking platforms. Because of the great amount of morphological variability

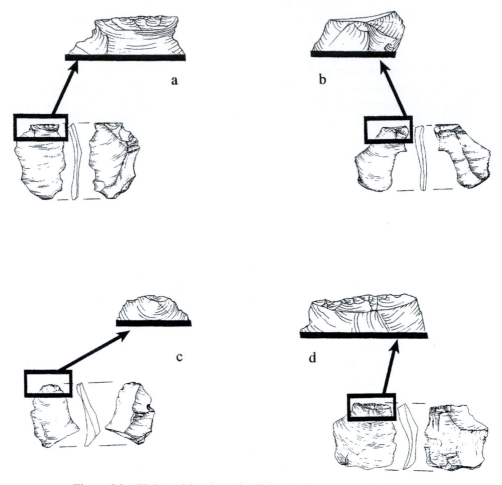

Figure 5.3   Flakes with enlarged striking platform areas showing variability in shape.

in striking platforms it is almost impossible to define the striking platform angle. An angle is formed by the intersection of two lines or two planes. The surfaces of striking platforms are usually curved or rounded, and do not intersect to form an angle. How does one measure the angle on a rounded surface? A common definition for striking platform angle is the angle formed by the intersection of the striking platform surface and the ventral surface (Dibble and Whittaker 1981; Shott 1993). Unfortunately, the striking platform surface is usually curved or contains many facets and it is often the case that the ventral surface is also curved. This results in the possibility that many striking platform angle measurements can be derived from the intersection of the curved surfaces depending upon where the lines forming the angle are selected. Figure 5.4 shows several potential angle measurements for a single specimen.

Three Different Measurements for Platform Angle

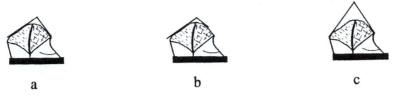

a   b   c

Platform

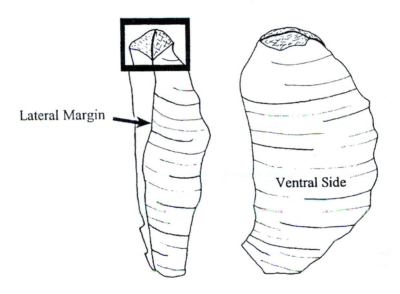

Lateral Margin

Ventral Side

Figure 5.4   Schematic diagram of flake striking platform surface being measured for striking platform angle. Note the different angle measurements potentially derived from the same curved striking platform surface.

Given the possibility that a researcher can consistently select lines to derive striking platform angles, the angle has to be accurately measured. I have tried a variety of instruments and techniques to make accurate striking platform angle measurements and found none to be effective. Not only do different people consistently record different values for the same specimen, the same person consistently records different values when asked to measure the specimen multiple times. Owing to the complexity of striking platform angles, it seems logical to skip measurement and to record other striking platform characteristics that may encompass the source of striking platform variation.

Another striking platform characteristic cited is the number of striking platform facets; replication of facet counts, however, can be difficult. Perhaps part of the difficulty is that striking platform facets are seldom defined. What constitutes a striking platform facet? By definition a facet is a flat surface or plane. The striking platforms shown in Figure 5.3 have many flat surfaces in many different sizes. How many facets are found for each striking platform? Abraded, ground, and even chipped striking platform areas have small angular scars that may produce facets too small to count. Without a definition of striking platform facet(s) it is not easy to record their number consistently. Defining striking platform facets in such a way that students or other researchers can measure the same thing is illusive.

For the reasons stated above, using striking platform angle or number of striking platform facets in debitage attribute analysis is not encouraging; they are very time consuming processes and produce results that are notoriously difficult to replicate. The underlying technological behavior purported to be expressed by these attributes, such as amount of time invested in tool production, can be recovered from other striking platform characteristics in a more reliable manner. Odell (1989) also provides a discussion on replicability problems associated with debitage striking platform characteristics.

Striking platform width and thickness

Variables that have been found to be useful and replicable are striking platform width and thickness. Figure 5.5 illustrates how striking platform width and thickness are measured. The width of a striking platform is measured by first locating the striking platform. The striking platform contacts the ventral surface, the dorsal surface, and each lateral margin of the flake. The striking platform width is the distance across the striking platform from lateral margin to lateral margin. Striking platform thickness is defined by a line perpendicular to the striking platform width; it is the greatest distance on the striking platform from the dorsal to the ventral surface following that line. Both of these striking platform variables are ratio in scale and easy to replicate.

Striking platform types

Striking platforms are surfaces that are usually impacted by a percussor to detach a flake. Striking platforms are sometimes prepared or made by manipulation of the objective piece. This manipulation can be performed by rubbing, grinding, abrading, chipping, or crushing the edge of the objective piece. Striking platforms are isolated and created for impact by tool makers who understand the relationship between striking platform characteristics and the

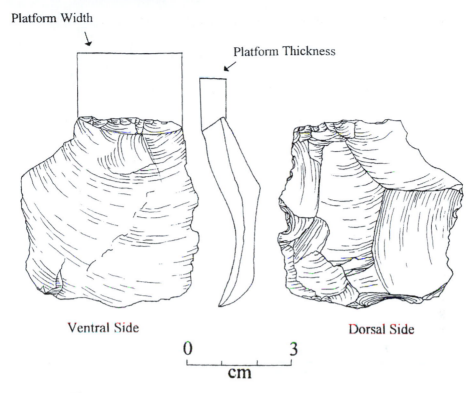

Platform Width

Platform Thickness

Ventral Side   Dorsal Side

0   3

cm

Figure 5.5   Locations on a flake striking platform for measuring platform width
and platform thickness.

size and shape of the detached piece desired. Striking platform preparation is
the basis for another attribute, striking platform type, that I find very useful
because it incorporates a great variety and range of variability. Since striking
platforms have infinite variability there are potentially an infinite number of
striking platform types. I prefer to use a very simple striking platform typology
that can be supplemented with other information such as striking platform
width and thickness. The striking platform typology I prefer is a nominal scale
that has four states: cortical, flat, complex, and abraded. Each striking platform type recognizes some characteristic(s) of the objective piece from which
the detached piece was removed. Figure 5.6 illustrates examples of each
striking platform type.

A cortical striking platform (Figure 5.6a) is simply composed of the unmodified cortical surface of the objective piece. Flake debitage that has a cortical
striking platform may or may not have dorsal cortex present. For instance, a
rounded river cobble of flint may be entirely encased with a cortical surface. This
cobble can be chipped or flaked to remove a detached piece (Figure 5.7). The
initial detached piece will have a striking platform that is entirely cortical. The
striking platform in this case would be classified as a cortical striking platform.

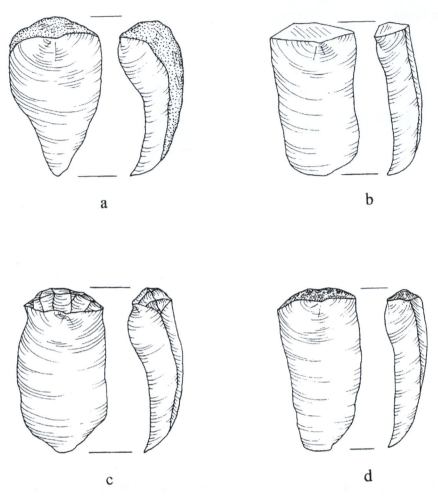

Figure 5.6   Schematic diagram showing four generalized flake striking platform types: (a) cortical striking platform; (b) flat striking platform; (c) complex striking platform; (d) abraded platform.

That first detached piece will also have a dorsal surface with cortex present at 100%. It is possible that the outside of the objective piece (river cobble) will continue to be impacted to remove additional flakes. The subsequent flakes removed from this objective piece will have cortical striking platforms if flakes are produced from impact along the cortical edge of the objective piece. However, as flakes are removed in this manner it is entirely possible that some flakes will have neither dorsal cortex nor a cortical striking platform.

Flat striking platforms (Figure 5.6b) are recognized as smooth flat surfaces which have been impacted to remove a detached piece. In most cases flat striking platforms are the result of detaching pieces from nonbifacial tools (Figure 4.7, 3b). Debitage with flat striking platforms is usually removed from

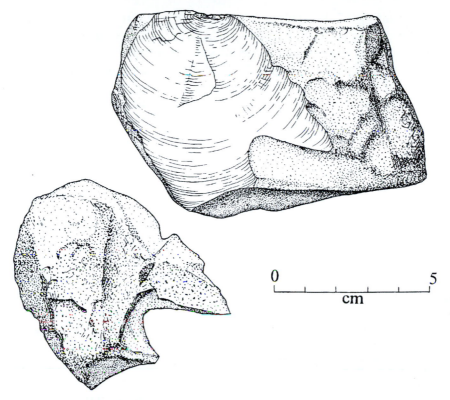

Figure 5.7   Flake removed from a river cobble with a cortical surface. The striking platform on the detached piece also has a completely cortical surface.

unidirectional cores. However, small debitage with flat striking platforms may have been removed from a flake blank or some other objective piece with a smooth flat surface. Flat striking platforms tend to articulate with the dorsal surface of the detached piece to form an angle that approaches 75°–90° (Figure 5.6b).

Striking platforms that are neither cortical nor flat are either complex or abraded. Striking platforms with a rounded surface or a surface composed of multiple flake scars are considered complex striking platforms (Figure 5.6c). If this type of striking platform is additionally smoothed by abrasion or rubbing, it is classified as an abraded striking platform (Figure 5.6d). The difference between these two types can sometimes be distinguished by their surface texture. Complex striking platforms usually have an angular surface created by removal of several striking platform preparation flakes; there may be tiny step fractures on the striking platform surface as well. The combination of flake scars on the complex striking platform may create a rounded or convex appearance in addition to or instead of an angular appearance. Abraded striking platforms reveal additional preparation in the form of

abrading or grinding of the striking platform surface. Often tiny step fractures or multiple flake scars on a striking platform will alter the direction of
force being applied by the hammer or percussor. To eliminate the uncertainty
of direction of force created by multiple flake scars and/or step fractures on
the striking platform it is often abraded or ground. Some researchers believe
that abrading or grinding the striking platform is indicative of more care
being taken by the knapper to remove the precise shape of detached piece in
order to achieve better results. Such care is often taken when the objective
piece is in its final stages of production or when there has been a great deal of
investment made in production of the tool. It is also believed that striking
platform abrasion will provide better purchase or less chance of the pressure
flaker slipping from the contact surface.

Debitage size

Debitage size has long been an important characteristic for lithic analysts.
It is generally believed that the size of debitage is directly related to the size
of the objective piece, and therefore can provide a good indication of the size of
the objective piece. Since artifact production is a reductive or subtractive
process, the size of debitage produced from the process generally becomes
progressively smaller as the artifact nears completion. As the stone tool
decreases in size it necessarily follows that the debitage removed from the tool
during production also grows progressively smaller. It is not possible to
remove a flake that has a larger linear dimension or mass than the largest
dimension of the objective piece or tool being made. However, this does not
necessarily mean that larger flakes are always removed from an objective piece
before any smaller flakes are removed; smaller flakes are often removed to "set
up" the removal of a larger flake. However, the change in flake sizes during
removal will follow a general pattern of decreasing size. This is true for core
reduction to produce usable flakes and for tool production to obtain a finished
product.

   Based on the above, many lithic analysts use size to determine the stages of
artifact production and core reduction, and weight is probably the most
reliable size characteristic for discrimination of reduction stages (Amick *et al.*
1988; Ammerman and Andrefsky 1982; Gilreath 1984; Magne and Pokotylo
1981; Odell 1989). Furthermore, flake debitage weight measurements are
normally easy to make and replicable. Shott (1994:80) suggests that weight is
important for predicting degree or stage of reduction because it covaries
closely with other linear dimensions, a conclusion supported by other researchers (Lyons 1994). Mauldin and Amick (1989:77) have shown that
debitage weight correlates with length and several measurements of debitage
width, all of which relate to the size of debitage.

One of the basic and most elementary types of debitage size analysis under-taken is the recording of length, width, and thickness. These characteristics are often recorded as both descriptive information – with little or no other analysis in some cases – and as analytical data for more complex interpretation in other cases (Flenniken 1981:66; Gero 1989:102). Size measurements on debitage are usually recorded for whole or unbroken specimens or those specimens with intact striking platforms. Whole specimens retain diagnostic characteristics that allow the investigator to record replicable measurements. Broken flakes may not have striking platforms or proximal or distal ends, and therefore their lengths cannot be measured in a replicable manner. However, some size measurements, such as weight and size grade, can be replicably recorded for whole or broken specimens. The flake size measurements described below should be recorded with the flake positioned so that the proximal end is up and the distal end is down, and the ventral surface is facing the observer. This will allow for uniform discussion regarding right and left margins.

Flake length

Flake length is usually measured as a straight line distance from the proximal to the distal end; this straight line is perpendicular to the wide axis of the striking platform at the center of the striking platform (Figure 5.8a). The wide axis of the striking platform is defined by the locations on the proximal end of the flake where the striking platform intersects with the lateral margin on the proximal end. Sometimes the flake length line is oriented in such a manner that the line perpendicular to the wide axis of the striking platform intersects a lateral margin before reaching the distal end (Figure 5.8b). In this case the flake may be longer than the recorded flake length. This is why I prefer to use maximum flake length, which is measured to the distal end of the flake as a line perpendicular to the flake length line at the most remote point on the distal end (Figure 5.8c). Maximum flake length is a superior measurement for all debitage pieces with an intact striking platform because, in most circumstances, it is quite easy to make such a measurement consistently. Furthermore, broken flakes with intact striking platforms can be identified in the analytical assem-blage by recording the kind of termination on the distal end: feathered, hinged, and plunging terminations indicate that the flake is intact and step termina-tions indicate a broken flake.

Flake width

The width of a flake can be recorded at a number of different locations on the specimen, but it is usually recorded as a straight line distance perpendicular to the flake length line. When this straight line distance intersects the flake at its widest point, it is called the maximum flake width (Figure 5.9c). Some

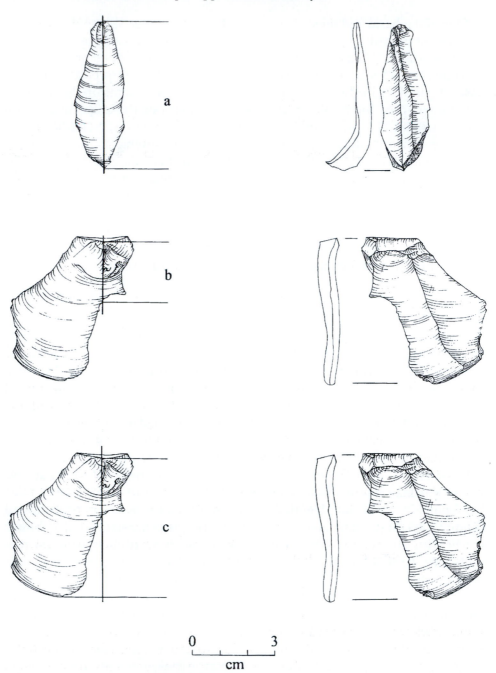

0   3
cm

Figure 5.8   Flake length measurements: (a) length corresponding to a line perpendicular to striking platform width; (b) length taken on an irregular shaped flake where the line perpendicular to striking platform width is less than 3 cm; (c) length measured as the maximum distance from the proximal to distal end along a line perpendicular to striking platform width.

Ventral Side   Dorsal Side

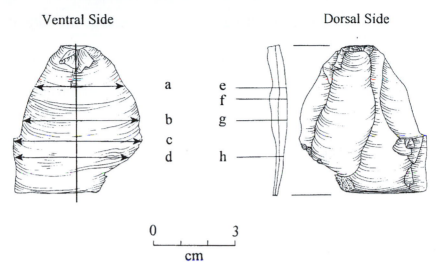

Figure 5.9   Flake width and thickness measurements: (a) flake width at $\frac{1}{4}$ maximum length; (b) flake width at $\frac{1}{2}$ maximum length; (c) maximum flake width; (d) flake width at $\frac{3}{4}$ maximum length; (e) flake thickness at $\frac{1}{4}$ maximum length; (f) maximum flake thickness; (g) flake thickness at $\frac{1}{2}$ maximum length; (h) flake thickness at $\frac{3}{4}$ maximum length.

researchers prefer to record flake width at the mid-point or the straight line distance along a line perpendicular to the flake length line at a point equal to exactly half of the maximum length (Figure 5.9b). Flake width measurements can also be taken at the quarter point (Figure 5.9a) and at the three quarters point (Figure 5.9d) along the flake length line.

Given the definitions of flake width, it is not possible to obtain a replicable measurement if the flake does not have an intact proximal end. However, as with flake length, flake width can be recorded for any specimen with a proximal end, provided that the termination type is also recorded. A step termination indicates that the specimen was broken and that width measurements might differ for the whole specimen.

Flake thickness

Flake thickness is measured in the same manner as flake width. Flake thickness is the distance from the dorsal side to the ventral side of the flake, perpendicular to the flake length line. Common measurements are maximum flake thickness (Figure 5.9f), thickness at mid-point (Figure 5.9g), and thickness at various points along the length of the flake. An additional thickness measurement is sometimes taken at the bulb of force. Some researchers feel that relative bulb size in relation to other size characteristics can determine the type of technology (hard hammer, soft hammer, pressure) used to detach the flake (Crabtree 1972), and therefore flake thickness at the bulb of force can have significant value.

Size characteristics of debitage can be good indicators of various tool production behavior. Odell (1989:186) has examined debitage size characteristics to determine if any are useful for discriminating between biface production on the one hand and core reduction on the other. Maximum length and maximum width of flakes were found to be good discriminatory characteristics in this regard. Width of the flake at mid-point was found helpful in discriminating bifacial stages. It must be remembered that each of these debitage size characteristics can be influenced by other factors. The specific kind of technology used, the relative abundance of lithic raw material available to make the tool, and the size and shape of stone from which the tool is produced are factors that can affect size characteristics.

Flake size class

Another size characteristic often recorded in debitage studies is size class or size range. Size classes are often obtained by sifting the debitage through a series of nested screens. Screen mesh sizes frequently used for this kind of size analysis are $\frac{1}{2}$ inch, $\frac{1}{4}$ inch, and $\frac{1}{8}$ inch (Ahler 1989; Andrefsky *et al.* 1994b; Kalin 1981; Patterson 1990; Root 1992). Size classes can also be derived from linear data such as length, width, thickness, or weight. Sometimes a single measurement such as length is combined with a second measurement to obtain a ratio value that provides a better overall shape characterization as it relates to size. For instance, if only maximum length is used to divide a debitage population into size classes there would potentially be a great amount of variability in shape and ultimately the size of specimens found in the same size class. Specimens that were 10 cm long and 0.5 cm thick would be in the same class as specimens 10 cm long and 4 cm thick. A value derived by dividing length by thickness or by weight is a way to obtain size classes in the population that depict shape more accurately. Figure 5.10 illustrates another method to obtain size classes. In this case, circles with different diameters are used to place specimens in classes; flake debitage is placed in the smallest diameter circle possible without touching the edge. In this kind of size sorting it is best to standardize how the specimen is compared in relation to the circle. For instance, all specimens might be placed in the circle with the ventral side down in order to standardize the measurement. A very long and narrow blade-like specimen might fit into a small size class if it were passed through the circle from the proximal to the distal end. However, this same specimen would not fit into a small size class if it were laid over the circle with the ventral side down. It is therefore essential to consider flake orientation when making size class measurements in this manner.

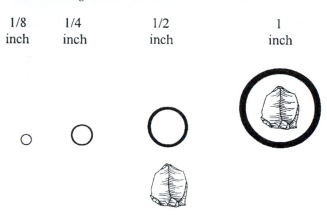

| 1/8 inch | 1/4 inch | 1/2 inch | 1 inch |

Figure 5.10   Flake size grades in diameters of 1 inch, $\frac{1}{2}$ inch, $\frac{1}{4}$ inch, and $\frac{1}{8}$ inch. The specimen shown is graded at $\frac{1}{2}$ inch because it is smaller than the 1 inch grade and is greater than the $\frac{1}{2}$ inch diameter grade.

Debitage dorsal cortex

Before measuring dorsal cortex it is important to define what cortex is. Cortex can be produced by either chemical or mechanical weathering of the stone surface. Chemical weathering usually occurs as a result of exposure to moisture and/or heat causing the actual composition of the rock to change. It is also usually apparent by a change in color and texture. For example, different kinds of chert that undergo chemical weathering normally develop a white patina that gradually turns chalky in texture. The Cliffs of Dover, England are chemically weathered dark-colored cherts that appear chalky and white as a result of exposure to moisture and sun. Chert nodules weathered in this manner may be cracked open to reveal a smooth hard inner core that has not been weathered. The chemically weathered stone surface is the cortical surface. Sometimes the cortical surface does not change color and is more difficult to recognize. Mechanical weathering usually changes only the texture of the stone surface. An example of mechanical weathering would be a nodule that has been rolled in a river or abraded by sand thereby producing a smooth polished stone surface. The smooth or polished surface is the cortex in this case. When mechanical weathering is prolonged, chemical weathering may occur as well. If a flake debitage specimen contains a dorsal surface with mechanical or chemical weathering it is said to have cortex present.

The amount of cortex present on the dorsal surface of flake debitage has been used as an indicator of the reduction stage for tools (Johnson 1989; Morrow 1984; Sanders 1992; Walker and Todd 1984; Zier *et al.* 1988) and nontools (Draper and Lothson 1990; Plastino 1994:99; Stafford 1980). This is based on the assumption that the weathered exterior of lithic raw materials – the cortex – will be the first area removed in either tool production or core reduction. As flakes are removed the exterior must be detached before the interior can be detached. Of course, cortex amount will vary depending upon the amount of cortex present on the objective piece, the technique of reduction, and the kind of artifact being produced. Tomka (1989:141) has shown, for instance, that dart point production produces a relatively greater number of flakes without cortex than does biface production or multidirectional core reduction. This is apparently related to the fact that a dart point is initially made from a flake blank that has a dorsal surface with or without cortex, and a ventral surface without cortex. As such, the initial objective piece used for dart point production has less cortex present than the initial objective piece for either biface or multidirectional core production when a cortical nodule is used. The form in which raw materials occur also has an effect upon the amount of dorsal cortex found on debitage regardless of the kinds of tools being produced. For example, projectile points made from small river pebbles produce a higher frequency of debitage with dorsal cortex than the same projectile points made from flake blanks (Tomka 1989).

Sullivan and Rozen (1985:756) have cautioned that value assigned to dorsal cortex amount may be problematic because of unstandardized measurement techniques and terminology. They note the lack of consistency in the use of nontool debitage terminology (primary, secondary, and tertiary) as a significant problem. Several other studies have demonstrated that the amount of dorsal cortex can be reliably measured, however, and that the amount is useful in some cases when discriminating between reduction stages or sequences (Magne and Pokotylo 1981). Odell (1989:185) has found the amount of dorsal cortex useful in distinguishing the extremes of bifacial reduction stages from one another – the earlier part of a reduction sequence from a later part, for instance. Mauldin and Amick (1989:70) have found dorsal cortex amount useful as an indicator of early reduction as well. Their study shows that most cortex is removed by halfway through the reduction sequence during bifacial blank production.

Dorsal cortex amount

As previously discussed, it is important to develop mutually exclusive and replicable cortex measurements and any replicable technique is acceptable. Figure 5.11 illustrates the dorsal surfaces of seven debitage specimens. In the best of all possible situations dorsal cortex amount can be express as an absolute percentage of the dorsal surface. If the entire dorsal surface were covered in cortex the cortical amount would be 100%. If 7.5 cm^2 of the dorsal surface were covered by cortex and the dorsal surface were 10.0 cm^2, the dorsal cortex amount would be 75%. Unfortunately, it is not easy to obtain an absolute value for the area of a dorsal surface and the area covered by dorsal cortex. One way to do this effectively is by using a computer digitizer to map

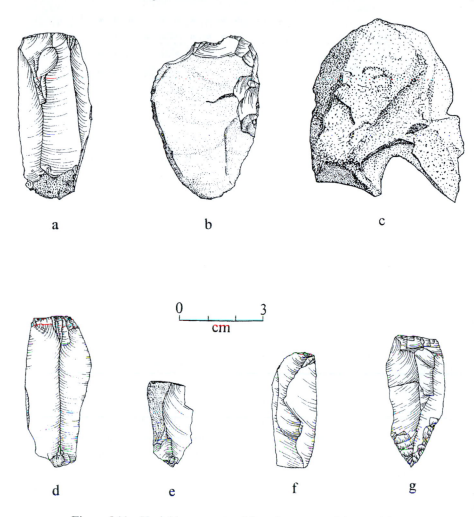

Figure 5.11   Variable amounts of dorsal cortex on flakes and flake tools: (a–e) have dorsal cortex present; (f, g) have no dorsal cortex present.

the surface of the specimen; another way is to measure the dorsal surface by using a nominal scale. Dorsal cortex amount can be expressed as either present or absent. If a nominal scale were used, all the specimens in Figure 5.11 would have a value of present (+) except specimens f and g with values of absent (−). Cortex amount can also be measured on an ordinal scale. If values were precisely defined, an ordinal scale would be a good compromise between ratio and nominal ways to characterize cortex amount. However, precision is one of the problems with ordinally ranking cortical values. In order to reduce that error it is best to eliminate as many subjective elements as possible. With regard to replicability one of the best ordinal scales I use is the four rank scale.

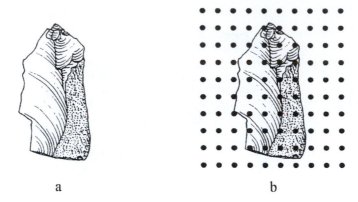

a   b

Figure 5.12   Dot grid superimposed over the dorsal surface of a flake to
determine relative amount of dorsal cortex. The specimen would be given a score
of 1 using the ordinal scale described.

If the entire dorsal surface is covered with cortex it gets a value of "3," the
highest rank in this scale. If absolutely no dorsal cortex is present the flake gets
a value of "0," the lowest rank. Both of these are relatively unambiguous and
easily replicable. The next two values fall between 0 and 100% dorsal cortex. A
value of "2" is given for debitage that has less than 100% but greater than 50%
dorsal cortex; a value of "1" is given for debitage with greater than 0% but less
than or equal to 50% cortex. The difference between the cortical values of "1"
and "2" are usually easy to distinguish. Most debitage that falls within this
range has either considerably less or considerably more than 50% cortex. In
either situation the cortex amount can be easily estimated. The only problem
with this scale is when the dorsal cortex amount is very close to 50%. In this
case I superimpose a grid sheet composed of dots or grid squares over the
specimen and count the number of dots on the cortical portion and the number
of dots not on the cortical portion of the dorsal surface (Figure 5.12). If the
greater number of dots are located over the cortical portion the specimen is
given a value of "2." This ordinal scale for dorsal cortex amount is relatively
easy to use and takes only a few seconds to perform unless most of the
specimens under analysis have approximately 50% dorsal cortex. The specimens in Figure 5.11 were quickly measured using this technique. Table 5.1 lists
the cortical amounts for each specimen after this was done.

Dorsal flake scars

Dorsal flake scars are the impressions found on the dorsal surface of a flake
debitage specimen caused by the removal of previous flakes from the objective
piece. Figure 5.13 illustrates several examples of dorsal flake surfaces with flake
scars. By definition, the dorsal surface on all flakes contains either flake scars

Table 5.1 *Dorsal cortex scores for speci-mens illustrated in Figure 5.11*

Specimen	Dorsal cortex value	Amount of cortex
a	1	≤50%
b	2	>50%
c	3	100%
d	1	≤50%
e	1	≤50%
f	0	none
g	0	none

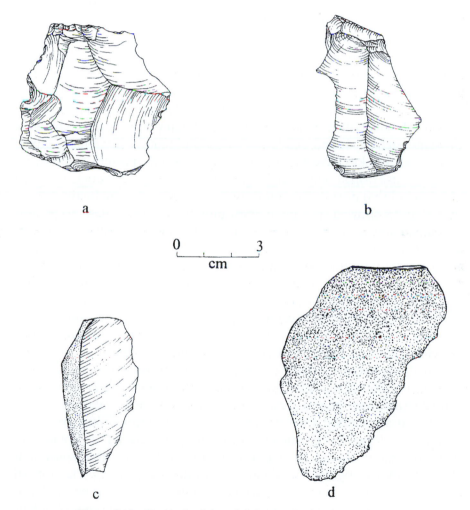

Figure 5.13 Example of dorsal flake scar variation. Using the ordinal method described the flakes would be given the following scores: (a) 3; (b) 2; (c) 1; (d) 0.

or cortex or both. Some researchers count dorsal flake scars or removals to determine the sequence of core reduction. Other researches count dorsal ridges or arises that are also produced by the previous removal of flakes from the objective piece. Counting the number of flake scars found on the dorsal surface of debitage has been used quite extensively by archaeologists to define stage of reduction and type of objective piece (Gilreath 1984:3; Johnson 1987:193; Magne 1985). Lyons (1994:33) states that dorsal scar count should indicate the stage of production because a piece in its earliest stages has only a few large flake scars and a piece nearing completion has many small scars from previous removals. McDonald's (1994:68) results from bifacial experiments also showed that few dorsal flake scars occurred in the earliest stages and many flake scars on the later stages. However, other researchers warn that this attribute can be difficult to measure consistently and may not be a good indicator of reduction stage (Baumler 1988:262; Shott 1994:80).

Dorsal scar counts are influenced by a variety of characteristics other than type of objective piece or sequence of reduction. The size of the objective piece, flaking technique used, type of raw material being worked, and the type of artifact being made all affect the number of dorsal scars on debitage. In experimental studies, dorsal scar counts have been found to be quite variable. Mauldin and Amick (1989:73) believe that dorsal scar counts tend to correlate with debitage size; they found that larger flakes tend to have six or more dorsal scars, and smaller flakes have one or no dorsal scars. This pattern complicates the attempt to use dorsal scar count alone to define stage of reduction. Odell (1989:178) found that dorsal scar counts did not discriminate reduction stages well. His analysis showed that the highest number of dorsal scars were produced in the middle of the reduction sequence in projectile point manufacturing experiments.

Identifying and counting dorsal flake scars is not easy, and it is not known for sure why dorsal flakes scars vary in number. However, under certain circumstances the number of dorsal flake scars may reveal information about reduction stages and/or type of objective piece. One of the easiest methods of assessing flake scars is to eliminate as much clutter as possible from the dorsal surface before counting. Clutter is defined as all of the small flake removals that have resulted from striking platform preparation, breaks, modification after detachment, and shattering. After eliminating clutter, a four value ordinal scale can be used to measure the relative amount of flake removals. An ordinal scale is preferable to an interval scale because it is nearly impossible to replicate actual counts of dorsal flake removals consistently. Figure 5.13a provides an example: how many dorsal flake removals are evident on this specimen? Clearly, different investigators would arrive at different numbers. The ordinal scale used to determine number of flake removals assigns a value of "0" to those flakes with a completely cortical dorsal surface and no flake removals (Figure 5.13d). It is relatively easy to recognize flakes with a single dorsal flake removed, and in all such cases, there will be some amount of dorsal cortex remaining; these flakes are given a value of "1" (Figure 5.13c). The value of "2" is assigned to flakes with two dorsal flake scars, and these may or may not have dorsal cortex (Figure 5.13b). Those flakes with more than two dorsal flake removals are given a value of "3" (Figure 5.13a).

Debitage curvature

Gilreath (1984) has shown that the amount of ventral curvature on debitage removed in the bifacial reduction process decreases as the biface approaches finished form. The same trend has been found by Andrefsky (1986a) with debitage analysis from the production of small triangular projectile points. Debitage curvature measurements have also been examined to identify differences between hard- and soft-hammer percussion. Hayden and Hutchings (1989) have found that hard and soft hammers generally produce debitage with the same amount of curvature during biface production. However, they found that a number of soft-hammer debitage specimens did have curvature values far in excess of any hard-hammer debitage specimens. They concluded that curvature found in soft- and hard-hammer debitage is not necessarily distinctive, although it can be (1989:245). Curvature on experimentally derived debitage populations reported by Lyons (1994:78) illustrated uniform curvature measurements for debitage derived from core and biface production, although his data did show a slight increase in ventral surface curvature in the later stages of reduction.

There are many ways to calculate curvature of debitage, but it is important to consider the overall size of the specimen in the calculation. Simple measures such as the height of the curve on the ventral surface will be skewed toward larger pieces (Figure 5.14). Flake curvature can be defined as the arc created at the height of an isosceles triangle that best fits into the length of a flake. Only three measurements are required to derive this curvature value: maximum length (L), thickness at midpoint (T) (both explained previously), and angle height (A) (Figure 5.14). Angle height can be measured by pressing flat edge calipers together along the dorsal and ventral sides. In this manner, the proximal and distal ends of the flake should be resting on the lower caliper edge plane. A parallel plane is made by the upper caliper surface. This plane rests on the dorsal surface of the flake. The perpendicular distance between the two planes is the angle height (A). Figure 5.15 is an abstract representation of flake curvature in the form of an isosceles triangle. Curvature is calculated as:

$$c = 2(90 - a)$$

where:
$$a = \tan^{-1} H/M$$
$$M = L/2$$
$$H = A - T$$

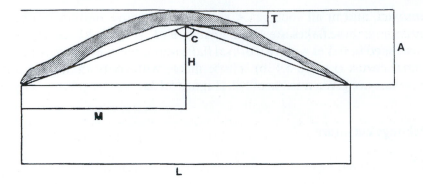

Figure 5.14   Schematic diagram of a flake in cross section illustrating different measurements for derivation of flake curvature. Adapted from Andrefsky (1986a:50).

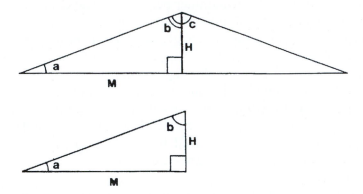

Figure 5.15   Abstract representation of flake curvature in the form of an isosceles triangle showing relevant measurements. Adapted from Andrefsky (1986a:50).

A detailed explanation of the calculation is found in Andrefsky (1986a). Briefly, this measurement is calculated by deriving the height "H" of the ventral curve by subtracting the thickness at midpoint "T" from angle height "A" (Figure 5.14). The value of "M" is half the flake length "L." From the known values of "H" and "M," a value for angle "a" is derived by taking the arc tangent of "H" divided by "M." Angle "b" is derived by subtracting angle "a" from 90°. This value is doubled to obtain the curvature measurement "c."

Summary

There are an infinite number of attributes that can be recorded for flaked stone debitage. The debitage characteristics described and discussed above represent some of the most common attributes recorded in debitage analysis. I have mentioned some of the attribute trends found in specific debitage studies. For instance, debitage gets progressively smaller, in general, as individual tools become progressively closer to completion; similarly, cortex amounts tend to become progressively less on debitage specimens during later stages of core reduction. These trends, however, should be viewed from the perspective of a debitage population and not from that of an individual flake. In actual fact, if the size of any two flakes is compared, the larger flake may not necessarily have been removed before the smaller flake. The same can be said for dorsal cortex amount. However, if the entire population of debitage were considered, those trends in size and cortex would probably be significant. Another thing to remember is that the particular context of the lithic assemblage will be very important for interpretations about debitage characteristics. The context of debitage can drastically alter predicted relationships among debitage characteristics even if a population approach is taken in the analysis. If, for instance, the cortex amount were compared between two different assemblages of debitage, it would be important to know what kinds of lithic raw materials were used, as well as the relative abundance of each type of raw material. The amount of cortex found on the dorsal surface of debitage can be the direct result of the amount of cortex found on the raw material. If raw materials were collected in flake blank form and then reduced into tools, there is a high probability that the debitage would have very low amounts of dorsal cortex regardless of the reduction stage. Conversely, debitage produced from the reduction of cobbles with complete cortical surfaces would produce debitage with greater amounts of dorsal cortex.

It is also important to remember that there are not yet any formulas or expected patterns for making behavioral interpretations based upon debitage analysis owing to the fact that the context of lithic production has such a profound effect upon individual debitage characteristics and upon debitage assemblage characteristics. Because of this, debitage analysis should be conducted so that multiple lines of evidence are used to support various interpretations about production and reduction of objective pieces. Different characteristics of debitage should be brought to bear on any particular topic being studied. Additionally, it may be beneficial to explore some characteristics, such as size, in several different ways (weight, length, size grade, etc.).

The next chapter examines different ways in which various investigators have analyzed debitage. Most has been done by classification of specimens. Short discussions regarding each technique of debitage analysis are provided so that the reader can better understand the advantages and disadvantages of using various techniques under different circumstances.

6

APPROACHES TO DEBITAGE ANALYSIS

As in chapter 5, this chapter is primarily a review of the literature on flake debitage analysis. It is not intended to be a "cook book" or a manual for selecting flake debitage attributes and analytical techniques. Instead it reviews various analytical approaches to flake debitage analysis in an attempt to show the relationship between various debitage attributes and stone tool production behavior. The examples used in this chapter have been selected to illustrate how flake debitage attribute data might be compiled for analysis. However, more sophisticated quantitative analysis and tests of association have not been applied on the data. I have chosen not to apply more sophisticated quantitative methods because any number of methods could be used to tabulate data depending upon the question(s) or issues being addressed. Since this chapter is primarily a review of flake debitage analysis approaches and not a problem or question oriented study, specific quantitative functions have not been performed.

The analysis of debitage has been conducted on many different scales with a variety of different techniques. Some researchers analyze debitage from the perspective of an individual artifact, and others from the perspective of a population. Analysis from an individual artifact perspective is used to make one-to-one associations between the artifact and past behavior. An example would be that after analysis a detached piece may be identified as a bipolar flake, and such a flake would indicate that bipolar technology was practiced at the site – even if no bipolar cores have been found. Analysis from a population perspective examines an entire range of debitage variability found in an assemblage to make inferences about past behavior. This kind of analysis assumes that tool production results in a wide range of debitage forms, and that the variation in forms within the debitage assemblage are more revealing than any single detached piece. Some kinds of debitage analysis seek to classify debitage into types that are then used as data for either individual or population analysis. Other kinds of debitage analysis examine only debitage attributes. As with individual debitage specimens, attributes such as cortex amount or striking platform type can be analyzed and interpreted individually or as a population.

This chapter considers debitage analysis from several different perspectives, but begins with the description and discussion of a series of debitage typologies. These typologies are derived from analysis or examination of debitage attributes discussed in chapter 5. Such typological analysis is presented from the perspective of the individual specimen. This is followed by an explanation of various types of population analysis using both debitage types and debitage attributes as data for input into the interpretation of complete assemblages.

The reader should be aware that the debitage attribute analysis described here represents some of the more widely used attributes in debitage analysis. Not all of the attributes discussed would be effective for any particular data set nor would I advocate the use of all of the attributes discussed. Nor does this review of debitage attribute analysis include all possible attributes. The approaches to debitage attribute analysis in this chapter are presented in a manner to allow readers to determine for themselves the usefulness and applicability of some of the more widely accepted approaches.

Typological analysis of debitage

Many lithic researchers prefer a typological approach to debitage analysis as opposed to an attribute approach because they feel that attribute analysis is too time consuming (Ahler 1989:86) or that attribute definitions are too subjective (Sullivan and Rozen 1985). A typological analysis of debitage assigns debitage into groups or types based upon one or more characteristics. Typological analysis of debitage has been conducted in many different ways that depend upon the needs of the researcher and the kinds of questions being addressed. Typologies have been developed to distinguish the kind of hammer used (Crabtree 1972; Hayden and Hutchings 1989), the stage of reduction (Daugherty *et al.* 1987; Mauldin and Amick 1989), the type of artifact produced or worked (Frison 1968; Raab *et al.* 1979), and the technology used (Parry 1987; Shott 1993; Sullivan and Rozen 1985). The advantage of using some kinds of typological analysis is the immediate behavioral inference gained from recognition of a single piece of debitage. For instance, if a notching flake (Titmus 1985) were identified in an assemblage it could be inferred that notched points were made at the site even if none was found. Similarly, if a bifacial thinning flake (Raab *et al.* 1979) or a channel flake (Wilmsen and Roberts 1978) were discovered it would indicate that a biface was thinned or a Folsom point was made at the site. The realization that an individual flake contains significant behavioral information is a powerful argument for using debitage typological analysis.

The triple cortex typology

Probably one of the most frequently used typological analyses for debitage is what can be called the "triple cortex" approach, by which analysts classify the debitage as either primary, secondary, or tertiary. Generally, these types are based upon relative amounts of cortex found on the dorsal surface of the flake: primary flakes have more dorsal cortex than secondary flakes, and they in turn have more dorsal cortex than tertiary flakes. Flakes with more dorsal cortex are representative of earlier reduction stages than those flakes with less dorsal cortex. This seems reasonable, but not all researchers use the same criteria to determine the differences between primary, secondary and tertiary. Sullivan and Rozen (1985:757) demonstrate how some researchers identify primary flakes as having as little as 50% dorsal cortex, while others use 100% dorsal cortex as the criterion for primary flakes. Secondary flakes are shown to have no dorsal cortex by some researchers, but as much as 100% by others. Sullivan and Rozen also note that different scales of measurement are used by various researchers, which causes problems in replicability. They note that the two major problems with the triple cortex approach are (1) lack of an available procedure to replicably partition varying expressions of cortex, and (2) unstandardized proportions of cortex that define each of the three types (1985:756). The first leads to unreliable data with regard to actual cortex amount on the dorsal surface of flakes. The second may produce a substantial incomparability between studies, where primary flakes in one study would be called secondary flakes in another, or tertiary flakes in a third.

Another problem associated with the triple cortex approach to debitage classification is the lack of any distinction between what constitutes primary, secondary, and tertiary (Daugherty *et al.* 1987:92–104; Sappington 1991:69–76; Draper and Lothson 1990:70–9). In some cases it is not clear if these flake types represent detached pieces from bifaces, cores, flake tools, or all these categories of stone tools. This distinction is important because it has been shown that production or reduction of different kinds of objective pieces will produce detached pieces with differential amounts of dorsal cortex (Tomka 1989). We should also be aware that it has not been clearly demonstrated that flakes with more cortex are necessarily removed earlier in the reduction sequence than flakes with less cortex (Mauldin and Amick 1989; Odell 1989).

Even with these problems, the use of the triple cortex typology continues. Since the Sullivan and Rozen article first appeared in 1985, most researchers are careful to define what they mean by primary, secondary, and tertiary detached pieces. This makes their study replicable even if it may not make their designations interchangeable with other studies that use the same terms for debitage. The data in Table 6.1 were derived from the reduction of three cores with different amounts of cortical surface present. The amount of dorsal cortex found on detached pieces from each of the cores was stratified into four groups based upon the method described in chapter 5. The triple cortex typology uses cortical amount on detached pieces to characterize primary, secondary, and tertiary flakes. If the data in Table 6.1 are interpreted using the triple cortex approach primary flakes may be defined as debitage with values of "3" and "2" (greater than 50% dorsal cortex), secondary flakes with a value of "1" (less than

Table 6.1   *Number of flakes with various cortex amounts for three cores stratified by four stages*

Objective Piece	Cortex amount				
	0	1	2	3	Total count
Core A 1/4	0	3	7	3	13
Core A 2/4	4	8	1	0	13
Core A 3/4	11	2	0	0	13
Core A 4/4	12	0	0	0	12
Core B 1/4	0	1	5	1	7
Core B 2/4	2	4	1	0	7
Core B 3/4	3	3	1	0	7
Core B 4/4	6	1	0	0	7
Core C 1/4	4	3	0	0	7
Core C 2/4	7	0	0	0	7
Core C 3/4	6	1	0	0	7
Core C 4/4	6	0	0	0	6

or equal to 50% dorsal cortex), and tertiary flakes with a value of "0" (no dorsal cortex). Objective piece A was a cobble covered with a cortical surface. Objective piece B was a cortical cobble split roughly in half, and objective piece C was a large flake blank with about 20% dorsal cortex. Each of the objective pieces was reduced as a core to obtain as many large flakes as possible. The debitage from the reduction processes was collected as each piece was removed from the core, then segregated into quarters based upon count. In other words, objective piece A produced a total of fifty-one detached pieces with proximal ends: the first thirteen detached pieces were included in the first quarter of the assemblage, and the next thirteen in the second quarter; the third quarter contained the next thirteen pieces, and the final quarter the last twelve proximal flakes.

One of the first trends apparent in the data is that the amount of dorsal cortex found on debitage varies depending upon the amount of cortex originally present on the objective piece. In general, objective pieces with more cortex relative to surface area tend to produce more debitage with a greater amount of dorsal cortex. This may seem obvious, but if the triple cortex typology is used to determine stage or sequence of reduction, it would be misleading to make those determinations without some proviso for raw-material characteristics. For instance, the first quarter of the detached pieces from any of the cores could certainly be considered "primary" reduction debitage. However, the first quarter of objective piece C has no detached pieces with 50% or more dorsal cortex, and the first quarter of objective piece A produced ten out of thirteen detached pieces with dorsal cortex of 50% or more.

The data also reveal that dorsal cortex is found on some debitage from all quarters of the assemblage for objective pieces A and B. Objective piece C has a lower frequency of debitage with dorsal cortex. However, one of the seven detached pieces from the third quarter of objective piece C contains dorsal cortex. This clearly illustrates that dorsal cortex alone is not a reliable indicator of reduction stages on any single piece of debitage. If secondary flakes represent the "middle" of a reduction sequence, it would be reasonable to expect that they were detached during the second or third quarter of a reduction sequence. However, all three of the objective pieces have secondary flakes or flakes with a cortex value of 1 from the first quarter of reduction. Of the twenty-six secondary flakes from the three objective pieces, seven were removed during the first quarter of reduction, twelve during the second quarter, six from the third quarter, and one from the fourth quarter. This means that 54% of all the "secondary" flakes were not removed from the middle of the reduction sequence.

The results presented in Table 6.1 are by no means conclusive; these data are presented to illustrate how the triple cortex typology is used and also to demonstrate how some of the factors may affect typology. The data do show a trend of greater cortex amount in earlier detached pieces, provided that cortex was originally present on the objective piece. This suggests that the attribute "dorsal cortex amount" may be a more sensitive indicator for core reduction stages than the triple cortex debitage typology. This might be particularly true if debitage is examined for trends in the population and not as individual pieces.

The application load typology

Another classification scheme used by lithic analysts is the load application designation. Using this scheme researchers classify flakes as derived from either hard-hammer percussion, soft-hammer percussion, or pressure flaking (Cotterell and Kamminga 1987, 1990; Crabtree 1972). Flakes with a diffuse bulb of force and a pronounced lip have been called soft-hammer percussion flakes (Crabtree 1972:74; Frison 1968:149). Brittle fracture studies (Lawrence 1979; Tsirk 1979) have shown that flakes with diffuse or no bulbs and pronounced lips are caused by bending forces, and in many cases are the result of soft percussors or hammers. However, not all researchers agree. In a set of replication studies Patterson and Sollberger (1978) concluded that flake lipping is not a good indicator of soft-hammer percussion flaking.

Pressure flakes have been identified in many lithic studies as a specific type of detached piece which is apparently discriminated from soft-hammer and hard-hammer percussion pieces (Daugherty *et al.* 1987:92–104; Draper and Lothson 1990:70–9; Sappington 1991:70). Unfortunately, there do not seem to be any good mutually exclusive definitions of a pressure flake. According to some researchers who do identify pressure flakes in their assemblage of debitage, pressure flakes are generally smaller, thinner, and weigh less than flakes detached by percussion (Ahler 1989:91; Root 1992:87). Other than statements regarding these size characteristics, I have not found definitions of pressure flakes. Yet smaller, thinner, and lighter flakes have been produced by percussion flaking as well as pressure flaking in experiments with bifacial production (Andrefsky 1983, 1986a) and with core reduction (Ammerman and Andrefsky 1982). In fact, the majority of debitage produced from almost any kind of lithic reduction activity is small debitage (Henry *et al.* 1976; Kalin 1981; Patterson 1982, 1990; Patterson and Sollberger 1978; Stahle and Dunn 1982). Accordingly, it can be very difficult to segregate reliably a detached piece produced by pressure techniques from those produced by percussion techniques solely on the criterion of size.

Hard-hammer percussion is believed to produce flakes with pronounced bulbs of force, no lipping, and slightly crushed striking platform areas (Crabtree 1972:44). Cotterell and Kamminga (1987:686) recognize pronounced bulbs as diagnostic of conchoidal fracture, and tend to agree that hard hammers are most likely to cause pronounced bulbs. However, they do say that conchoidal flakes can be produced with bone or antler pressure flaking. Even though soft-hammer and hard-hammer flaking techniques produce detached pieces that overlap in their range of bulb morphology and amount of lipping, these characteristics may be effective discriminators in most cases.

One of the ways that relative bulb size can be measured is to compare flake thickness at the bulb to flake thickness at mid-point. The difference between the two measurements gives an indication of relative bulb size. Figure 6.1 illustrates the locations of these two measurements on different sized detached pieces.

To determine if application loads are sensitive to relative bulb size, data were gathered from hard-hammer and soft-hammer detached pieces and the relative bulb sizes recorded as described above. Table 6.2 lists relative bulb sizes for the first twenty-six flakes with intact striking platforms for two cores of similar size. One was reduced with hard-hammer percussion and the other

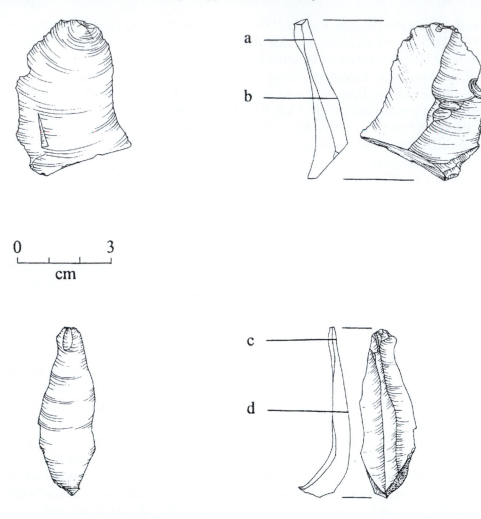

Figure 6.1   Thickness measurements: (a) bulb thickness; (b) thickness at midpoint; (c) bulb thickness; (d) thickness at midpoint.

with soft-hammer percussion. It should be noted that these data represent only a small sample and may vary as the sample is increased, or they may vary with other conditions such as relative density of hammers or type of raw material being reduced. A two-sample t-test comparing relative bulb thickness indicates significant differences between the samples at a 90% confidence level ($f = 1.47$; $df = 50$; $p < 0.10$). Another way to view the relative bulb size values would be to compare the summed values for each objective piece. The hard-hammer detached pieces have a value of 1.7, and the soft-hammer ones a value of 0.5. This indicates that relative bulb size assemblage values are over three times greater with hard-hammer percussion than with soft-hammer techniques. The hard-

Table 6.2   *Bulb size differences between hard- and soft-hammer percussion*

Hard-hammer flake	Thickness at midpoint	Bulb thickness	Relative bulb size	Soft-hammer flake	Thickness at midpoint	Bulb thickness	Relative bulb size
1	1.1	1.2	0.1	1	0.5	0.7	0.2
2	1.2	1.1	−0.1	2	0.3	0.4	0.1
3	0.7	0.7	0	3	0.3	0.3	0
4	1.5	1.4	−0.1	4	0.2	0.3	0.1
5	0.5	0.6	0.1	5	0.5	0.6	0.1
6	0.6	0.7	0.1	6	0.6	0.7	0.1
7	0.6	0.7	0.1	7	0.4	0.6	0.2
8	1.5	1.4	−0.1	8	0.3	0.3	0
9	1.1	1.2	0.1	9	0.2	0.3	0.1
10	1.2	1.3	0.1	10	0.8	0.7	−0.1
11	0.6	0.7	0.1	11	0.4	0.3	−0.1
12	0.7	0.9	0.2	12	0.3	0.4	0.1
13	0.6	0.8	0.2	13	0.4	0.3	−0.1
14	1.8	1.9	0.1	14	0.8	0.8	0
15	0.6	0.8	0.2	15	0.3	0.2	−0.1
16	0.6	0.8	0.2	16	0.8	1.0	0.2
17	0.3	0.3	0	17	0.4	0.5	0.1
18	1.5	1.6	0.2	18	0.9	1.0	0.1
19	0.9	0.9	0	19	0.2	0.1	−0.1
20	1.8	1.7	−0.1	20	0.4	0.4	0
21	1.4	1.6	0.2	21	0.2	0.3	0.1
22	1.0	1.1	0.1	22	0.4	0.3	−0.1
23	0.6	0.5	−0.1	23	0.6	0.3	−0.3
24	1.6	1.7	0.1	24	0.3	0.3	0
25	0.5	0.5	0	25	0.2	0.2	0
26	0.7	0.7	0	26	0.2	0.1	−0.1

hammer assemblage appears to be more variable than the soft-hammer assemblage with regard to relative bulb size trends. For instance, five of the hard-hammer detached pieces have negative bulb size values. However, three of the five occur within the first half of the assemblage (flakes 2, 4, and 8), and two of the five occur in the last half of the assemblage (flakes 20 and 23). The soft-hammer assemblage tends to have more detached pieces with negative values in the second half than in the first half. Five of the eight detached pieces with negative values occur in the second half of the assemblage. Also, the three detached pieces that occur in the first half of the assemblage represent three of the last four detached pieces from the first half (flakes 10, 11, and 13). These data suggest that relative bulb size may get smaller with soft-hammer percussion as the core is progressively reduced. Such a trend is not apparent with hard-hammer percussion.

The technological typology

A popular phrase in lithic studies is "technological analysis" or "technological classification." This refers to a debitage typology that separates detached pieces into groups based upon some characteristic(s) of stone tool technology. Some of the more popular types used in this analysis are bifacial thinning flakes or flakes of bifacial retouch (Raab *et al.* 1979), retouched scraper flakes (Frison 1968), bipolar flakes (Flenniken 1981), striking platform preparation flakes (Draper and Lothson 1990), and notching flakes (Daugherty *et al.* 1987). Probably the most famous critique of debitage technological analysis is by Sullivan and Rozen (1985), who focused primarily upon problems associated with bifacial thinning flakes, but made it apparent that other technological types were equally problematic (1985:757). The bulk of their critique emphasized the lack of consistent definitions and the use of different attributes for identification of types by various investigators (1985:757–8). It is confusing to have multiple investigators use the same term for differently defined items. However, as long as any particular study adequately defines various technological types there is no reason to assume the study is wrong simply because of terminology.

As stated above, the term bifacial thinning flake has been widely used as a technological type of debitage, and is defined by attributes such as striking platform type, relative thickness, shape, and size. Even though there may be no universally accepted definition of bifacial thinning flakes, it is commonly believed that these flakes represent detached pieces from bifaces for the purpose of trimming the face of the objective piece. The bifacial thinning flake may not actually "thin" the biface, but trimming does occur. Depending upon the size and shape of the biface, and the method with which it was trimmed, the bifacial thinning (or trimming) flakes will be of various sizes and may have different values for attributes such as striking platform, curvature, bulb of force, lipping, and dorsal scars. Figure 6.2 illustrates various examples of bifacial thinning flakes.

Another good definition of bifacial thinning flakes is also one of the earliest (Frison 1968:149–50). Frison calls these technological types "flakes of bifacial retouch." He indicates that the striking platforms on these flakes are usually faceted and that ridges between flake scars appear on the dorsal surface because the flake includes a small part of one face of the bifacial tool. He also indicates that the striking platform is composed of part of the dulled bifacial edge. Another working definition of a bifacial thinning flake is that it contains most or all of the following characteristics: curved longitudinal cross-sections, extremely acute lateral and distal edge angles, feathered flake terminations, narrow faceted striking platforms, a lip, little or no cortex, and a small flattened or diffuse bulb of force (Root 1992:83). Raab *et al.* (1979:179), Crabtree (1972:96), and Andrefsky (1986a:49) provide illustrations of biface thinning flakes.

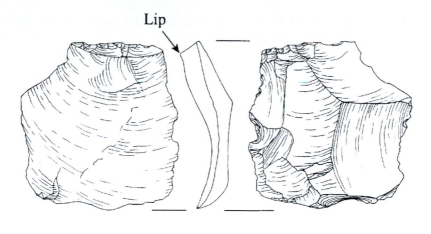

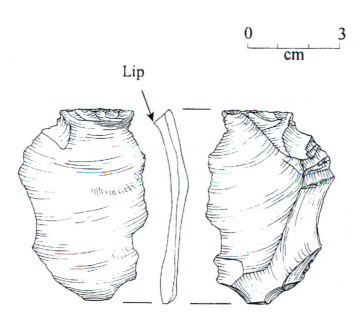

Figure 6.2   Examples of biface thinning flakes. Note the complex striking platform and pronounced lips.

Bipolar flakes are another important technological type of detached piece (Binford and Quimby 1972; Goodyear 1993; Hayden 1980; Honea 1965; Shott 1989; White 1968). This debitage type is produced by smashing an objective piece between a hammer and an anvil stone. Bipolar technology may produce a considerable amount of shatter, and the detached pieces can have considerable morphological variability. Some detached pieces may have more than two faces and therefore the appearance of bipolar cores. It is believed that bipolar technology is a method used to maximize lithic raw materials (Andrefsky

1994b; Knudson 1978). It has been described as a technique to obtain usable cutting edges from small nodules of objective pieces (Parry and Kelly 1987) and also as a technique used to recycle raw materials that have already been made into artifacts. Other researchers believe that bipolar objects were used as wedges for splitting wood and bone (Gramly and Rutledge 1981; Lothrop and Gramly 1982; MacDonald 1968).

Cotterell and Kamminga (1987, 1990) believe that bipolar flakes originate from compression forces and that the Hertzian cone splits during the crack initiation phase. Flenniken discusses bipolar cracking as shearing (1981:29–32). Because bipolar flaking technology has the potential to shatter an objective piece into many different shapes of debitage, it is difficult to characterize the full range of potential morphological variability found in bipolar flakes. However, there are several characteristics that originate from compression forces that make some bipolar flakes easier to recognize. Logically, some bipolar flakes should show evidence of load application to both ends, and this load application may appear as crushing at the points of applied force. At opposite ends of the bipolar flake there should be evidence of crushed or sheared striking platforms. Also, since the compression forces have cracked the objective piece, bipolar flakes should not have bulbs of force on either end. Pronounced compression rings originating from either end should meet near the center of the flake. Figure 6.3 illustrates these bipolar flake related characteristics.

There are several other technological types of debitage reported in the archaeological literature. Most do not have definitions that are as universally applicable as bipolar flakes and bifacial thinning flakes. However, many are adequate for a particular context of study. For instance, Frison's report on a bison butchering and processing station was able to match debitage types to specific types of tools used at the site. In addition to bifacial trimming flakes he identified several different kinds of scraper retouch flakes (Frison 1968). Shott (1995:64) also recognizes scraper retouch flakes, and defines them simply as "small, with correspondingly small, flat striking platforms." However, although most scraper retouch flakes appear to be small, small flakes are produced from all kinds of tool production and retouching. Figure 6.4 illustrates some examples of endscraper retouch flakes. Since endscrapers are resharpened by using the ventral surface of the flake as a striking platform, they almost always have flat striking platforms, and they seldom have dorsal cortex. The ventral surface of the scraper retouch flake is often concave and the curvature tends to occur near the distal end. Newcomer and Karlin (1987) recognize unifacial retouch flakes, similar to endscraper retouch flakes, that are produced when tool makers resharpen or produce unifaces. In experiments with making and notching projectile points, Titmus (1985) was able to identify specific flakes associated with projectile point notching. During Witthoft's (1971) analysis of a Paleoindian site assemblage, several flakes were found that

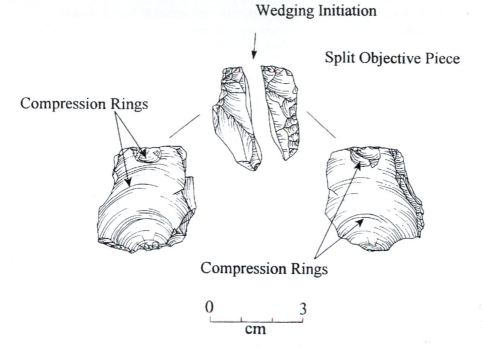

Figure 6.3 Example of bipolar flaking showing split objective piece and compression forces originating from opposite ends.

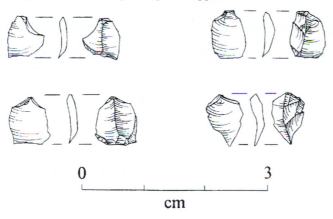

Figure 6.4 Examples of flakes removed to retouch an endscraper. Note the curved distal ends.

probably represent the detached piece from channel or flute removal. It is reasonable to expect that in a specific study with known contexts, different technological flake types will be reliably identified.

Debitage typologies based upon technology can be very valuable for making behavioral interpretations. A good example is provided by Parry and Kelly (1987) who use the relative proportion of bifacial thinning flakes from all flakes

Table 6.3   *Percent of biface thinning flakes in two areas of North America*

	Plains data (North Dakota)		
	Early	Middle	Late
Percent of biface thinning flakes	27	15	9
	Southwest data (Black Mesa)			
	Early	Early/Middle	Late/Middle	Late
Percent of biface thinning flakes	15	19	2	0

Source: Data taken from Parry and Kelly (1987).

found in their selected assemblages in an attempt to demonstrate changes in tool production preferences over time, and then link various kinds of tool production efforts to relative amounts of sedentism. Table 6.3 shows relative percentages of bifacial thinning flakes over time in the southwestern United States and northern Plains. Populations in both areas are known to have become gradually more sedentary. The trend with decreasing relative amounts of bifacial thinning flakes suggests that bifacial technology decreases with increased amounts of relative sedentism.

The free standing typology

Another typological approach to debitage analysis is what can be called the free-standing approach. This uses objective, replicable criteria that may have nothing to do with the final interpretations about the debitage being studied. Some researchers classify debitage on the basis of raw-material types, size grade (Ahler 1989), weight classes (Ammerman and Andrefsky 1982), and condition (Lyons 1994), and use these types of classification schemes in conjunction with analysis that examines other debitage characteristics. For instance, debitage types based upon size classes may be evaluated in relation to cortex amount on specimens within each size class (Larson *et al.* 1988), or debitage types based upon weight group may be evaluated in relation to the count of items in each type (Andrefsky 1983). Interpretations about technological characteristics can be made about an assemblage from these kinds of comparisons.

An example of a free-standing typology is the Sullivan and Rozen "interpretation-free" typology (1985:758). Their classification scheme used a monothetic divisive dendrogram to separate a population of debitage into four types. A dendrogram that recognized the presence or absence of three variables was used to classify debitage (Figure 6.5). All debitage was first evaluated for a

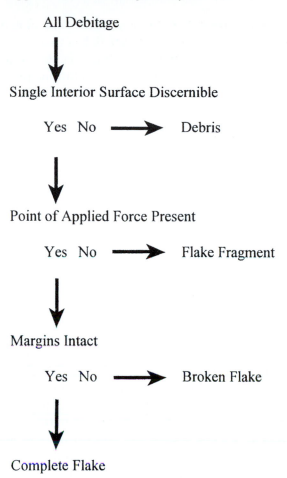

All Debitage

Single Interior Surface Discernible

Yes No ⟶ Debris

Point of Applied Force Present

Yes No ⟶ Flake Fragment

Margins Intact

Yes No ⟶ Broken Flake

Complete Flake

Figure 6.5 Debitage classification flow chart identifying four types of debitage. Adapted from Sullivan and Rosen (1985:759).

discernible single interior surface (ventral surface). If a single interior surface was absent the specimen was classified as debris; if present the specimen was further evaluated to discover a point of applied force (striking platform). If the point of applied force was absent the specimen was classified as a flake fragment; if present the specimen was evaluated for margins, and if margins were not intact the specimen was classified as a broken flake, or a complete flake if the margins were intact. The four types of debitage in the Sullivan and Rozen scheme were complete flake, broken flake, flake fragment, and debris.

Although the Sullivan and Rozen typology was highly criticized (Amick and Mauldin 1989b; Ensor and Roemer 1989; Prentiss and Romanski 1989), most of the criticism was leveled against the interpretations made from the typology and not the typology itself. In fact, experimental studies have shown that some of the Sullivan and Rozen interpretations about technology were incorrect.

For instance, Sullivan and Rozen (1985:763) indicate that core reduction produces relatively higher percentages of complete flakes than other kinds of flakes, and that tool production produces fewer complete flakes and relatively higher frequencies of flake fragments. Contrary interpretations resulting from other controlled experiments of core reduction and tool production indicate that tool production (particularly biface production) produces relatively greater frequencies of complete flakes than does core reduction (Baumler and Downum 1989; Tomka 1989). Even though the interpretation-free approach used by Sullivan and Rozen met with problems when technological interpretations were made, their contribution has had a significant and positive impact on lithic analysis, particularly in the areas of terminological clarity and replicability of attributes and debitage typologies.

Some researchers believe that it is possible to determine the difference between unidirectional core reduction and multidirectional core reduction by looking at the debitage assemblage. Of course, any number of debitage analyses can be conducted to try and discriminate between the two types of core reduction. A free-standing typological analysis is one way to approach a problem of this kind. An example of the use of a free-standing debitage typology would be to use the debitage types identified in the morphological typology from Chapter 4. By using this typology, all debitage is either flakes (Figure 4.7, 4e), flake shatter (Figure 4.7, 4f), or angular shatter (Figure 4.7, 4g).

Another example of a free-standing typology might be one based on definitions by flake weight, maximum length, and maximum thickness. The general shape of the detached piece can be determined when maximum length is divided by maximum thickness; an indication of overall size can be achieved by analyzing flake weight. By using these measurements a typology with six types can be derived. The length to thickness ratio can be stratified into two units (ratios <5 and ratios ≥ 5). Each of these units can be stratified into weight groups (<5 g, 5 g to 20 g, >20 g). Table 6.4 lists the counts and relative percentages of each of these six types of detached pieces for a unidirectional core and a multidirectional core. Both of the cores have little or no representation in the large and very thin flake category (ratio ≥ 5 and >20 g), and both of the cores are evenly split between relatively thick flakes (ratio <5) and relatively thin flakes (ratio ≥ 5). Detached pieces from the multidirectional core have a fairly uniform representation in all categories other than large flakes (>20 g). The highest representation is in the group of small flakes with a ratio of ≥ 5 (31.4%). The detached pieces produced from the reduction of the unidirectional core appear to be more uniform in size and not as uniformly distributed as the multidirectional core pieces. Approximately 63% of the detached pieces from the unidirectional core fall within the 5–20 g weight range regardless of length to thickness ratios. Figure 6.6 graphically depicts the flake type distribution for both cores types. Other free-standing typologies might show better discriminating patterns than the typology presented here, but this typology is a

Table 6.4 *Relative frequency of flake types for unidirectional and multi-directional cores*

Flake type	Unidirectional Cores		Multidirectional cores	
	count	percent	count	percent
Ratio <5 Weight <5 g	3	11.1	8	15.7
Ratio <5 Weight 5–20 g	8	29.6	11	21.6
Ratio <5 Weight >20 g	3	11.1	5	9.8
Ratio ≥5 Weight <5 g	3	11.1	16	31.4
Ratio ≥5 Weight 5–20 g	9	33.3	11	21.6
Ratio ≥5 Weight >20 g	1	3.7	0	0
Total	27		51	

good example of how free-standing approaches to classification of debitage can be used.

Debitage typological summary

The various debitage typologies presented above represent only some of the more common kinds of typological analysis. As with all kinds of phenomena, there is an infinite number of typologies. Selecting the kind of typology and the kind of typological analysis is dependent upon the needs of the researcher. If a certain type of debitage or a debitage attribute is highly correlated with a type of technology, the presence of that type of debitage or attribute provides a solid reason for making a technological inference. If, for instance, instead of comparing differences in debitage from unidirectional and multidirectional cores, the researcher were more interested in the debitage differences between biface production and unidirectional core reduction, other ways to approach the analysis can be selected. The six different debitage types could still be used, but it might be more effective to include technological debitage types such as bifacial thinning flakes in the analysis. Since pieces are detached from cores differently than they are from bifaces, it might also be effective to compare striking platform types on debitage pieces.

The data generated from free-standing debitage types for Table 6.4 are effective only if they are compared in a population structure, such as the one illustrated (Figure 6.6). For instance, no single flake greater than 5 g or single flake less than 5 g is effective in and of itself, for determining the kind of

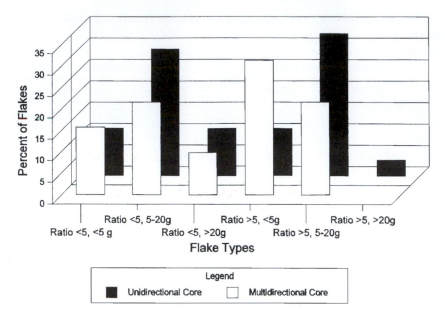

Figure 6.6 Flake type frequencies from unidirectional and multidirectional cores. Flake types are based upon length to thickness ratios and weight groups.

technology that produced the debitage. However, when all debitage is examined as a population and compared to other populations, the debitage population trends reveal a great deal about the type of technology used. The following section provides a review of other types of debitage population analyses.

Aggregate analysis of debitage

Aggregate debitage analysis is conducted by stratifying the entire assemblage of debitage by some uniform criterion and then comparing the relative frequencies of debitage in each stratum. When different assemblages are stratified using the same criteria, differences and similarities in the populations can be used to make interpretations about each population. One of the key elements is size variability, and almost all forms of aggregate analysis incorporate some aspect of debitage size into the analytical formula (Ahler and VanNest 1985; Ammerman and Andrefsky 1982; Raab *et al.* 1979; Stahle and Dunn 1982). As discussed above, because chipped stone tool production and core reduction are reductive processes, the objective piece always gets smaller as the production process goes from beginning to end, and debitage will necessarily get progressively smaller as well. Since aggregate analysis examines the entire population of debitage, individual detached pieces that are larger than previously detached pieces should become apparent as anomalous specimens. This is in contrast to individual flake analysis that cannot generally control for anomalous specimens.

In addition to the relation of flake size to objective piece size, the size of debitage is responsive to the type of load application on the objective piece. In other words, flake size is determined by the location of impact and the type of hammer used on the objective piece. For instance, percussion flaking generally produces larger-sized detached pieces than does pressure flaking (Ahler 1989:91). Similarly, detached pieces initiated on the edges of objective pieces tend to be smaller than detached pieces initiated away from the edge (Speth 1975:205–6; Whittaker 1994:96–7). As a result, variability in load applications has a great deal to do with the size of debitage. It is for these reasons that debitage aggregate analysis almost always incorporates some aspect of the detached piece size.

Linear size debitage analysis

Debitage size is sensitive to any number of morphological dimensions. Length is one way to partition debitage assemblages into size groups, and can be a relatively easy way to structure assemblages. Since many researchers record the length of debitage, it may also be an effective way to obtain multiple comparative collections for analysis. If length alone does not appear to be a good way to characterize the size variability of detached pieces within a particular assemblage, length can be divided by thickness or width to obtain a better overall perception of shape and size.

Raab *et al.* (1979) used length groups based on increments of 1 cm to determine debitage signatures related to settlement strategies for sites in the Ozark Mountains of Arkansas in central United States. They ultimately determined five different length groups that ranged from less than 1 cm to over 4 cm. The debitage size groups were plotted against the mean value of striking platform angles found on flakes within each size group. Figure 6.7 illustrates the distribution of flake characteristics by length and mean striking platform angle for a replicated assemblage and three sites from the Ozark study. The replicated assemblage contains debitage from the entire reduction trajectory. Two of the three excavated sites have reduction trajectories similar to the replicated assemblage. Raab *et al.* (1979) suggest that longer reduction trajectories reflect the total range of bifacial production from earlier to later stages and are reminiscent of base camps. Short trajectories, on the other hand, represent temporary use sites where only part of the bifacial reduction sequence might take place. Site 3CW139 was interpreted as a temporary use site based upon the short reduction trajectory.

However, the length-group analysis of debitage used by Raab and his colleagues required that the debitage be stratified to include only those unbro-

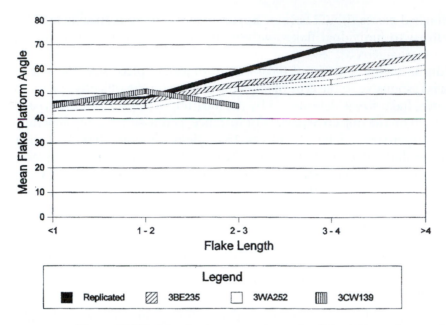

Figure 6.7 Bifacial reduction comparison using flake debitage characteristics from a replicated assemblage and three excavated assemblages. Based upon data from Raab *et al.* 1979:181).

ken specimens with an intact striking platform in order to make accurate length measurements. Therefore, a potentially large percentage of the debitage assemblage may not have been included in the analysis. In such cases it would be wise to conduct a second type of analysis to incorporate more of the excavated assemblage.

Screened size graded debitage analysis

One of the first types of aggregate analysis to appear in the literature was an analysis of debitage that was segregated by a series of nested sieves or screens (Henry *et al.* 1976). Using application load experiments, hard-hammer, soft-hammer, and pressure flaking loads were evaluated by frequency counts of six different debitage sizes. Maximum thickness and weights of individual specimens were also taken. The results of the analysis demonstrated significant differences in flake size between percussion and pressure techniques – pressure flakes were generally smaller than percussion flakes.

Stahle and Dunn (1982), also using nested screens to segregate debitage size grades, attempted to discriminate different stages of projectile point production. Nine different size grades were used from $\frac{1}{8}$ inch to $1\frac{1}{2}$ inch mesh size in $\frac{1}{8}$ inch increments. Their results were plotted on a cumulative frequency curve

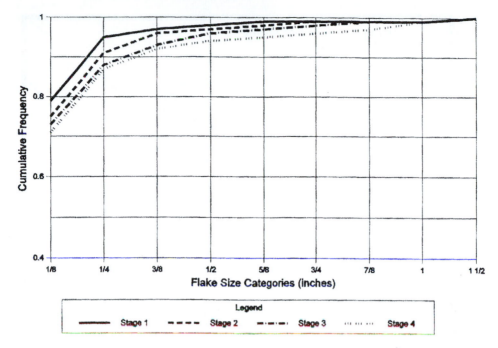

Figure 6.8 Cumulative frequency distribution of flake sizes by bifacial stages of reduction. Data derived from Stahle and Dunn (1982:19).

and showed good segregation between early and late reduction stages in point manufacture (Figure 6.8). In addition to testing for different stages of reduction, they also explored assemblages with debitage mixed from several different stages and discovered that size grade analysis was not as effective when applied to mixed assemblages.

Ahler (1989) also used screened size grade analysis of debitage. His approach used nested screens made of sieve cloth in increments of $\frac{1}{16}$, $\frac{1}{8}$, $\frac{1}{4}$, and $\frac{1}{2}$ inch. Ahler minimized examination of individual specimens and relied almost totally upon size grades and their aggregate weights and counts, a technique quite different from some others. This allowed for the processing of extremely large samples of debitage in a relatively quick manner, and for the processing of all debitage regardless of shape or size. By contrast, Henry *et al.* (1976) weighed each specimen and measured maximum thickness, a process that required each piece to be handled separately and could take a great deal of time and effort if the number of specimens in a study were great.

Ahler's analysis focused upon twenty-two different assemblage variables by using percentages of different size grades by weight and count, as well as ratios of different size grades and combinations of size grades. His twenty-two variables included: (1–4) percentage of total weight in size grade 1–4 (the total is based on four size grades); (5–7) percentage of total weight in size grades 1–3 (the total is based on three size grades); (8–11) percentage of total count in size

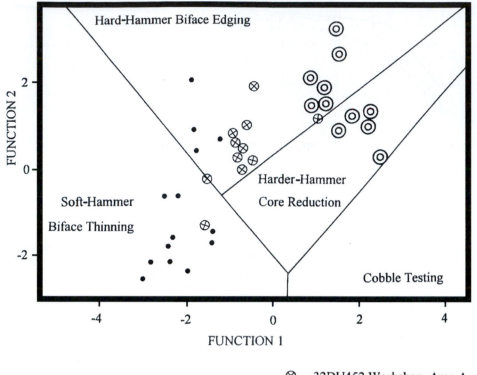

Figure 6.9 Discriminant scores for archaeological samples from three site areas plotted on a territorial map of discriminant functions from experimental reduction data. Adapted from Ahler 1989:105).

grades 1–4 (the total is based on four size grades); (12–14) percentage of total count in size grades 1–3 (the total is based on three size grades); (15–18) percentage of flakes with cortex in size grades 1–4; and (19–22) mean flake weight in size grades 1–4. It is not clear why these twenty-two size grade attributes were chosen, and it is apparent that each piece of debitage in his study had to be handled so that weight and cortex could be recorded – defeating one of the stated advantages of the technique. However, the twenty-two attributes were used in a discriminate function analysis to obtain signatures for activities such as bipolar core reduction, hard-hammer edging, soft-hammer thinning, and cobble testing, among others. These signatures were then compared against excavated data to determine the kinds of activities that might have taken place at a site.

An example of his results is shown in Figure 6.9 where quarry area assemblages and workshop area assemblages are superimposed upon a discriminate function map of different technological activities. Ahler's results show slight

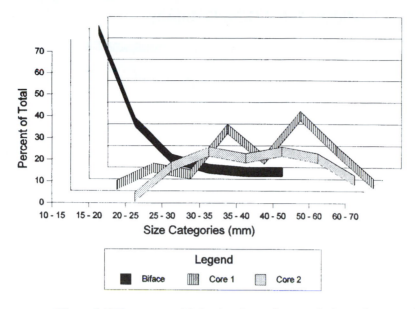

Figure 6.10 Frequency of flake size classes for two platformed cores and one biface.

clustering of excavated debitage assemblages with experimental debitage assemblages. Like some of the other screen sized studies he obtained reliable results when assemblages were not mixed. However, when excavated assemblages contained debitage mixed from several different kinds of reduction activity, the size grade signatures could not correctly discriminate activities.

Another example of screened size graded aggregate analysis is included in some of Patterson's work with bifacial reduction debitage (Patterson 1979, 1982, 1990; Patterson and Sollberger 1978). On the basis of his experimental data Patterson (1990) illustrated that biface reduction activities have a different signature from platformed core reduction. Figure 6.10 shows the difference in flake size distributions for a biface and a platformed core. Patterson concluded that biface reduction debitage has a characteristically high relative percentage of flakes in the small size grades, with progressively fewer detached pieces in larger size grades, and that this pattern differs from the product of platformed core reduction (1990).

Weight increment analysis of debitage

Another form of debitage assemblage analysis uses weight increments instead of screen sizes to partition the debitage into groups. Ammerman (1979), one of the first to use this form of analysis, initially developed the procedure to

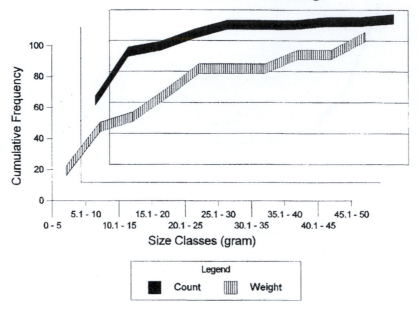

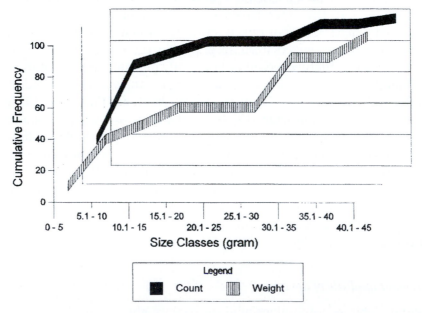

Figure 6.11 Cumulative frequency curves for count and weight from a unidirectional core and a multidirectional core.

characterize entire excavated assemblages of obsidian from southern Italy. The analysis was later refined in an attempt to determine various stages of production in an exchange system (Ammerman and Andrefsky 1982). Screen sized analysis requires a two-step approach in which debitage is first sifted through screens into various size grades and then every piece from each size grade is measured for cortex and weight amounts. Data for weight increment analysis are gathered by simply weighing each piece of debitage.

After the debitage is weighed the population is partitioned into groups by size based upon weight. Group sizes are arbitrary and can be designed around specific debitage populations for any study area. For instance, the Italian materials were partitioned into groups based upon 0.5 g increments (<0.5 g, 0.5–1.0 g, 1.1–1.5 g, 1.6–2.0 g, etc.) (Ammerman and Andrefsky 1982). Another study examining projectile point reduction processes from the eastern United States used 0.1 g size increments (Andrefsky 1983). The number of detached pieces and the total weight in each size group are tallied, and can then be displayed as cumulative frequency curves for count and weight to produce a graphic image of the debitage population. Figure 6.11 shows cumulative frequency curves for counts and weights of debitage from the reductions of a multidirectional core and of a unidirectional core. Note that both core types show the majority of specimens or counts of specimens occur within the smaller size classes. Approximately 70% of the specimens are under 15 g in size. The weight of individual specimens does not peak as quickly for either core type, but multidirectional core debitage weight appears to peak earlier than the weight of unidirectional core debitage.

The two separate curves for count and weight can be combined to produce a single image that combines information from both the population count and the population weight. This is done by converting the graph into a concentration curve (Kendall and Stuart 1969:48). Concentration curves are created by plotting the cumulative percentage of count on the y-axis and the cumulative percentage of weight on the x-axis. Figure 6.12 illustrates the data from Figure 6.11 after conversion into a concentration curve. Each point on the graph represents a weight class with specimens. The distribution of points shows the curve for each assemblage so that count and weight can be assimilated into a single image. One interesting aspect of this graph is that the debitage from each core type appears similar with regard to specimen weights and counts. In other words, both debitage populations have about the same amount of weight and counts within the same size groups. This form of weight increment analysis can be used on entire assemblages of debitage, or the debitage can be partitioned into groups to reduce complexity. In other words, assemblage debitage may be stratified into raw material types and/or technological types before weight increment analysis is conducted.

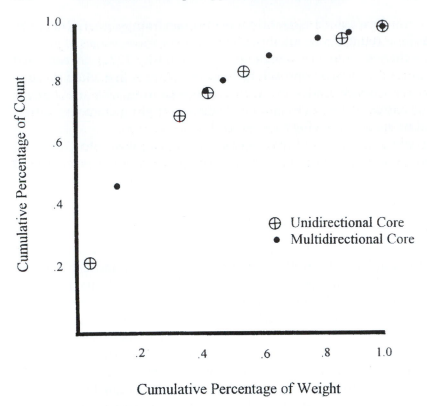

Figure 6.12 Concentration curves showing cumulative frequency of counts and weights combined. Both core types reveal similar distributions based upon weight and number of flakes.

Summary

The production of debitage is sensitive to a number of different kinds of technological behavior. Debitage attributes and combinations of attributes may vary depending upon constraints associated with tool production, tool use, tool maintenance, and tool discard. There is no "cook book" formula for the type and scale of analysis that should be conducted on a debitage assemblage to derive a specific type of behavioral interpretation. I have found that the most convincing interpretations made from debitage analysis are those using results from different debitage attributes and/or debitage types. Similarly, both individual and aggregate debitage analysis used in combination with one another can lead to strong interpretations.

When possible, the analysis of debitage assemblages should be conducted in combination with other evidence from the site that might support interpretations derived from the debitage. It is particularly important to use the chipped stone tools from assemblages to support behavioral interpretations derived from debitage analysis. For example, if the results of debitage analysis indicate that only the initial stages of bifacial core reduction occurred at a site, it would not be unrealistic to find early-stage bifaces in the assemblage. Early-stage bifacial cores that were broken during reduction and discarded at a site could also reasonably be expected if only early-stage reduction, based upon debitage analysis, had taken place at the site. Such data patterns are typical of raw material access areas or quarry locations used by prehistoric tool makers. The next chapter goes beyond the analysis of chipped stone debitage and explains some of the different ways researchers conduct and employ analysis of chipped stone tools.

APPROACHES TO STONE TOOL ANALYSIS

Chapter 4 introduced a classification scheme that separated chipped stone artifacts into two primary groups, debitage and tools. Tools are considered to be all those chipped stone objective pieces that have been modified by intentionally altering their form and those detached pieces that show signs of modification as a result of use. The discussion thus far has dealt primarily with debitage or chipped stone artifacts that are not tools. Now the discussion turns to tools, specifically bifaces (Figure 4.7, 3a), flake tools (Figure 4.7, 4c), and cores (Figure 4.7, 4d).

Since chipped stone tools include specimens that may have been altered by usewear only, it is important to re-emphasize the point that the analysis in this book is restricted to macroscopic approaches. Macroscopic approaches frequently require the use of a hand lens of about $10 \times$ to observe some of the smaller attributes on stone tools. A small hand lens is particularly helpful in recognizing striking platform characteristics and retouch patterns. If magnification is required that is greater than that provided by a hand lens, a researcher needs to consider microscopic analysis. Excellent studies of microscopic lithic analysis exist in the published literature (Hayden 1979a; Keeley 1980; Odell 1977; Vaughan 1985).

Macroscopic analysis of stone tools is considerably less time consuming than microscopic analysis. However, the level of detail related to tool use that can be collected is also considerably less from macroscopic approaches than from microscopic approaches. For example, it is almost impossible to determine the differences between some kinds of tool-use damage and some kinds of intentional retouching of tool edges by macroscopic analysis. This is particularly true if an edge is used, dulled, retouched, and used repeatedly. The differences between intentional retouching and usewear are difficult to discriminate on flake tools that have been backed or dulled intentionally for safe hand prehension. The reader should be aware, however, that the same kinds of discriminatory difficulties occur with microscopic analysis as well. This is particularly true when dealing with backed tools and tools that have been resharpened over a series of uses. In other words, the same tools that are difficult to analyze macroscopically are difficult to analyze microscopically. The macroscopic analysis of tool edges discussed in this chapter makes no attempt to segregate usewear from intentional retouch wear. All specimens with alteration along an edge or edges are considered tools. The analysis described below examines variations of macroscopic alteration patterns on such artifacts.

Core analysis

Cores can be considered objective pieces which are primarily used as sources of raw material. As previously shown (chapter 2), cores come in a great variety of forms and sizes. The effort expended in shaping cores to obtain various kinds of detached pieces is also extremely variable; formalized cores may go through several stages of preparation before they are ready to have usable pieces removed. Informal cores, on the other hand, may undergo no preparation. In these cases, usable pieces are detached from the core in an opportunistic manner. One advantage of formalized core technology over informal core technology is maximization of cutting edge. Because formalized cores tend to produce uniform detached pieces in a systematic and patterned manner, the number of detached pieces per mass of core is usually greater than with informal cores. Formal core shapes also allow the removal of predictable sizes and shapes of detached pieces.

Cores represent the end product of a sequence of objective piece preparation, reduction of detached pieces, and continued preparation and reduction. This sequence of removals alters the form of the core so that the core recovered from the archaeological record may not reflect the complete history of the specimen. In fact, core morphology represents only the last phase of use before deposit in the archaeological record, which is why it is important to analyze the detached pieces as well as the cores when trying to understand the trajectory of core reduction. In the next section the techniques of flake blank analysis that emphasizes core variability and morphological properties of the objective piece are discussed.

Classification of cores

The morphological typology presented in chapter 4 separated cores into either unidirectional (Figure 4.7, 5e) or multidirectional (Figure 4.7, 5f) forms. Unidirectional cores usually have a single flat surface or striking platform and pieces are detached in one direction away from the striking platform. The detached pieces are removed roughly parallel to one another. This definition subsumes more formalized core types recognized around the world including, but not limited to, Mesoamerican polyhedral cores, the Alaskan microblade cores, and Shirataki cores from Japan. Like unidirectional cores, multidirectional cores include a wide range of forms from relatively complicated Levallois cores to simple radial and bipolar cores. The primary characteristic of multidirectional cores is the removal of flakes in more than one direction and, therefore, the use of more than one striking platform.

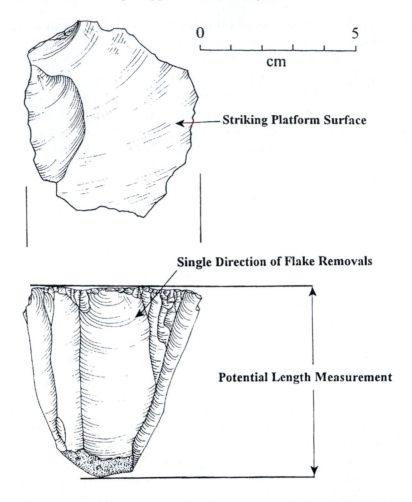

Figure 7.1   Unidirectional core showing potential technique for measuring core length.

Since cores can often have a great deal of morphological variability within any technological type and among different types, it can be difficult to obtain consistent size measurements on these specimens. The literature contains numerous references to the size of cores, but few have explained how size is measured (Cox 1986:93–5; Lothrop and Gramly 1982:14; McNerney 1987). Length, width, and thickness of cores are frequently given as size measurements for both unidirectional cores and multidirectional cores (Johnson 1987; Shott 1989). Because formal definitions for any of these core measurements are difficult to find, comparisons of core sizes are difficult to make. It seems reasonable to define core length as the longest measurement perpendicular to the striking platform and parallel to the removal of detached pieces (Figure 7.1). Unfortunately, this definition can present a problem when talking about multidirectional cores, where more than one striking platform is used to remove detached pieces. The attributes of core width and thickness can also be difficult to measure. Because of the multitude of core shapes a consistent definition for the width or thickness of cores is illusive. It follows that, if these attributes cannot be consistently defined, it is not possible to compare these characteristics consistently among different cores.

For these reasons I prefer to characterize core size not by length, width, and thickness, but by a combination of weight and maximum linear dimension. Most cores, regardless of how amorphous their shape, have one linear dimension that is easily recognized as the greatest; that dimension multiplied by the weight provides a uniform measure of size. Figure 7.2 shows how the maximum linear dimension (MLD) is measured on several different shapes of cores. Note that the length perpendicular to the striking platform and parallel to the detached pieces on specimen b is considerably smaller than the maximum linear dimension.

Specimen b is an example of a Yubetsu microblade core from Japan (Kobayashi 1970; Yoshizaki 1961) based upon the manner in which such cones are prepared. There are several different kinds of microblade cores in Japan, and all would be considered unidirectional because detached pieces are removed from a single striking platform in roughly the same parallel direction. The size value for the Yubetsu core is 50 since it has a MLD of 2.6 cm and it weighs 19.4 g.

The Yubetsu core reduction technique is quite distinctive from other microblade reduction strategies found in east Asia and the North American Arctic. Initially, a biface is prepared and then it is either snapped in half or split by removing a large flake. In either case, the flat surface created by the break is used as the microblade striking platform (Figure 7.3a). Detached pieces are removed perpendicular to the striking platform and are parallel to each other. The original bifacial edge is used as a crest or ridge from which the first microblade is detached. The removal of the first microblade produces two ridges for the removal of subsequent microblades.

Another microblade core reduction strategy from Japan is known as the Hokoru technique (Kobayashi 1970; Morlan 1970). It is similar to mi croblade reduction strategies found in Alaska and British Columbia (Ackerman 1996; Anderson 1970; Magne 1996; Mobley 1991). The Hokoru technique begins with a split cobble or an angular mass of lithic material. The objective piece is systematically prepared to give the core a wedge shape. The wedge-shaped appearance is formed as a result of the angle created between the striking platform and the surface of the core (Figure 7.3b). This angle is usually in the range of 60° to 80°.

Specimen a in Figure 7.2 is an example of a Levallois core. This core is shaped to produce a Levallois surface for the removal of a large detached piece or Levallois flake. The conical shaped core allows for relatively easy reworking

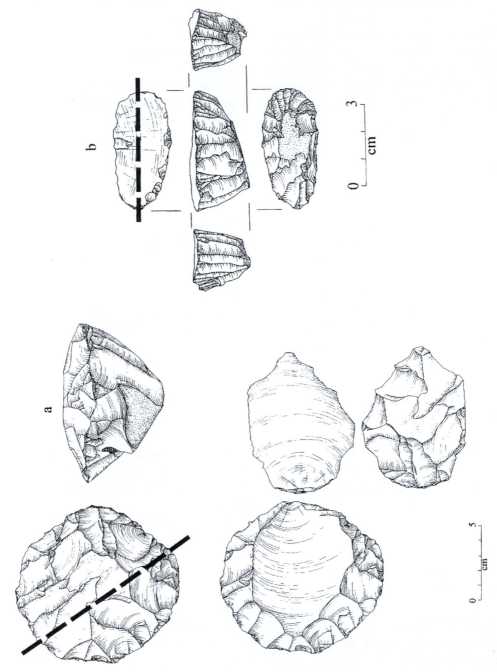

Figure 7.2 The dashed line illustrates the maximum linear dimension on two different shapes of cores: (a) multidirectional core; (b) unidirectional core.

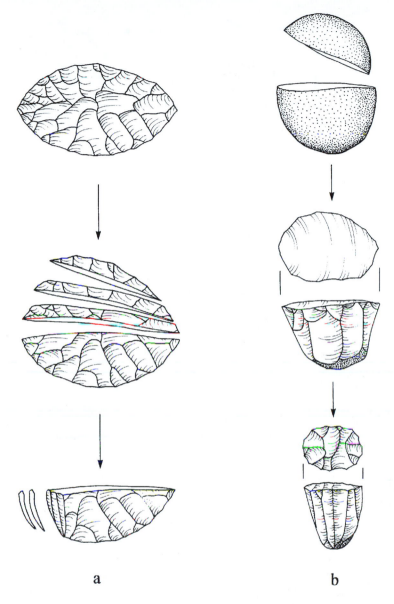

Figure 7.3 Schematic diagrams of microblade core reduction: (a) Yubetsu technique; (b) Hokora technique. Adapted from Kobayashi (1970).

to prepare the Levallois surface multiple times. Figure 7.4 shows the classic sequence of reduction and core preparation first described by Bordes (1961). Note that the Levallois core contains flakes removed in a multidirectional pattern. The size value for the Levallois core depicted in Figure 7.2a is 5429 (9.5 cm × 571.5 g).

Debitage analysis associated with Levallois reduction has generated some

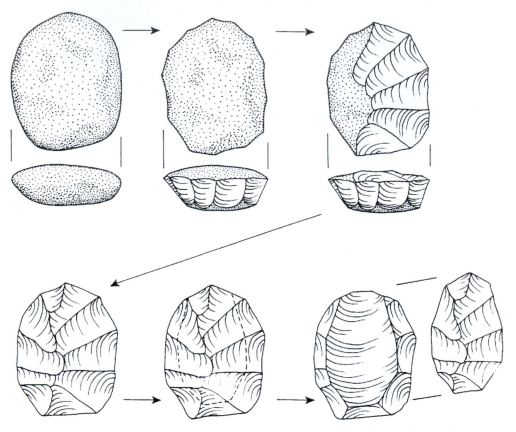

Figure 7.4   Schematic diagram of classic Levallois core reduction. Adapted from Mellars (1996:62).

confusion in the 1970s about exactly how the Levallois core is reduced (Boeda 1993; Bordes 1980; Copeland 1983). Bradley (1977) and then others began systematic analysis of reduction techniques to gain a better understanding of Levallois technology (Boeda 1986; Geneste 1985; Van Peer 1991, 1992). These studies have defined a number of different techniques associated with Levallois core reduction. However, there appears to be an underlying, unifying theme that runs through all Levallois reduction strategies. Levallois reduction technology is based upon the preparation of a core that has a single convex upper surface from which detached pieces can be systematically removed. This core is conical in shape so that as Levallois flakes are removed, the core maintains its shape so that subsequent removals can be made with minimal repreparation of the core (Figure 7.5). Mellars (1996:61) describes this theme:

> This is defined by a basic division in the initial stages of preparation and shaping of Levallois cores into two main components: first, the preparation of a continuous

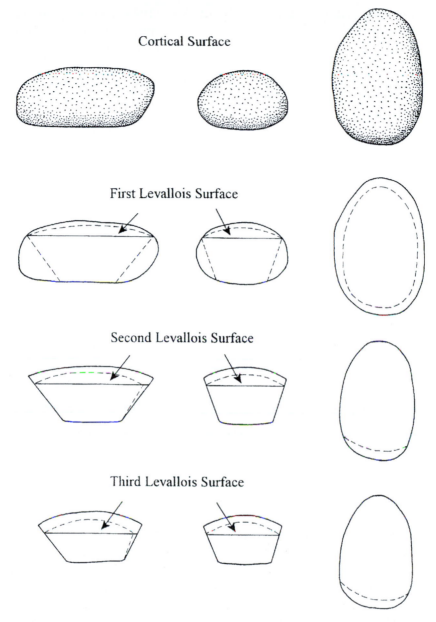

Figure 7.5 Schematic diagram showing conical shape and size of Levallois core during reduction. Adapted from Van Peer (1992).

striking platform extending around most of the perimeter of the selected nodule – normally produced by successive blows delivered more or less vertically on the upper face of the core and extending over a substantial part of the lower face; and second, by the systematic shaping of the upper surface of the core by blows delivered from various points around the perimeter of this prepared striking platform . . .

Following Boeda (1988, 1993), Mellars (1996) characterizes two general strategies of Levallois core reduction – lineal and recurrent. Lineal is defined as the traditional Levallois technique as characterized by Bordes (1961) and illustrated in Figure 7.4. This technique is designed for the removal of a single large flake from the prepared top surface (Figure 7.5). This technique initially shapes the core so there is a continuous striking platform around the perimeter of the upper surface. The upper surface is then shaped so that a single large Levallois flake can be removed. After removal of the Levallois flake the upper surface is again shaped so that another flake can be detached. The sequence of preparation and removal may continue up to five times (Mellars 1996:67).

The recurrent Levallois technique is designed so that multiple flakes can be removed from the upper surface of the Levallois core before it requires reshaping. Figure 7.6 illustrates a sequence of three Levallois flake removals using the recurrent strategy. Boeda (1988) notes that Levallois flakes may be removed from one end or both ends of the core. The recurrent technique has also been documented with a centripetal removal pattern where flakes are detached from various positions around the perimeter of the core toward the center (Figure 7.7).

Another multidirectional core reduction pattern is illustrated in Figure 7.8 with examples of bifacial cores. Note the location for measuring the MLD on these bifacial cores. These cores have detached pieces removed from several directions on both faces of the specimen. They are prepared by first edging a cobble or flake blank by detaching pieces from alternating faces (Figure 7.9). The flake scar produced by the removal of an edging detached piece is used as the striking platform surface for the subsequent removal of a flake on the opposing surface. Once edging is complete, larger detached pieces are removed to create a convex surface on both faces of the core. Ridges created by previous flake scars, along with the convex surface, allow the removal of successive flake blanks from both faces of the bifacial core.

The size values for the eight core specimens in Figures 7.1, 7.2, and 7.5 are listed in Table 7.1. using the technique described above. Note that the unidirectional core depicted in Figure 7.1 has the second highest weight value, yet because it is relatively short it is ranked fourth in size with a size value of 679. This shows how any one dimension alone may not be a good indicator of core size.

Core technology and raw material size

The size of lithic raw materials has been shown to be an important factor related to the kind of technology practiced by prehistoric tool makers (Bar-Yosef 1991; Dibble 1991; Kuhn 1992; Lothrop 1989). In general, large blanks tend to be used for the production of large tools and small blanks for small tools. Similarly, different blank shapes tend to have an effect on the shape of

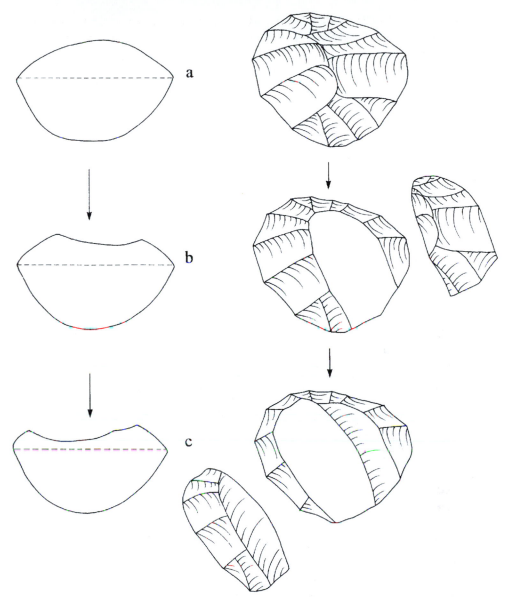

Figure 7.6   Schematic diagram illustrating the sequential removal of Levallois flakes on a conical Levallois core: (a) Levallois surface; (b) first Levallois flake removal; (c) second Levallois flake removal. Adapted from Mellars (1996:68).

finished flake tools. The idea of fitting technology to the size of available lithic raw material has important implications for core reduction strategies. Fish (1981) suggests that Levallois core reduction is directly related to available nodule size in some European and Near Eastern Middle Paleolithic sites. Levallois core technology does not seem to have been practiced in areas where

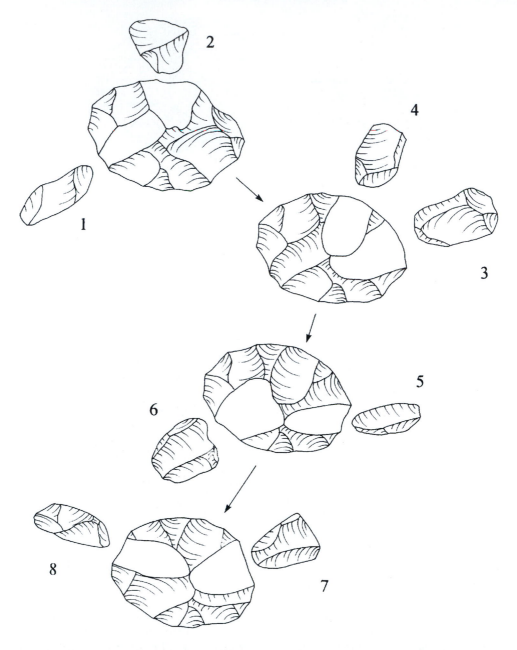

Figure 7.7   Schematic diagram showing the centripetal recurrent Levallois strategy recognized by Mellars (1996:71). Numbers indicate the sequence of flake removals.

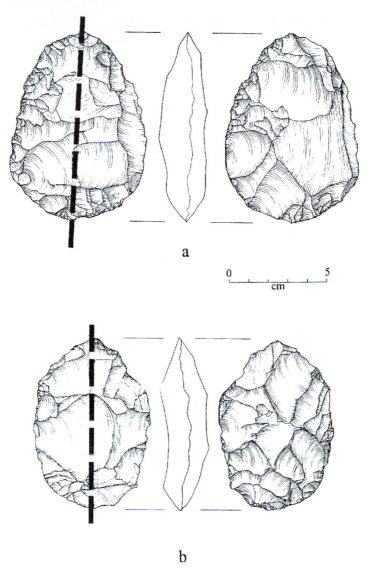

Figure 7.8   Examples of bifacial cores showing maximum linear dimension with a dashed line.

raw material nodules are small. This implies that Levallois core reduction requires relatively large objective pieces, and without those pieces a different strategy of flake blank production is practiced.

Bipolar cores, found in all regions of the world, seem to be an especially good example of technology matching the size of raw materials available for use in an area. Bipolar cores (Figure 7.10) are typically amorphously shaped and can be easily confused with angular shatter (Figure 4.7, 4g). Several

Table 7.1   *Size values for cores illustrated in Figures 7.1, 7.2, and 7.8*

Core fig. no.	MLD (cm)	Weight (g)	Size value	Size rank
7.1	3.8	178.8	679	4
7.2a	9.5	571.5	5429	1
7.2b	2.6	19.4	50	5
7.8a	7.7	144.3	1111	2
7.8b	6.7	123.3	826	3

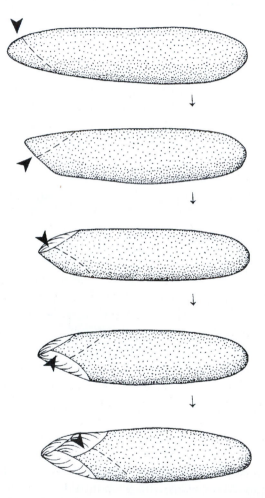

Figure 7.9   Schematic diagram showing the sequence of bifacial edging on a nodule.

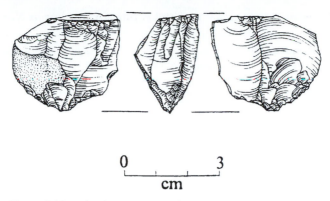

0   3

cm

Figure 7.10   Bipolar core example showing flake scars originating from opposite ends.

archaeologists (Goodyear 1993; Knudson 1978; Shott 1989) have suggested that bipolar technology is used to maximize or exhaust the utility of raw material before discarding it. However, if bipolar cores were used as a maximizing strategy for raw material consumption, these cores should be relatively smaller than other kinds of cores. The sizes of bipolar and freehand cores from six sites in eastern Washington were compared to test this proposition (Andrefsky 1994b). In all cases, bipolar cores were significantly smaller than freehand cores. Bipolar cores had a mean size of 43 cm^3. This was 34 times smaller than freehand reduced cores that had a mean size of 1,455 cm^3. This pattern seems to be true in areas where raw materials that have high chipping quality are rare or absent. In areas where raw material with high chipping quality are abundant, the pattern of core production is frequently different.

In northern Bosnia, where highly chippable lithic raw materials are abundant, bipolar technology was not frequently employed. On the basis of length measurements of cortical flakes Montet-White determined the average sized cobbles used in core reduction (1988:363–4), and then compared mean core size to mean cobble size to determine the amount of cobble reduction in her study area. Table 7.2 shows length, width, and thickness measurements for cobbles and cores from four sites. The cobbles were reduced by only approximately half of their original size – a fact that suggests raw materials were not being maximized or conserved. The cores from this lithic-rich study area were primarily single platformed and subconical or prismatic in shape (1988:366).

Kuhn's work on Mousterian assemblages from Italy also demonstrates how core reduction strategies are linked to raw material size (1995). In his study, cores were divided into two general classes, centripetal and parallel or platformed. Centripetal cores were defined as those cores that had flakes removed from the perimeter towards the center (Figure 7.11a). Parallel cores were those with flakes removed along a single axis of the core (Figure 7.11b). Centripetal cores have detached pieces removed from multiple directions

Table 7.2   *Mean measurements of cores and cobbles from sites in Northern Bosnia*

Site-core	Length (cm)	Width (cm)	Thickness (cm)
Ukrina cobbles	7.2	6.5	5.4
Kadar cores	4.1	3.3	2.2
Willendorf I-N cores	4.8	3.0	1.5
Willendorf II-5 cores	4.5	4.3	2.2
Willendorf II-6 cores	4.4	4.4	2.3

Source: Data taken from Montet-White (1988:367).

and parallel cores have unidirectional detached pieces. The selection of one or the other core reduction strategy was determined by the kinds of raw material sizes available for blank production and also by the kinds of detached pieces needed to perform various tasks. Centripetal cores were used to maximize the size of flakes being detached and parallel cores were used to maximize the number of flakes being detached (Stiner and Kuhn 1992). Figure 7.12 illustrates the ratio of detached pieces to objective pieces for both centripetal and parallel cores. There are almost three times the number of detached pieces associated with parallel cores as compared to centripetal cores.

Core technology and prehistoric mobility

Although cores may be considered primarily as objective pieces used as sources of raw material it is not unreasonable to expect that cores may have had other functions as well. Given the dynamic character of lithic artifacts with regard to their uselife and morphology, it would not be unthinkable to find cores that were used as cutting or scraping tools (Beyries 1988). Nor would it be uncommon to find tools such as bifaces or points that were used as sources of raw material (cores). In fact, it has been suggested that bifaces are excellent types of cores for certain peoples (Andrefsky 1991; Kelly 1988), particularly mobile populations. Mobile hunting and gathering bands may reduce the risk of being unprepared for a task by transporting finished tools such as bifaces and formalized cores with them as they travel.

Some bifaces have been shown to be highly efficient cores with less overall weight in proportion to amount of cutting edge (Kelly 1988). Preference for bifacial cores in mobile populations is consistent with the belief that mobile groups prefer multifunctional, readily modifiable, and portable tools to decrease the risk of uncertainty. Bifacial cores may be considered highly formalized cores that have undergone a great deal of effort in their production. By

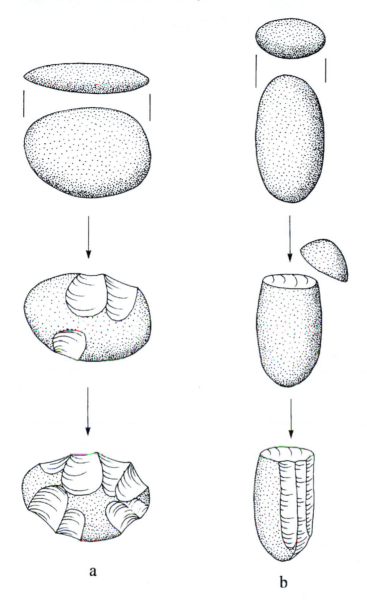

Figure 7.11 Schematic diagram illustrating two general kinds of core reduction strategies: (a) centripetal reduction; (b) parallel reduction. Adapted from Stiner and Kuhn (1992).

shaping an objective piece into a biface, the tool maker becomes familiar with the consistency and quality of the raw material, two characteristics very important in stone tool production. It may be argued that raw materials shaped into bifaces contain a much more reliable source of usable stone than do cobbles or even flake blanks that have not been worked. It would make

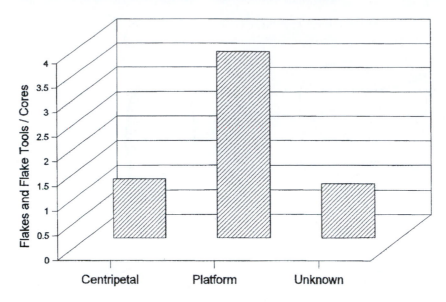

Figure 7.12   Relative percentage of flakes for centripetal and platform core types in Mousterian assemblages. Adapted from Stiner and Kuhn (1992).

sense for mobile groups to travel with bifacial cores rather than nodules or flake blanks.

Parry and Kelly (1987) have gathered core data from five different regions of North America that have shown decreased residential mobility over time. Table 7.3 lists the ratio of bifaces to cores for these regions. Note that in all cases preference for bifaces or bifaces used as cores decreased as mobility decreased. This pattern supports the belief that relatively more mobile groups tend to select bifacial core technology over potentially more cumbersome types of core technology.

This pattern is not necessarily universal, however, and depends upon a range of other factors. It has been shown that raw-material abundance and quality play a major role in the production of various core types (Andrefsky 1994a:30). Informal core technology, such as rotated mutidirectional core reduction, tends to be used in situations where poor-quality materials are all that are available in either high or low abundance. Formal core technology, such as bifacial core reduction, tends to be practiced in areas where high-quality raw materials occur in low amounts. When high-quality raw materials occur in great abundance both formal and informal core technology will be used. Figure 7.13 shows the relationship between raw-material abundance and quality as it relates to formal and informal core technology.

It has also been shown that core reduction strategies may become more intensified as a consequence of raw-material availability. For instance, instead of changing core type or technology type, some prehistoric tool makers simply

Table 7.3 *Differences in core and biface use based upon relative sedentism from various areas of North America*

		More mobile			Less mobile
Ratio of bifaces to cores	Arizona data:	Archaic 5.75	BMII 2.38	PI 0.45	PII 0.04
Ratio of bifaces to cores	Colorado data:	Archaic 5.75	BMII 2.83	PI 0.95	PII 0.75
Ratio of bifaces to cores	New Mexico data:	Preceramic 0.80			Puebloan 0.14
Ratio of bifaces to cores	North Dakota data:	Paleoindian 3.52	Archaic 3.92		Plains Village 1.34
Ratio of bifaces to cores	Mesoamerica data:	Archaic 1.09			Early Formative 0.03

Source: Data assembled from Parry and Kelly (1987:Tables 12.1–12.5).

extended or increased the reduction of cores to obtain more usable raw material (Marks *et al.* 1991). Clearly alluding to this, Table 7.4 lists core and debitage data for sites located both near and farther away from raw material sources. The mean core weight for sites near raw material sources is 158 g. This is three times greater than core weights located on sites away from sources of lithic raw material. These data suggest that core reduction intensity may be influenced by proximity of lithic raw materials. In turn, raw-material proximity may have a direct relationship to raw-material abundance.

It seems clear that the various factors associated with core reduction technology may be related on several different levels. Factors such as raw-material size and proximity have as much to do with core reduction technology as the type of tools being manufactured and the kinds of settlement patterns exhibited by the tool makers and users. It also seems clear that the kind of core technology used by prehistoric people may not be entirely evident when examining the end products of that technology (discarded cores). To understand more fully the processes of stone tool production, use, maintenance, and discard, it is important to include debitage in the analysis, as previously discussed, and also to include detached pieces that are modified to form flake tools and bifaces. The following sections discuss the latter in detail.

Flake tool analysis

Flake tool artifacts were described in chapter 4 in the morphological typology section (Figure 4.7, 4c). These tools show evidence of modification either from

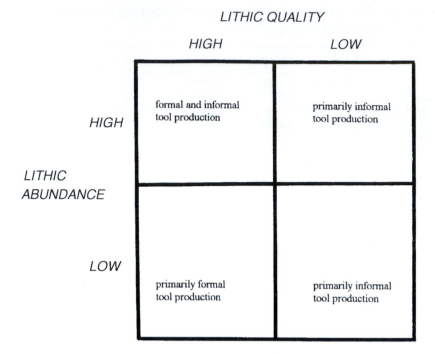

Figure 7.13   Contingency table illustrating the relationship between abundance and quality of lithic raw material and the kinds of tools produced. Adapted from Andrefsky (1994a:30).

intentional retouch of edges or from usewear along the margins. Flake tools must also come from detached pieces that show evidence of flake or blade properties. Flakes tend to have only two primary surfaces, dorsal and ventral. As discussed previously, ventral surfaces are usually smooth and never have evidence of previous flake removals. Ventral surfaces also do not show evidence of cortex except in the cases where a shallow flake is struck off an objective piece with a thick cortical surface. In such a case the entire flake may be composed of cortex. Dorsal sides contain flake scars and/or the original cortical surface of the raw material.

There is a wide range of flake tool shapes and sizes; some are illustrated in Figure 7.14. Variability in flake tool morphology originates from three primary sources: (1) functional requirements, (2) tool uselife, and (3) raw material differences. Functional requirements refer to the tool shape in relationship to specific task requirements. It is well known that different edge angles on chipped stone artifacts are more practical for performing certain tasks. A very acute or sharp edge angle is more effective for cutting soft materials such as meat than are wider edge angles. Edge angles that approach 75–90° are better for scraping hides than are the more acute edge angles. Artifacts with wider

Table 7.4   *Mean assemblage values for debitage and cores from Middle Paleolithic sites in the Avdat-Aqev area*

Sites away from lithic sources	Mean debitage length (mm)	Mean debitage thickness (mm)	Mean core weight (g)
D15	49.1	8.9	46.9
D35,1	49.1	8.5	77.6
D35,c	52.4	8.2	49.8
D52	45.4	9.6	43.7
Sites near lithic sources			
D44	54.1	11.3	159.5
D42	57.8	13.7	124.7
D40	70.3	12.4	190.0
D46	68.1	12.5	156.0

Source: Data derived from Marks *et al.* (1991:132).

edge angles can be pulled or pushed over the hide surface with little chance of cutting the hide. Thus a tool maker may make a choice of flake tool morphology based upon function. Flake tool uselife also accounts for variability in tool morphology. This refers to the change in tool shape as a result of flake tool use, resharpening, and reconfiguration (see chapter 2). Burins provide a good example of how the uselife of a flake tool changes its form. These tools are believed to be graving instruments or instruments used to chisel very hard materials such as bone. The cutting edge or bit of a burin is made by removal of small flakes or spalls, a process that rejuvenates the dull bit. Burins are believed to be hafted so that more leverage can be applied to the hard material being worked. As the burin becomes dull from use it is constantly resharpened while in the haft. By the time the burin is discarded it looks quite different than when it was first manufactured. However, although the haft element may stay the same throughout the life of the tool, uselife has altered the overall flake tool morphology. Another source of flake tool formal differences is raw-material variability. The shape, size, quality, and abundance of raw materials may affect the ultimate form of a flake tool (Andrefsky 1994b; Dibble 1991; Kuhn 1992). This source of variability is primarily related to the shape of the overal flake blank. For instance, if flake tools are made from blanks procured from small river pebbles, such tools may appear very different from flake tools made from blanks detached from formalized unidirectional cores. This may be the case even if the flake tools are produced to perform the same task, such a cutting vegetable fibers.

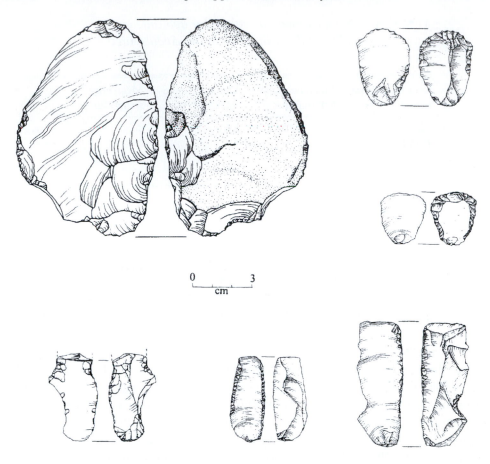

Figure 7.14   Examples of general flake tool variability.

Each of the three sources of variation in flake tools is discussed below by examining blank form production, haft element configuration, and working edge attributes. Several different flake tool attributes and attribute measurements are introduced that can be used to identify tool variability related to the different sources of morphological variation.

Flake blank production

The analysis of flake tool types might best be approached by considering how the flake blank was produced. Whether obtained from river nodules, tabular stone slabs, multidirectional cores, or unidirectional cores the origin of the flake blank can explain a great deal about the shape of the flake tool and possibly about the most prominent flake tool attributes that relate to artifact

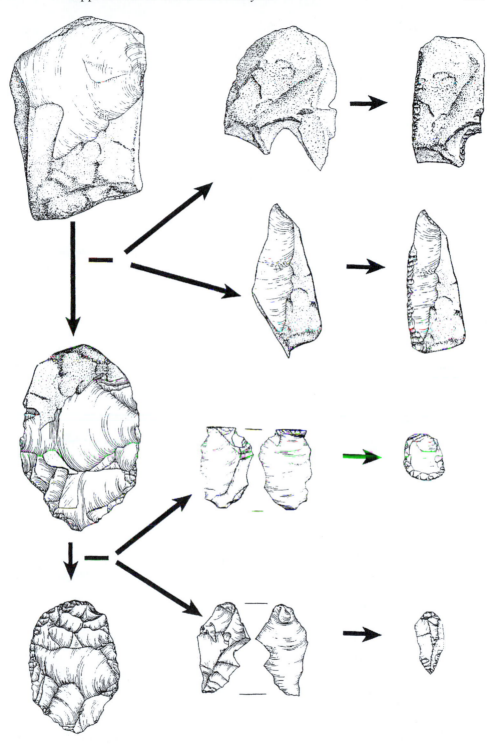

Figure 7.15   Schematic diagram of a reduction trajectory for a cobble reduced to a bifacial core, illustrating flake blanks removed and potential flake tools produced.

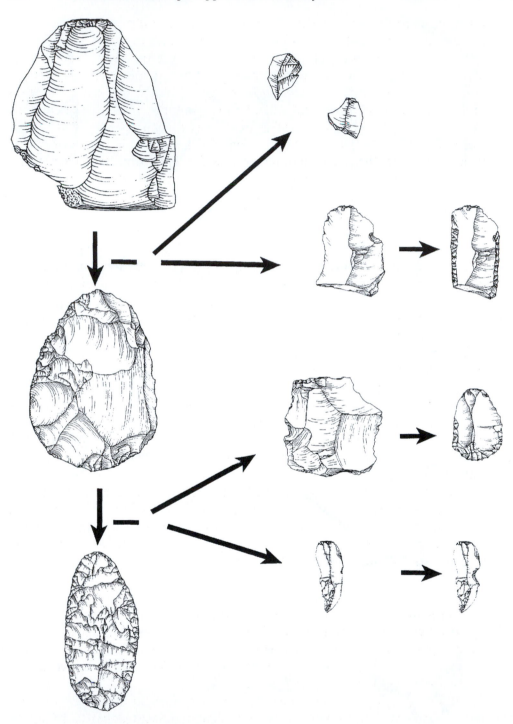

Figure 7.16   Schematic diagram of a reduction trajectory for a large flake blank reduced to a bifacial core.

function. The original raw-material size and shape certainly places constraints on the form of tool to be produced. However, this problem is frequently eliminated during the initial trimming of the raw-material objective piece. For instance, a river cobble covered with cortex can be trimmed and shaped into a multidirectional core such as a bifacial core or a centripetal core. The same kind of core can be produced from a large flake blank of chippable material removed from a bedrock outcrop. Figures 7.15 and 7.16 illustrate the reduction trajectory for each of these two raw-material sources. The detached pieces trimmed during the early shaping process for both objective pieces have obvious differences in shape, and may reveal much about the original shape of the raw material. However, once the raw materials are trimmed, the flake blanks detached from each core may be very similar. From a technological point of view, some flake blanks produced from core types derived from different raw material shapes might be considered to have originated from an identical technology. At this point, therefore, it may be worth exploring some of the potential differences in flake blank characteristics as they relate to technological differences.

Variability in core types was discussed earlier in this chapter. One way to evaluate the effects of core technology on flake blank form is to examine differences between multidirectional and unidirectional core reduction. As previously stated, multidirectional cores have more than one striking platform or surface and unidirectional cores have only a single striking platform surface. A typical example of a multidirectional core would be a bifacial core. The edge of the bifacial core is used as a striking platform, where pieces can be detached from either surface; Levallois cores would fit this definition as well (Bradley and Sampson 1986; Mellars 1996; Rolland 1988). Figures 7.15 and 7.16 illustrate the reduction trajectory of bifacial cores showing the various flake blanks removed for production of flake tools. Flake blanks produced from multidirectional cores generally tend to spread progressively wider from the proximal to the dorsal end, yet can be relatively parallel sided. As with all core reduction processes, the detached pieces tend to get progressively smaller as the reduction process goes from earlier to later stages.

During unidirectional reduction trajectory, pieces are detached from a single striking platform or flat surface in a single direction after the core has been prepared (Figure 7.17). Sometimes the core striking platform must be rejuvenated or resurfaced because of flake removal errors. This can be done by removing a long flake from just beneath the existing striking platform that runs perpendicular to the direction of the detached pieces. These rejuvenations flakes are sometimes called core tablets (Mobley 1991; Morlan 1970). Generally, flakes produced from unidirectional cores have parallel lateral margins and uniform width and thickness values at different places along the longitudinal axis. These kinds of flake blanks are often called blades, microblades, or microliths (Ackerman 1992; Andrefsky 1987; Kobayashi 1970; Mellars 1974;

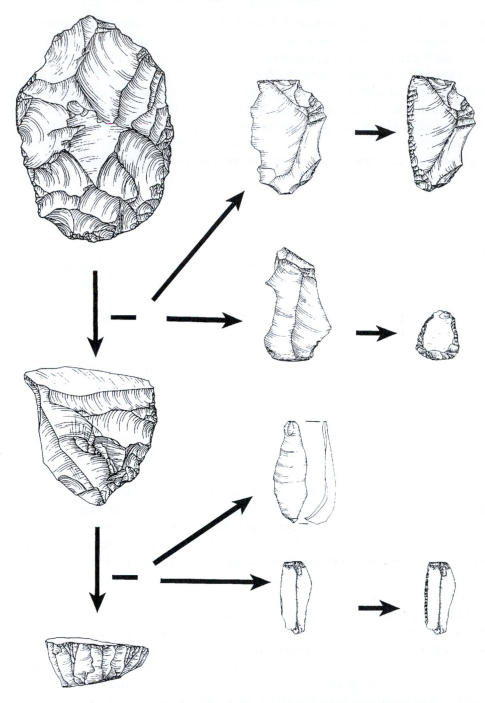

Figure 7.17   Schematic diagram of a microblade core reduction strategy. The microblade core is produced from splitting a biface. Note how uniform the lateral margins are when compared to flake blanks produced from bifacial cores.

Myers 1989). Note the difference in shape and size of the flake blanks produced from unidirectional cores (Figure 7.17) and multidirectional cores (Figures 7.15, 7.16). Differences in blank form may have important implications for the style and function of the flake tools produced. Flake blanks produced from the initial preparation of the unidirectional core appear very similar to the flake blanks produced from the multidirectional core. Only after the unidirectional core has been prepared with a single striking platform do the trends in flake blank morphology change.

In any basic analysis of flake tools one of the first sets of data recorded are the attributes related to the flake blank. These attributes represent the overall size and shape of the tool, and are the same attributes recorded for flake debitage as described in chapter 5. The only difference in the measurement of the attributes of flake debitage and flake blanks may be that modification may have altered the size and shape of the specimen.

The difference in detached pieces from unidirectional cores and multidirectional cores, such as Levallois cores, can be measured in several different ways. The thickness and width values at the quarter, half, and three quarters point along the length for individual specimens detached from unidirectional cores are relatively uniform when compared to the same point values for specimens detached from bifacial cores. This is indicative of the fact that the unidirectional detached pieces are uniform in shape and roughly parallel sided, as stated above. Detached pieces from bifacial cores tend to spread wider as they get closer to the distal end of the flake.

Another technique that has been applied to flake blanks to determine differences between unidirectional and multidirectional cores is the measurement of dorsal scar orientation on whole flakes. Baumler demonstrates such a technique for flakes from the Middle Paleolithic in what was Yugoslavia (1988); the technique superimposes four quadrants over a complete flake blank, as illustrated in Figure 7.18. Quadrant 1 is oriented over the proximal end of the specimen, with quadrant 3 directly opposite at the distal end of the flake. Quadrants 2 and 4 cover the right and left margins respectively. Any dorsal flake scars removed from the same direction as the detached piece gives quadrant 1 a positive value. Any flakes originating in the opposite direction of the detached specimen give quadrant 3 a positive value. Quadrant 2 is scored by flake scars originating from the right margin and quadrant 4 is scored by flake scars originating from the left margin. The greatest possible value for a flake blank would be 4, when each quadrant has a positive value. Such a flake blank is considered to have been produced from a multidirectional core. Unidirectional cores tend to have a value of 1. The specimen in Figure 7.18b, removed from a radial core, has a value of 4; and the specimen in Figure 7.18a, removed from a unidirectional core, has a value of 1.

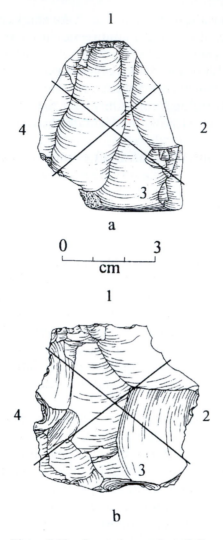

Figure 7.18   A superimposed quad diagram over the dorsal surface of flakes: (a) specimen has a value of 1; (b) specimen has a value of 4.

Flake tool prehension

Artifacts are identified as flake tools on the basis of modification to the flake blank. Such modification is usually in the form of intentional retouch or chipping of the edge or edges. A second kind of modification is the unintentional retouch or wear of the tool edge from use. In either case a flake blank with a modified edge would be considered a flake tool. Modification on edges of flake tool artifacts can originate from being used as either the handle or the blade. The handle would constitute the area on the tool that was held or grasped, and the blade would be the tool area that was used to work or modify another material. Prehension of the tool can be either by directly holding the stone artifact in the hand or by hafting the stone tool to a handle. Usually when sharp chipped stone tools were used with manual prehension, the sharp areas of the tool in contact with hands were dulled or backed in some way to prevent the tool user from getting injured. Hafting of flake tools was done to protect the tool user from injury, but also to increase the amount of force that could be applied to the worked material (Frison and Todd 1987; Montet-White 1988; Rule and Evans 1985). The haft element or handle was usually made of wood or bone. These materials were fitted with either a socket or a notch into which the flake tool was mounted and then lashed and/or glued in some manner. Figure 7.19 shows various examples of haft element mounting.

Haft element mounting usually produces greater amounts of wear than hand-held prehension (Odell 1980). Hand-held prehension of flake tools is usually evidenced by backing to dull sharp edges. In contrast, haft element prehension is usually apparent from dulled and polished edges over a relatively large area (Beyries 1988). There may also be evidence of crushing and polishing on dorsal ridges that were covered by the haft element. When the application of force is repeatedly applied by the hafted artifact in an action (such as the graving or incising of bone, or the sawing or drilling wood) the worn surfaces of the flake in contact with the haft element become polished. Flake tools hafted into a handle frequently show an abrupt change in wear on the edges of the specimen where the haft element stops. This abrupt change is created not only by crushing and polishing from the haft element, but also from modification of the blade, that may still be attached to the haft element while it is repeatedly resharpened. This resharpening activity may accentuate the differences in edge form between the blade and haft areas.

Hafting characteristics

Some flake tool analysts record information about the haft element since hafting is known potentially to change the morphological character of the artifact (Shott 1993:49). Since it is rare to find flake tools with both backed edges for hand prehension and abrupt edge modification from haft element mounting, recording these characteristics as either present or absent is an adequate place to begin.

Backing is usually identified as an intentionally dulled edge, accomplished by chipping or from grinding or abrading the edge. Frequently both retouching and abrading are used to dull the edge. Polish is usually not apparent on the edge if the tool is being held in the hand. Often backed tools will have only a single lateral margin dulled. Dulling on both lateral margins is more typical of hafting because a greater relative percentage of the flake blank has to be

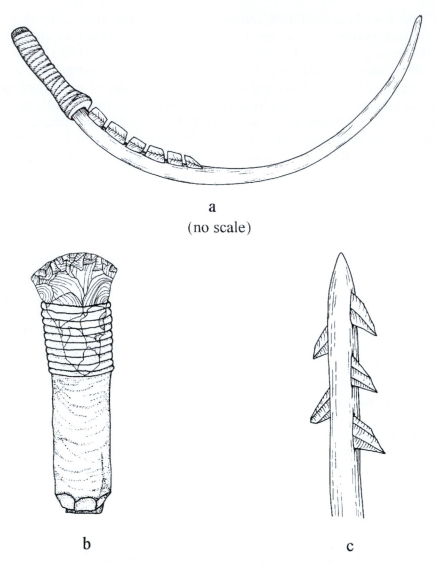

a

(no scale)

b   c

Figure 7.19   Schematic drawing of flake tools in various hafting contexts: (a) blades mounted on a sickle; (b) scraper inserted into a handle; (c) microliths used as point barbs.

encased in the half element in order to produce more support and leverage. Figure 7.20 illustrates an example of a backed flake tool.

The presence or absence of a haft element or haft area is another attribute that may be recorded for flake tools. As discussed previously, haft elements are evidenced on flake tools by grinding and polishing on the edges as well as on the dorsal ridges of a flake tool. Often there will be the just mentioned abrupt change on the flake blank edges between the haft element area and the blade

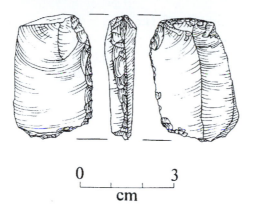

0   3

cm

Figure 7.20   Example of a backed blade showing dulled edge for hand prehension.

area; many examples of this are found in the literature (Beyries 1988:220; Cahen *et al.* 1979:681; Gallagher 1977; Nissen and Dittemore 1974; Rule and Evans 1985). Not all hafted flake tools show evidence of hafting along both margins of the tool; some were simply hafted or in contact with a haft element along a single margin. Blades or microblades inserted into slots cut along the sides of bone points or harpoons would be examples of such single-sided hafting. In this case the blade segments may not be backed, but are inserted while still extremely sharp, and are then glued into place with a mastic of some kind.

Once a flake tool has been determined to show evidence of hafting there are a variety of attributes that can be recorded to help explore the relationship between hafting and overall tool shape. One of the first attributes of interest is the haft length. Using the same characteristics that helped identify the presence of the haft element (changes in edge characteristics) the length can be measured from that point of change to the farthest point on the haft element, which may be the proximal or distal end of the original flake blank (Figure 7.21). Sometimes this point will be the center of the striking platform if it is still intact (Figure 7.21a). If the haft element ends with a snapped or truncated base the left and right lengths are measured to the point where the margin intersects with the basal truncation on either side (Figure 7.21c). If only one edge of the flake blank was hafted, the haft length is recorded for either the left or right sides of the tool. Identification of left and right sides should be made with the flake tool oriented with the ventral surface up and the haft element towards the bottom and the blade towards the top (Figure 7.21). This orientation permits uniform recording of right and left margins for all the flake tools being studied. It is not uncommon to get different haft lengths for each margin of the tool.

On flake tools with evidence of hafting on the left and right margins

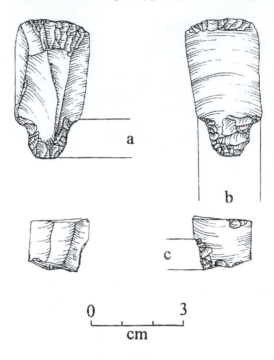

Figure 7.21   Various haft element measurements: (a) haft length on a
nontrucated flake tool; (b) maximum haft width measurement; (c) haft length on a
flake tool hafted on the left margin only.

maximum haft width can be recorded (Figure 7.21b). This is a straight line
distance from the left to the right margin at the widest point on the haft
element. For those flake tools which have only been hafted on a single margin,
such as microblade inserts, a maximum haft width is not recorded. Maximum
haft thickness is recorded instead, in the same manner as maximum haft
width. However, the measurement for haft thickness is taken at the thickest
point between the left and right margins from the dorsal to the ventral
surfaces.

Sometimes the flake blank is intentionally retouched to fit a socket or notch
on the haft. To lash the handle better, notches are sometimes flaked into the
edges of the tool. Retouching or notching of the haft element is recorded as
present or absent for the right and left margins of the flake tool. Since it is not
always possible to determine intentional retouching verses accidental or inci-
dental retouching, any flake retouching is identified for this attribute. Retouching is usually evident as the systematic removal of flakes marked by the
presence of tiny flake scars, usually with feathered terminations.

The tool margins may also be coded for the presence or absence of abrasion.
Unlike retouch, abrasion is characterized by a crushed surface that may have
numerous step fractures. Abrasion may be recorded for both the right and left

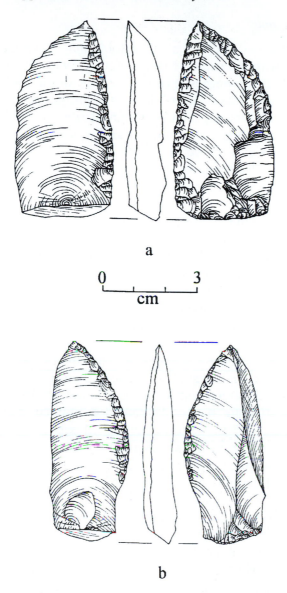

Figure 7.22   Flake tools showing the location of retouched edges: (a) two retouched edges; (b) one retouched edge.

margins of the tool haft area. It can additionally be recorded as present or absent on the ridges of the dorsal surface of the blank.

Polish may be recorded for the right and left margins, and the dorsal surface of the flake tool haft area. Unlike abrasion, polishing completely or partially obliterates evidence of the tiny flake termination scars on the haft area and the tool margins or dorsal ridges are smooth, often lustrous, and reflect light.

Blade elements on flake tools

Researchers have shown that individual flake tools may have had several different edges for use with a variety of tasks (Keeley 1980, 1982). A single artifact, therefore, might be a composite tool. One edge of the tool might be used for slicing leaves and another edge of the tool might be used for shaving bark from twigs. General tool edge and retouch attributes on flake tools should be recorded. Depending upon the research questions being investigated, some investigators may record only a few of these characteristics. Yet in some regions of the world, even more flake tool characteristics are recorded for analysis. Described below are flake tool attributes I often record.

The first attribute is the number of tool edges found on the blade area. Since flake tools often have more than a single worked edge on the blade element, each worked edge must be initially recognized and all subsequent analysis must relate specifically to each worked edge. As an example, the specimen in Figure 7.22b contains only one tool edge and the specimen in Figure 7.22a contains two tool edges. Each retouched edge of the flake tool is identified by relative location. With the proximal end oriented downward and the ventral surface facing the observer, tool edges are identified as being located on the right margin, left margin, proximal end, and/or distal end. In some cases the same tool edge may be continuously located on more than one margin. The tool edge is located on the right margin for the specimen in Figure 7.22b.

Each tool edge is also characterized by its outline morphology. Four descriptive states for this attribute are usually recorded: pointed, straight, concave, and convex. Figure 7.23 illustrates examples of each of these outline morphologies; specimen a (Figure 7.23a) has a convex edge morphology and specimen b has a pointed edge morphology. Specimen c (Figure 7.23c) has a straight edge on the right margin and a concave edge morphology on the left margin. The concave retouch on specimen c is evident from the dorsal side only. When viewed from the ventral surface the concave worked edge is not apparent.

Although edge angles are difficult to measure consistently, they can be important characteristics when related to the kind of material the tool was used to work and the technique employed to work it. Because of this, edge angles are recorded by using a three-state ordinal scale. These angles are estimated on the basis of gross shape and include: (1) angles $< 30°$, (2) angles between $30°$ and $60°$, and (3) angles $> 60°$. Figure 7.24 illustrates flake tools with estimated edge angles. Specimens a and d are endscrapers with edge angles $> 60°$. Specimen b shows a worked distal tip with an edge angle between $30°$ and $60°$; and the right lateral margin on specimen c has an edge angle of $< 30°$.

Edge length, the last of the general tool edge attributes I usually record for flake tools, is measured by taking the maximum linear distance along the

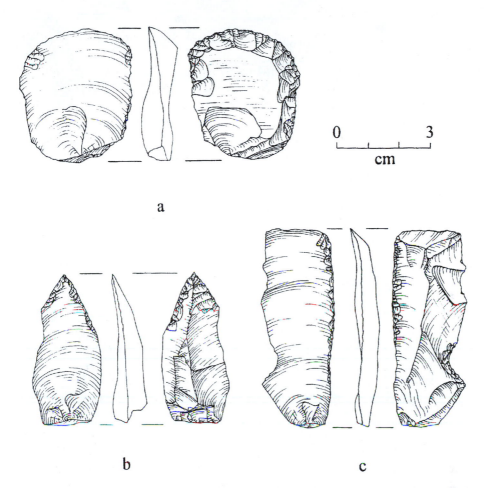

Figure 7.23   Examples of outline morphologies found on flake tools: (a) convex shape; (b) pointed shape; (c) straight shape on left margin and concave shape on right margin.

worked edge of the flake tool. This is performed by stretching a string along the worked edge of the tool following any contours; the string length is then measured to give a maximum edge length. Using a string allows accurate distance measurements on edges that may be curved or sinuous.

The pattern of edge damage or alteration along the margin of a flake tool has been shown to be significant as a functional indicator when using microscopy techniques (Keeley 1977; Odell 1977; Vaughan 1985). Other lithic analysts have used macroscopic techniques to infer flake stone functions (Parry 1987; Shott 1993a:50). Although not as reliable as microscopic techniques, macroscopic analysis of edge alterations may be as useful as the tool edge angles for determining relative density of materials worked.

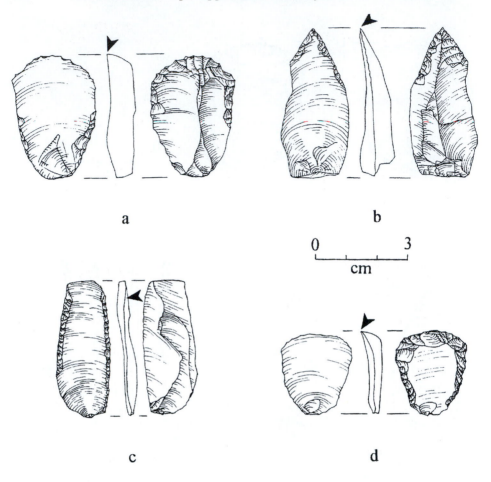

Figure 7.24   Estimated edge angles: (a) greater than 60°; (b) between 30° and 60°; (c) less than 30°; (d) greater than 60°.

Location relative to the flake surfaces is an important retouch attribute. Since flake tools are defined as showing evidence of both a dorsal and a ventral surface, retouch location refers to whether the alteration is found on one or both surfaces. Each worked edge on a flake tool (if more than one edge is worked) is evaluated as having either unimarginal or bimarginal retouch. A flake tool edge has bimarginal retouch if it is altered on the dorsal and ventral surfaces at the same edge location (Figure 7.23c). The tool is considered to have unimarginal retouch if it is altered on only one surface (dorsal or ventral) at the same edge location (Figure 7.23a).

Retouch type refers to the general pattern of retouch flake scars found on the worked edge. Some researchers believe that the pattern of retouch alteration on flake tool edges relates to task applications for which the tool was used

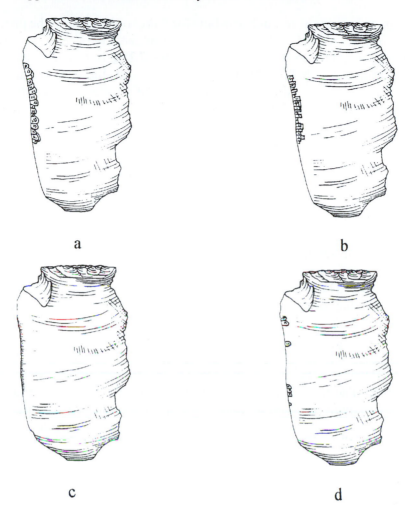

a

b

c

d

Figure 7.25   Schematic diagram of retouch type and retouch distribution:
(a) feathered retouch, continuous; (b) stepped retouch, continuous;
(c) smoothed retouch, continuous; (d) feathered retouch, clustered.

(Keeley 1980:24–61; Shott 1993:76). Retouch type is difficult to record consistently using either macroscopic or microscopic techniques because of the
variability found along the retouched edge. For this reason it is wise to keep
the number of retouch types to a minimum. I record retouch type as either
feathered, stepped, or smoothed. Feathered retouch (Figure 7.25a) is defined as
alteration found along the edge that is predominantly composed of flake scars
with feathered terminations. Stepped retouch (Figure 7.25b) is predominantly
composed of flake scars with step fracture terminations. Sometimes the termination of flake scars is obliterated or dominated by abrasion or polish; this
retouch is called smoothed (Figure 7.25c).

Another important retouch attribute for flake tools refers to the distribution of the retouch pattern. Retouch distribution may be either continuous or clustered. A continuous distribution (Figure 7.25a, b, c) is characterized by overlapping retouch flake scars that extend over the entire length of the worked edge. Clustered distributions show a discontinuous overlap of flake scars along the worked edge (Figure 7.25d).

Biface analysis

Bifaces are those objective pieces with two sides that meet to form a single edge that circumscribes the entire artifact (Figure 4.7, 3a). Both sides are called faces and both show evidence of previous flake removals. These tools may be considered objective pieces that have been extensively modified by flakes removed across the two surfaces of the tool. Bifaces come in numerous sizes and shapes and have hundreds of specialized names depending upon the shape and where they were found. Some bifaces are primarily used as cores, or as sources of usable flakes; sometimes bifacial cores are used as chopping or cutting tools. Other bifaces are primarily used as chopping and cutting tools. Still others are modified for hafting or attachment to a handle or shaft. These hafted bifaces may be used as projectile points for arrows or spears, or as tips for lances. The term biface refers to the shape of the artifact and does not necessarily imply a function. Different bifaces may have very different functions but some bifaces may have had several functions (Ahler 1971; Odell 1981).

Biface size

All bifaces have two sides that meet to form an edge, but there is usually a great range of sizes and shapes that lithic researchers must analyze in most assemblages. This is particularly true for North American assemblages where bifaces have so much variability that they have been used as fossil markers for prehistoric cultures (Broyles 1971; Coe 1964; Frison 1991; Ritchie 1965). Bifaces that have been worked to fit into a haft or handle are especially variable (Figure 7.26). I call these hafted bifaces, but they have been called projectile points, dart tips, and arrow heads, and a variety of other terms are common. The morphological typology separates hafted bifaces from those bifaces that were hand-held or nonhafted. This separation is based simply upon differences in morphological characteristics and is not meant to imply functional differences, although there may be functional differences between the two general forms. Bifaces with no haft elements may even represent earlier production stages of hafted bifaces. After bifaces are segregated into hafted and nonhafted

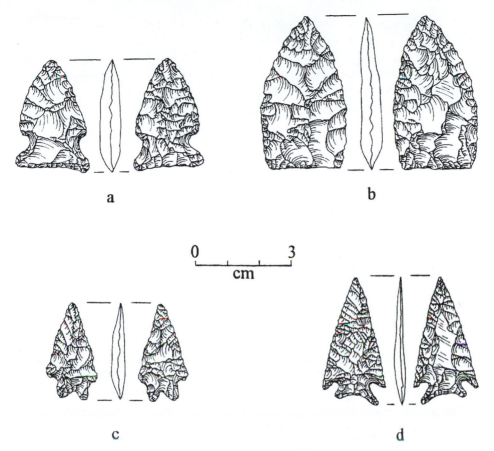

Figure 7.26   Examples of hafted bifaces: (a) side-notched; (b) lanceolate;
(c) basal-notched; (d) corner-notched.

classes, hafted bifaces can be further classified into types based upon shape, and nonhafted bifaces classified by size.

Nonhafted bifaces are considered primarily by size and to a lesser degree by shape because, in general, without a haft element most nonhafted bifaces have the same shape. The shape will vary somewhat but this variability can be accounted for by measuring a few size characteristics: weight, length, width, and thickness. Length is measured as the line that is often perpendicular to the pattern of flake scars across the surface of the nonhafted biface (Figure 7.27). It is usually the longest linear dimension of a biface. If the biface is perfectly round, and the flake pattern is radial toward the center, then length can be measured as a line anywhere on the biface that bisects it into two equal pieces.

Once the length of a biface is established it is relatively easy to measure width and thickness. Width and thickness can be recorded as maximum values or as values at certain distances along the biface length. Maximum biface width

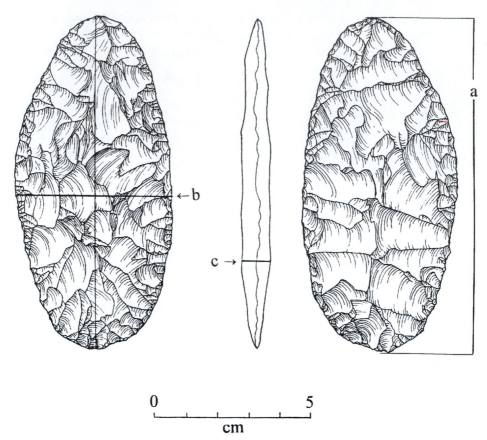

Figure 7.27   Measurements for nonhafted bifaces: (a) maximum length; (b) maximum width; (c) maximum thickness.

is defined as the line with the greatest value that is measured from one lateral edge to the other and is perpendicular to biface length. A width measurement can be taken at mid-point or mid-distance along the biface length or at any quarter point along the biface length (Figure 7.27). Maximum thickness is also measured as the greatest distance on a line that is perpendicular to biface length. However, unlike maximum width, maximum thickness is measured from one surface to the other. As with width, thickness can be measured at various points along the length of the biface.

Nonhafted bifaces may function as cores, knives, or scrapers. They may be specimens discarded during a phase of production, or they may be preforms for hafted bifaces. Size and general morphology are useful in segregating a nonhafted biface assemblage into classes that may be helpful for later interpretation. For example, suppose that well-flaked, thin, linear bifaces were known to have been used as preforms for side-notched hafted bifaces, and that thicker bifaces in the same length range were used as cores and scraping tools. Thick and thin are descriptions that relate to maximum width and/or maximum thickness as

Table 7.5   *Maximum length, width, and thickness values for pre-forms (pf) and small bifacial cores (bc)*

Biface type	Maximum	Maximum length	Maximum width	ML/MW thickness
bc	8.6	6.0	2.6	1.4
bc	8.4	5.3	2.1	1.9
bc	8.7	5.4	2.5	1.6
bc	8.5	5.8	2.4	1.5
bc	9.5	6.8	2.4	1.4
bc	9.6	6.5	2.3	1.5
bc	9.4	6.6	2.2	1.4
bc	9.7	6.1	2.2	1.6
bc	9.7	6.5	2.6	1.5
bc	9.6	6.9	2.5	1.4
bc	11.9	5.1	2.5	2.3
bc	10.1	5.1	2.2	2.0
pf	6.5	4.9	2.1	1.3
pf	6.6	4.8	2.0	1.4
pf	10.6	4.9	1.0	2.2
pf	9.7	5.4	1.5	1.8
pf	9.6	5.3	1.6	1.8
pf	10.1	4.8	1.3	2.1
pf	7.0	4.8	1.4	1.5
pf	7.3	4.9	1.6	1.5
pf	7.4	5.1	1.7	1.5
pf	6.9	4.9	1.9	1.4
pf	7.0	5.1	1.5	1.4

these relate to length. Therefore, measuring thickness alone on nonhafted bifaces would not be effective for discriminating the difference between biface preforms and biface cores. Some small bifaces may have thickness values less than some larger bifaces, yet the small ones may be relatively thicker when evaluated in overall shape.

The nonhafted biface assemblage listed in Table 7.5 is composed of preforms for large side-notched points (pf) and small bifacial cores (bc). Taken alone, none of the values discriminates the population into groups. Several of the preforms have the same length values as the cores. Similarly, several from each group have the same maximum width and maximum thickness values. However, when length is divided by width and is plotted against thickness, the relative proportions (shape) and sizes help to discriminate the two assemblages (Figure 7.28). Note that individual biface specimens have clustered into two groups using these ratio measurements – in this example the ratio of length to width. It would have been just as effective to use a thickness to width ratio, or perhaps a weight to thickness ratio. The ratio data combined with another dimension provide a better indication of tool shape and tool size.

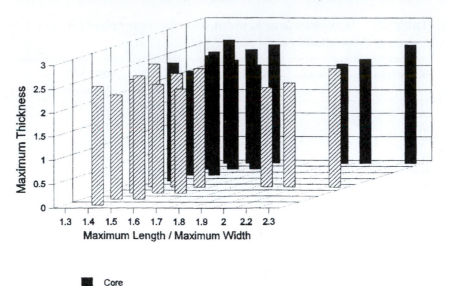

Figure 7.28   Distribution plot of bifacial cores and bifacial preforms, showing
maximum length divided by maximum width against maximum thickness.

Hafted biface morphology

As with most forms of chipped stone artifacts, analysis of hafted bifaces begins
with classification. This assumes that haft elements can be recognized in the
bifaces; in most instances this is a relatively easy endeavor. All the specimens in
Figure 7.26 have easily recognizable haft elements except for specimen b.
When this specimen is examined closely, however, minute differences in the
bifacial edges indicate the location of the haft element. These differences in
edges are usually a result of the hafting process.

A haft element, as described above, is the location on a biface that is used as
an attachment area onto a handle of some kind, in contrast to the blade or bit,
or the working end that is used as a tool for cutting, scraping, or puncturing,
among other things. The haft element is often inserted into a socket or notch
and then wrapped or covered with a mastic to form a tight bond. Because the
haft element is covered it is protected from day-to-day wear. The blade of a
hafted biface often becomes dull and is resharpened (Bienenfeld and Andrefsky
1984; Goodyear 1979). This resharpening process can occur while the biface
remains lodged within the haft. As a result, the hafted biface blade may
gradually change shape as a result of resharpening over the uselife of the tool.
The change in flake pattern or shape of the biface edge is one way to determine
if a biface has been hafted even if there are no obvious notches on the haft

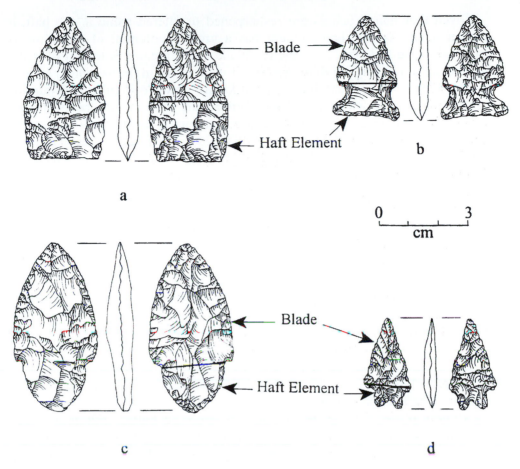

Figure 7.29   Location of blade and haft element on biface forms: (a) lanceolate;
(b) side-notched; (c) contracting-stemmed; (d) basal-notched.

element. Figure 7.29 illustrates the location of haft elements and blades on several common forms of bifaces.

In addition to changes on the blade as a result of resharpening, haft elements may also show evidence of wear as a result of rubbing while in the handle. Such wear may occur on the surfaces or faces of the haft element area or on the edges. Surface wear frequently appears as an abrasion that has obliterated the evidence of flake scars. The wear on edges of the haft element may also appear as a polish. Often there is intentional wear on the haft element that is believed to have been done to prevent cutting of bindings or wrapping used to hold the biface to the handle. In the American literature this kind of intentional wear is often referred to as basal grinding on projectile points. However, it is my opinion that most basal grinding on hafted bifaces is the result of wear while the tool is in the haft element. To my knowledge no microwear studies have been performed to evaluate the origin of such wear.

Given that hafted bifaces are resharpened or altered while in the haft, it makes sense that the haft element has a greater potential of retaining its original shape and size, and that the blade has a greater potential of being modified from its original shape and size. Furthermore, if the particular style of hafted bifaces is important as a fossil marker for prehistoric cultural groups or temporal units, it would also make sense that style should be evaluated primarily upon characteristics that do not change as a result of tool use or resharpening (Close 1978; Meltzer 1981; Sackett 1986). For this reason it seems preferable to classify the shape of hafted bifaces primarily from the variations found among haft elements.

The easiest way for any individual researcher to classify hafted bifaces from a single assemblage is to examine all the specimens as a group – to lay them on a table and begin sorting them into groups based upon perceived similarities and differences in shape. However, this can become cumbersome if the assemblage of hafted bifaces is extremely large. It may also present a replicability problem. For this reason, hafted biface typologies recognize formal attributes or characteristics of specimens and a set of rules to determine the most important attributes and the sequence of attributes to be observed for the particular typology. But when the data set is large, even formal attributes and rules governing attribute observation do not eliminate potential replicability problems of hafted biface classification. As a solution, many researchers use a numerical classification strategy that can be administered by a computer to designate hafted bifaces into types.

Numerical classification techniques for ordering hafted bifaces are well known in the archaeological literature (Andrefsky 1986b; Benfer and Benfer 1981; Corliss 1972; Hill and Evans 1972; Read 1974). These classification schemes come in a variety of quantitative forms, including cluster analysis, discriminate functions, and factor analysis. Even with all the experimenting done with numerical classification of hafted bifaces, there is no agreement on which attributes to use to define types. Some archaeologists believe that as few as seven or eight attributes are sufficient to identify types (Benfer 1967; Gunn and Prewitt 1975), and others believe that as many as nineteen are needed (Ahler 1971). From the many studies conducted on numerical classification of hafted bifaces some generalizations can be made regarding the choice of attributes. Binford was one of the first to claim that hafted biface form was most easily discriminated by differences in haft element and not blade (1963). This was supported by other studies that found haft elements to be more diagnostic than blades (Bacon 1977; Corliss 1972). The use of measurements that are too difficult to replicate consistently tends to add measurement error to classification analysis. As such, angle measurements should be avoided when classifying hafted bifaces (Benfer and Benfer 1981; Gunn 1981).

Some of the most common hafted biface attributes that I record are displayed in Figure 7.30 for a number of different hafted biface shapes, and

Table 7.6   *Attributes descriptions for measurements illustrated in Figure 7.30*

Attribute name	Description	
	From	To
BLL; blade length	Tip of biface	Tip of shoulder
NH; neck height	Neck	Base
HL; haft length	Top of haft element	Base
BLW; blade width	Shoulder	Shoulder
NW; neck width	Neck edge	Neck edge
BW; base width	Base edge	Base edge
SBC; shoulder to corner	Shoulder	Basal corner

Source: Descriptions adapted from Andrefsky (1986b:104).

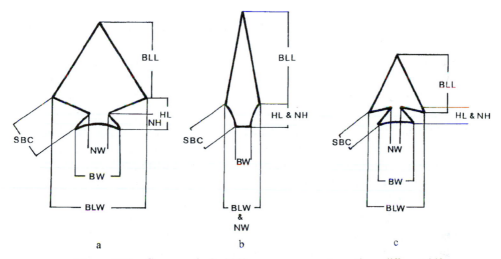

Figure 7.30   Common hafted biface measurements on three different biface forms. Adapted from Andrefsky (1984).

described in Table 7.6. These attributes are effective for the classification of extremely large assemblages (Andrefsky 1984), but they may not be the only ones necessary for any particular hafted biface assemblage. Numerical classification is, after all, purely an inductive technique; the adequacy of the results produced by a technique can be judged only by the appropriateness of the results for specific research questions (Dunnell 1971:190). In other words, theoretical assumptions, research methods, and questions that underlie a particular study are what give meaning to any numerically derived hafted biface types (Voorrips 1982:95–8). There is no measure of substantive significance for a quantitatively derived typology outside of a particular research context. A hafted biface typology is only meaningful if the criteria upon which it is established are shown to be relevant to a proposed archaeological question (see chapter 4).

During the course of biface discussion, stages of biface production were briefly mentioned. The concept of the various biface reduction stages has generated several other methods and techniques of biface analysis. The following section discusses how bifaces can be analyzed by using reduction sequences as a framework of interpretation.

Reduction sequences

One of the ways that researchers have organized bifaces is by reduction stage or sequence (Callahan 1979; Frison and Bradley 1980; Sharrock 1966). This method recognizes different forms of a biface as it is being chipped. Each of the forms is considered a stage in the evolution of the biface from a raw-material blank to a refined finished product. Other researchers do not recognize actual stages of bifacial production and instead conceive bifacial production as a continuum from raw-material acquisition to a final product (Muto 1971). Believers in either bifacial reduction continuums or reduction stages recognize an evolution in the shape of a biface from a relatively thick unshaped mass to a relatively thin uniformly flaked tool. Biface stages are recognized by the degree of workmanship exhibited by the specimen, that is, in turn, usually estimated by the relative thickness of the biface. In this regard biface thickness is discussed in relationship to biface width, and is often expressed as a width/thickness ratio (Callahan 1979). This is the linear width value divided by the linear thickness value. Maximum value or value at the mid-point of biface width and thickness can be used to derive the width/thickness ratio. A biface 3 cm wide and 1 cm thick would have a width/thickness ratio of 3.0.

Callahan's (1974, 1979) analysis of biface production distinguishes five bifacial stages before haft element production. Stage 1 is the blank. A bifacial blank may be a flake, cobble, or chunk of raw material, depending upon the type of biface being produced and the kind of raw materials available to the tool maker. Stage 2 is the initial edging of the objective piece, or when the objective piece is chipped around the circumference on both sides, and when the squared or rounded edges of the original piece are removed. The edging process produces an irregular bifacial edge that has few flake scars removed past the center of the objective piece. This process can be accomplished very quickly with little or no striking platform preparation for detaching pieces. Depending upon the original raw-material shape, Stage 2 bifaces may have width/thickness ratios as great as 5.0 on flake blanks or as low as 2.0 on cobbles being reduced. Stage 3 is primarily the thinning of the biface, when humps, ridges, and previous step fractures are removed while the biface is being thinned. Callahan suggests areas with the most convexity should be worked first during this stage of reduction (1974). Flake scars travel at least to the center of the biface during this stage and often carry past the center.

Table 7.7   *Technical description of biface stages*

Biface stage	Name	W/T ratio	Edge angle (degrees)	Description
Stage 1	Blank	N/A	N/A	Cobble or spall with probability of cortex
Stage 2	Edged biface	2.0 to 4.0	50 to 80	Small chips removed from around edges with few flakes scars across face(s)
Stage 3	Thinned biface	3.0 to 4.0	40 to 50	Flakes removed to center of biface, with most cortex removed
Stage 4	Preform	4.1 to 6.0	25 to 45	Large flat flake scars, flat cross section
Stage 5	Finished biface	4.1 to 6.0	25 to 45	Refined trimming of edges, possibly hafted

Width/thickness ratios are 3.0 to 4.0 in this stage. Stage 4 is secondary thinning of the biface. In this stage flake scars may be patterned and travel past the center of the surface, and striking platforms are prepared by grinding or beveling. Initial shaping of the biface also takes place during this stage simultaneously with thinning. Width/thickness ratios are greater than 4.0. Stage 5 is the final shaping of the biface before notching or hafting.

Whittaker (1994) also recognizes five different stages of biface production. Unlike Callahan, he calls the blank Stage 0, and ends with Stage 4 as the finished biface. Whittaker's Stage 1 is comparable to Callahan's Stage 2. This is the edging phase of production. The width/thickness ratio is approximately 2.0 when edging is complete. The edge angles range between 50° and 80°. Whittaker defines Stage 2 as a preform. At this point the emphasis shifts to thinning the biface. Flakes are removed at least to the center of the biface and cortex is removed. The edge angles are reduced to approximately 45° and the width/thickness ratio is 3.0 to 4.0. Whittaker defines Stage 3 as a refined biface. In this stage the biface is thinned by the removal of large, flat flakes and the outline shape of the biface is completed. The biface should have a flat cross-section with a width/thickness ratio of 4.0 or greater, and the edge angle is in the range of 25° to 45°. Stage 4 is the finished biface. This is the stage where a haft element is added if the biface is to be hafted. The form is slightly altered by refined trimming of jagged spots along the edge, and the removal of any striking platform remnants. If the biface is to be serrated, it will be done during this stage.

Whittaker and Callahan recognize very similar stages of biface production. Table 7.7 lists characteristics that are helpful in discriminating the various stages. I use Callahan's numbering sequence from Stage 1 through Stage 5, but the characteristics of each stage are similar in both Callahan's and Whittaker's models. The edge angles and width/thickness ratios are guides and should not be taken as definitive. These values will vary depending upon the type of biface

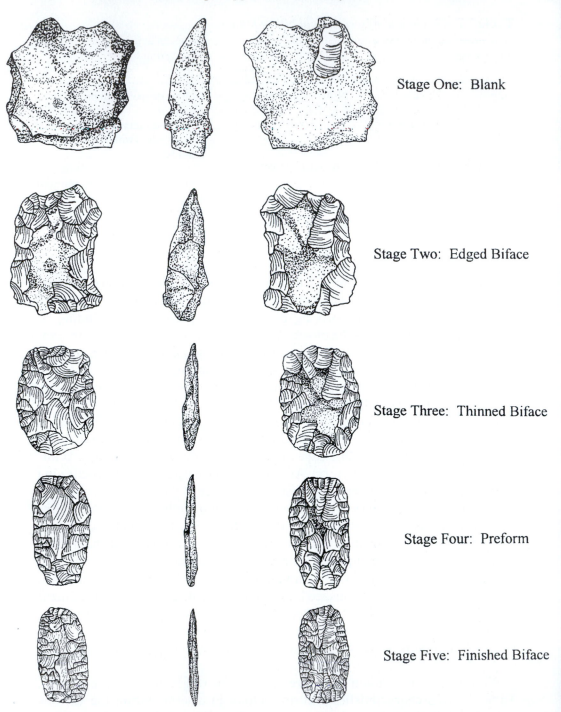

Stage One: Blank

Stage Two: Edged Biface

Stage Three: Thinned Biface

Stage Four: Preform

Stage Five: Finished Biface

Figure 7.31   Schematic diagram illustrating five biface stages for the production of a biface from a cortical cobble.

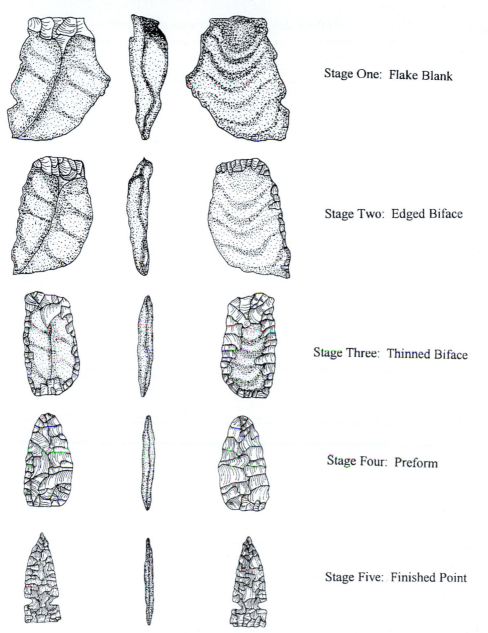

Stage One: Flake Blank

Stage Two: Edged Biface

Stage Three: Thinned Biface

Stage Four: Preform

Stage Five: Finished Point

Figure 7.32　Schematic diagram illustrating five biface stages for the production of a hafted biface from a flake blank.

Table 7.8   *Hypothetical biface data associated with quarry areas*

Biface stage	Early Archaic		Late Archaic		Early Woodland	
	count	percent	count	percent	count	percent
Edged bifaces	32	44	16	32	16	28
Thinned bifaces	28	39	16	32	15	26
Biface preforms	8	11	10	20	14	25
Finished bifaces	4	5	8	16	12	21
Totals	72		50		57	

being produced and upon the original shape of the blank. Figure 7.31 illustrates the five biface reduction stages for a biface produced from a large angular piece of tabular raw material. Figure 7.32 shows the five stages for a hafted biface produced from a small flake blank.

It has been shown that prehistoric stone tool makers organized their production of bifaces differently over time depending upon various factors. Some of them directly procured their raw-material and refurbished their tools at the raw material source area (Gramly 1980). Other tool makers only acquired blanks from quarry areas and produced finished bifaces elsewhere (Andrefsky *et al.* 1994a). The study of biface stages can help determine how prehistoric tool makers organized themselves in relation to stone procurement and tool production activities. For example, Root found that Paleoindian groups at the Knife River Flint Quarries in North Dakota primarily tested cobbles and made Stage 2 bifaces at stone quarries (1992:297); Stage 3 and Stage 4 bifaces were chipped at workshop locations away from the quarry area. Prehistoric groups later in time used the quarry location to make all stages of bifaces.

One way to use biface production stage data is to compare the relative frequencies of biface types (stages) over time. To illustrate this point, Table 7.8 shows hypothetical relative frequency data for biface types found at a quarry workshop site with three components. Since the acquisition of raw material for tool production and the actual production of tools constitute the primary activities conducted at quarry sites and quarry workshop sites, it makes sense that most of the bifaces recovered at such locations would be discarded owing to breakage. Unbroken bifaces, unless they were inadvertently lost by tool makers, were presumably carried from the quarry area and back to residences. In this example, the relative percentage of later-stage bifaces gets progressively greater during recent times. The data show that Early Archaic populations primarily edged bifacial blanks at the quarry workshop and reduced those blanks to finished products at another location. This is in contrast to Early Woodland populations that appear to have reduced bifaces all the way down to finished preforms for transportation away from the quarry. The differences in the extent of bifacial production at quarry locations over time has implications for proximity of bifacial use to the quarry area. Prehistoric populations

Table 7.9 *Chipped stone tool frequencies from the Santa Ynez river valley*

Bifaces	Cores	Other tools	Total
124	20	77	221

Source: Data taken from Bamforth (1991:223–5).

Table 7.10 *Count of intensively analyzed bifaces from Santa Ynez river valley*

Fragment type	Stage 2	Stage 3	Total
Complete	6	0	6
Proximal	5	8	13
Other fragment	12	3	15
Total	23	11	34

Source: Data taken from Bamforth (1991:225).

without good-quality chipping stone near their home ranges may have transported unfinished bifaces back to base camps so that detached pieces from final biface manufacturing could also be utilized. The Early Archaic population in this example may have preferred to transport Stage 2 bifaces so that detached pieces from later reduction could be used as flake blanks for other tool forms.

Some researchers believe that bifaces represent flexible tool forms that can be used for a variety of different functions (Odell 1981). Bifaces are also maintainable – they can be resharpened and they can be altered or reworked to suit specific needs (Kelly 1988). Other researchers have argued that bifaces are not only flexible, but portable as well, and represent ideal tools for populations conducting activities away from residential camps (Andrefsky 1993; Bamforth 1991). As a result of all these conditions, bifaces can potentially fulfill the tool requirements for unpredictable situations. With this model in mind, Bamforth attempted to characterize prehistoric use of the Santa Ynez River Valley/ Vandenburg region of California as a temporary use area occupied by relatively small groups of people (1991:228). Part of his analysis was based upon bifacial stage data. He first showed that biface preforms (Stage 2) and refined bifaces (Stage 3) were preferred over other types of tools in the project area (Table 7.9). Then, in a sample of bifaces that were subjected to heat alteration analysis (n = 34), Bamforth determined that bifaces used as tools and not as cores were heavily curated at the small temporary camps (Table 7.10). None of the Stage 3 bifaces in his sample was unbroken, and most of the Stage 2 bifaces were fragmentary. These data, combined with extensive debitage and flake tool

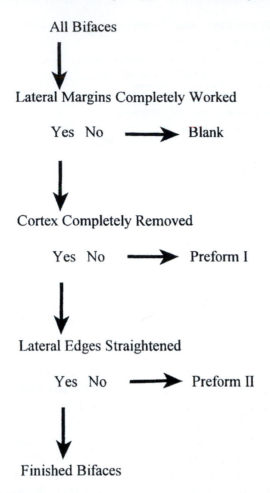

All Bifaces

Lateral Margins Completely Worked

Yes   No ⟶ Blank

Cortex Completely Removed

Yes   No ⟶ Preform I

Lateral Edges Straightened

Yes   No ⟶ Preform II

Finished Bifaces

Figure 7.33   Biface classification flow chart identifying four biface types. Adapted from Johnson (1989:124).

analysis, were used to support his interpretations of prehistoric land use in the project area.

Reduction trajectories

The bifacial stage classification scheme is not the only way to view biface production scenarios. Johnson recognized bifaces as either unfinished or finished, and defined several types of unfinished bifaces (1989:124). Figure 7.33 is a bifacial classification flow chart used by Johnson. In his scheme bifaces are classified as either Blank, Preform 1, Preform 2, or Finished. Using three characteristics to determine the type of biface defined in the flow chart, he noted whether or not the specimen had: (1) completely worked lateral margins, (2) completely removed cortex, and (3) straightened lateral margins. If a biface

Table 7.11   *Proportion of unfinished bifaces relative to distance from source*

Site	Source distance (km)	Number of bifaces	Proportion unfinished
Natchez	0	93	0.833
Little Tallahatchie	0	38	0.895
Lightline Lake	5	1034	0.695
Yalobusha River	5–12	76	0.802
Opossum Bayou	22–28	105	0.581
Line Creek	24–54	96	0.458
Upper Yocona			
Citronelle	50–61	11	0.272
Fort Payne	130–41	37	0.282

Source: Data taken from Johnson (1989:125).

does not have completely worked lateral margins it is considered a Blank. A biface with completely worked lateral margins with cortex still present is considered a Preform 1. If the cortex is completely removed, but the lateral edges are not straightened, the biface is classified as Preform 2. Those bifaces with straightened lateral edges are considered Finished specimens.

Johnson's (1989) analysis of bifaces attempted to understand the composition of assemblages from a regional perspective. He was interested in determining why some assemblages had more unfinished bifaces than other assemblages, and what this might mean with regard to interpretations about prehistoric behavior. Table 7.11 lists the proportion of unfinished bifaces from eight assemblages and their distance from raw-material sources. These data reveal that bifaces tended to be relatively less complete on sites closer to sources of raw material than on sites farther from raw-material sources. The farther a site is from the lithic raw material source, the fewer the number of rejects or unfinished bifaces there were in the assemblage (Johnson 1989:124). The only deviation in this pattern was the Yalobusha River assemblage, from which, Johnson suggests, the number of complete bifaces sample was artificially skewed. The site's location is fairly well known and it has been well sampled by relic hunters (1989:124). The proportion of unfinished bifaces does not decrease in a linear manner as distance from source areas increases. For instance, the Lightline Lake Site is only 8 km from a source area, yet drops in proportion similar to sites over 20 km from source areas. When the different types of bifaces were plotted using cumulative proportion curves for each of the assemblages, very distinct biface production trajectories were discernable (Figure 7.34). The cumulative proportion curves emphasize the drop-off rates in unfinished biface proportions. The sites appear to cluster into three groups: (1) sites at sources, (2) middle distance sites, and (3) long distance sites.

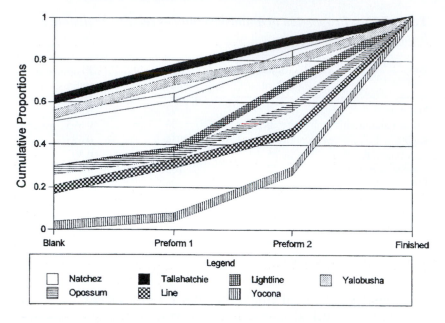

Figure 7.34   Cumulative proportion of various biface types from assemblages in Mississippi. Adapted from Johnson (1989:126).

Summary

The analysis of bifaces and other chipped stone tools should be organized around the specific research questions and goals of a particular study. The techniques reviewed in this chapter have been abstracted from specific research contexts to illustrate individual procedures and methods for conducting chipped stone tool analysis. Standardized tool measurement techniques are also described and illustrated. This chapter additionally provides discussion on how various analytical techniques relate to lithic technological practices. For instance, measurements on biface characteristics are associated with production stages, and measurements on edge retouch are related to tool prehension and use. Since few problem-oriented interpretations are addressed in this chapter statistical tests are minimized. However, most generalizations derived from lithic data require some kind of confidence or probability test as justification.

The next two chapters examine stone tools and debitage in problem-oriented contexts. The relationships among flake tools, cores, and bifaces are explored using specific case studies. Each of the case studies emphasizes a particular research context. Chapter 8 focuses upon artifact diversity and site functions. Chapter 9 emphasizes the role of lithic raw materials when making interpretations about prehistoric sedentism.

8

ARTIFACT DIVERSITY AND SITE FUNCTION

One of the ways that archaeologists have incorporated human behavior into their interpretations of archaeological sites is by determining the function or functions that have taken place at a site. Traditionally this has been done by identifying feature and artifact functions. Since a great majority of prehistoric sites from all parts of the globe do not exhibit well preserved features (such as living structures, storage facilities, or occupation floors) the interpretation of site function often falls to the recognition of artifact function. Artifact functions are then used to make inferences about site functions. This is an intuitively reasonable and very logical approach to determining prehistoric site function(s). If a site contains large numbers of butchering tools and the remains of butchered animals, it would be reasonable to assume the site has been a butchering location. Similarly, if we were to excavate a modern-day baseball field and found artifacts such as baseball bats, gloves, balls, dugouts, backstops, and the base paths, it would be reasonable to assume that the game of baseball had been played at that location. Unfortunately, it has become increasingly apparent to many archaeologists that the function of various artifacts, particularly stone artifacts, is not easy to interpret, and that many of the traditional interpretations of stone artifact functions are not necessarily correct. Without an accurate interpretation of artifact function, the logic behind site functional interpretations may be flawed.

It is suggested below that the function of chipped stone artifacts cannot easily and reliably be attributed to the morphology of the artifact, and that more and more evidence shows that lithic artifacts are multifunctional tools. Given the problems associated with interpreting artifact function from morphology it is necessary to make use of other methods to derive site function from stone tool assemblages. One way is to use populations of tools instead of single stone tool functions to derive site function. Notably, assemblage diversity is an important characteristic related to various aspects of site function. Stone tool assemblages from several areas of the world are used below to illustrate techniques of stone tool analysis that relate to site function models.

However, before exploring the relationship between artifact diversity and site function it is worthwhile reviewing some of the evidence associated with stone tool morphology and function. The discussion below on artifact form and function suggests that some stone tool forms may be associated with specific tool functions in some instances – but not in all. As a result it is important for researchers to support tool functional inferences with data other than tool morphology in most instances.

Artifact types and function

It is not hard to imagine that ever since archaeologists began naming stone tools after modern-day functional tools, some stone tools have been ascribed functions. A stone tool shaped in a similar fashion to an iron adze and called a stone adze was probably believed to function in the same way as an iron adze. Traditionally, artifact functions have been inferred by the morphology of the artifact. Terms such as arrow point, drill, scraper, perforator, and knife have been used to identify various morphological artifact types. These names imply an artifact function. Traditionally, such terms also imply a single function for each artifact type. For instance, scrapers were believed to be used for scraping hides and not necessarily anything else; similarly, dart points were believed to be used to tip projectiles and not necessarily for any other function.

The debate between Bordes and Binford regarding Mousterian lithic artifact variability was responsible for generating a great deal of literature on the function of lithic artifact types (Binford 1972; Binford and Binford 1966; Bordes 1979; Bordes and de Sonneville-Bordes 1970). Bordes believed that the variability found in an assemblage of Mousterian stone tool types was attributable to differences in prehistoric cultural groups depositing such tools. Variability within the same lithic assemblage was interpreted by Binford as differences in functional tool varieties associated with different activity areas. Most of the researchers working on this topic recognized that formal variation in stone tool types could be attributable to one of two factors, style and function (Dunnell 1978; Jelinek 1976; Sackett 1977). Once the formal variability associated with the style of a stone tool was defined, the remainder of variability became functional or nonstylistic. A problem with this approach was how to define style (Close 1978, 1989; Sackett 1982, 1986, 1990). Other archaeologists muddied the waters between style and function by determining that style was functional or that style had a function (Conkey 1978, 1980; Wiessner 1983; Wobst 1977). Function in this sense usually referred to the role of stylistic variability as a social group marker or as a means of information exchange, and not to design constraints on tools related to task or activity performance.

The notion that stone tool morphological variability related to functional constraints or to functional and stylistic constraints led investigators to evaluate the relationship between the form and function of stone tool types. Does stone tool form equate to a specific function? Jelinek suggests that the reason archaeologists have great difficulty determining stone tool characteristics associated with function is that the criteria they employ for the classification of lithic artifacts is neither explicitly functional nor morphological, but a mixture of both (1976:27). Jelinek's interpretation seems correct, but the problems for archaeologists are even more basic than the clarity of classification criteria. Until relatively recently there has been no adequate, objective way to assess the function of lithic artifacts. Until Semenov's (1964) pioneering work in micro-wear analysis of stone tools there was no independent way to determine the function of lithic artifacts. Since Semenov, a great many archaeologists have been able to determine effectively the function of lithic artifacts by microwear analysis (Ahler 1971; Bamforth 1988; Bienenfeld and Andrefsky 1984; Gould *et al.* 1971; Hayden 1979c; Kamminga 1979; Keeley 1974; Nance 1971; Odell 1977; Odell and Odell-Vereecken 1980; Siegel 1984; Vaughan 1985; Yerkes 1987, 1994). However, it should be realized that blind tests that evaluate the effectiveness of microwear analysis have not always produced satisfactory results (for prediction of tool use *vis-à-vis* type of material being worked) (Grace 1989; Keeley and Newcomer 1977; Newcomer *et al.* 1986). Some microwear studies have produced contradictory results (Hayden 1979a; Siegel 1984); several have specifically compared morphological artifact types to function and, for the most part, established that various morphological shapes of stone artifacts are functionally heterogenous (Ahler 1971:118–20; Keeley 1974:86–165; Nance 1977; Wylie 1975:27). In other words, artifact form does not appear to correlate with artifact function in all cases. This being the case, the following sections examine various lithic artifact forms and their functions and provide a brief review of the related literature. A more complete review of this topic can be found in Odell (1981) and Yerkes and Kardulias (1993).

Projectile point functions

One of the most commonly mentioned examples of form equating to function is the bifacial projectile point or hafted biface (Figure 4.7, 4a). This morphological type is often ascribed as having the function of a projectile. Projectile points are often assumed to be the tip or armature for a spear, dart, or arrow. It is not difficult to be persuaded that a hafted biface has a projectile function; hafted bifaces look very similar to tips found on modern-day projectile weaponry such as archery and lancing equipment. Figure 8.1 shows several examples of prehistoric hafted bifaces along with modern projectile point tips from archery hunting equipment. The similarity between the prehistoric and modern morphologies certainly suggests similar functions. In fact, many recent studies have found that some hafted bifaces were used as projectile tips of some kind (Churchill 1993; Patterson 1985; Peterkin 1993). However, it should also be noted that microwear functional analysis has demonstrated that hafted bifaces have been used as cutting and butchering tools in addition to their use as projectiles. Ahler's analysis of 114 hafted bifaces from Stratum 2 at Roger's Shelter, Missouri, indicated that less than 25% of the hafted bifaces were used as projectile points or armatures (1971:108). His study showed that hafted

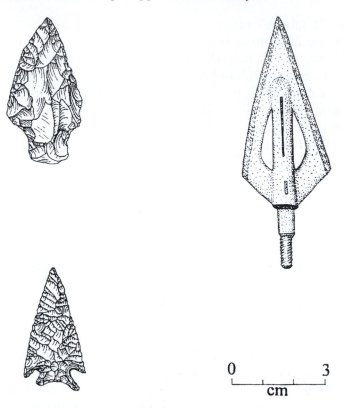

Figure 8.1   Example of prehistoric hafted biface types and contemporary archery hunting tips showing similarity in form.

bifaces were also used for slicing, cutting, sawing, whittling, scraping, splitting, and piercing. Nance (1971:365) has also conducted functional analysis on hafted bifaces and concluded they had multiple functions. Greiser's work with Plano hafted bifaces from Colorado led her to the conclusion that this form of artifact was purposely manufactured as a multifunctional implement for use as a projectile, butchering tool, and skinning tool (1977:114).

All of these studies specifically evaluated the function of hafted bifaces, and showed that they were used as projectiles at least some of the time, but that they may have been used primarily to perform other functions. This does not mean to suggest that some hafted bifaces were not specialized tools used exclusively as projectile tips. There are certainly cases where small arrow points or even large Paleoindian fluted points from North America were probably never used for functions other than as projectile armatures. However, even the late Paleoindian Dalton bifaces on the American Plains studied by Goodyear (1974) showed evidence of being used as cutting and slicing tools. In fact, during the uselife of these Dalton points the blades were dulled by cutting and ultimately sharpened to such a degree that they were reworked into a morphology traditionally recognized as a bifacial drill (Figure 2.16).

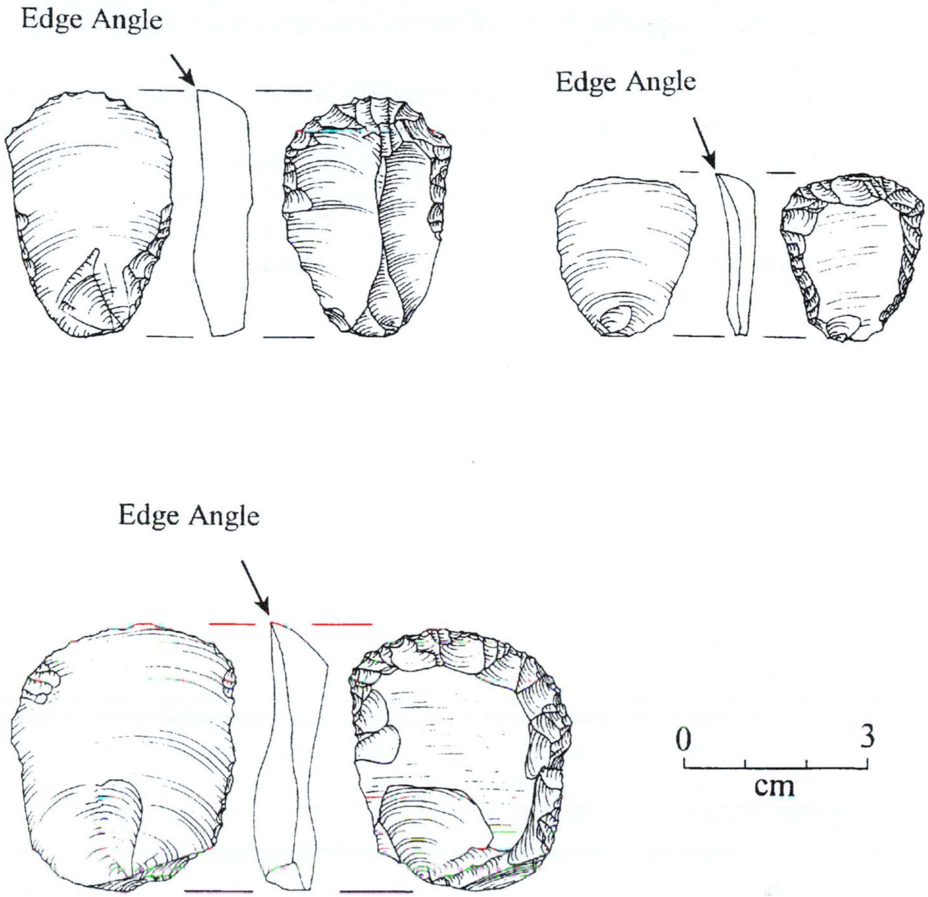

Edge Angle

Edge Angle

Edge Angle

0 _____ 3
cm

Figure 8.2   Illustrations of endscrapers showing cutting edge angle between 70°
and 90°.

Endscraper functions

Another form of artifact that has been repeatedly assigned a function in the
literature is the endscraper (Figure 4.7, 5c). Many researchers have ascribed the
function of animal skin working or scraping to the endscraper (Nissen and
Dittemore 1974; Stanford 1973), and this function has been observed in the
ethnographic record (Murdoch 1892; Nelson 1899). These stone tools are
usually hafted, and according to Hayden (1986:66), were held nearly parallel to
the skin surface, with the scraper blade both drawn toward and pushed away
from the worker, so that wear occurred on both the dorsal and ventral surfaces.
The endscraper cutting edge or bit approximates an angle of between 70° and
90°, and makes the edge effective for scraping but not acute enough to
accidentally slice or cut the material being worked (Figure 8.2). The wide edge

angle on endscrapers is probably one of the reasons most researchers ascribe a scraping function to this tool form.

Endscrapers are found in almost all parts of the world and in practically all periods when stone tools were primarily used. Meltzer conducted a discriminant analysis to assess whether endscraper form was the result of function or style (1981), and concluded that the form or shape of endscrapers was attributed to endscraper function. However, his analysis did not determine the type of function for which endscrapers were used. Dumont (1983:132–7) specifically evaluated the function of endscrapers recovered from Star Carr, England. He found that endscrapers were used for working hide, bone, wood, and antler, and his results contradict the popular notion that endscrapers were used solely as hide working tools.

Another functional study of endscrapers looked specifically at the action or mode of use for this form of artifact. Using microwear analysis on lithic tools from a Dutch Mesolithic site, George Odell compared classic morphological types to observed functional wear (1981), and found that endscrapers were used in many activities other than scraping. Endscraper activities identified in Odell's study include scraping, graving, boring, chopping, and use as a projectile. Other classic morphological types such as side scrapers and burins were also found to have been used for several different functions.

Siegel (1984) actually tested the proposition that endscrapers were used solely in hide working activities. His functional analysis was done on two populations of endscrapers, one from the Utkiavik site in Alaska and the second from the Lowie Museum collections at Berkeley, California. The results of his analysis showed that endscrapers were used on wood, clean bone, silty bone, silty hide, hide with hair, and antler. Siegel found that wood and not hide was the predominant material worked by endscrapers examined in his study.

Admittedly, there are problems associated with microwear analysis, particularly on stone tools that may have been used on more than one kind of material, but it is noteworthy that several microwear studies have shown that endscrapers were multifunctional tools. It is probable that endscrapers were not only used on several kinds of materials, but that they were used with several different kinds of actions or motions such as graving, boring, and slicing.

Microblades and microliths

Lithic tools manufactured on relatively small bladelets are commonly found in many parts of the world. They are sometimes called microliths in the European and Levantine Mesolithic (Gendel 1984; Jacobi 1978; Mellars and Reinhardt 1978; Myers 1989; Olszewski 1993; Woodman 1978). In the Arctic regions of northeast Asia and northwest North America these forms are known as microblades (Ackerman 1996; Anderson 1970; Andrefsky 1987; Chun and Xiang-Quian 1989; Kobayashi 1970; Morlan 1970; Serizawa 1976; Yoshizaki

1961). These bladelets have been classified into a variety of forms based upon overall size, number of edges, location of retouch, and type of wear. Generally, they are made on small parallel sided blades that are modified into a desired shape. They are usually not more than 2 cm wide nor are they usually more than 5 mm thick. In addition to being relatively small, they have the characteristic of very sharp and uniform edges produced from some kind of a systematic core reduction strategy.

Microliths from the European Mesolithic were long believed to have been used as hunting tools on projectiles (Clark 1932; 1969). Microliths with three sides or "triangles" were believed to have been used as point tips and as point barbs (Jacobi 1976, 1980; Mellars 1974, 1976; Radley *et al.* 1974). Triangular microliths found in Africa and southwest Asia have also been interpreted as barbs or points for projectiles (Clark *et al.* 1974; Deacon 1984; Olszewski 1993). Four-sided microliths have been interpreted as inserts for projectiles (Myers 1989). Microblades from the Arctic have traditionally been interpreted as projectile point components. The Arctic microblades are believed to have been used as side or lateral inserts along the length of a smooth bone shaft that had been slotted to accept the microblades. Ackerman (1994:110) recovered such a slotted bone point with an embedded microblade from the Lime Hills Cave in Alaska. Various examples of microblades and microliths hafted as projectile point tips, barbs, and inserts are illustrated in Figures 2.15 and 7.19.

Although evidence is mounting that microliths and microblades were used as projectile tips, barbs, and side inserts, there is also evidence that they were used for other functions as well. Garrod and Bate (1937) report the recovery in the Levant of a plant harvesting sickle or scythe with microlith inserts. Additionally, Curwin illustrates several examples of sickles excavated from various locations in Europe and the Middle East (1930); these sickles have rectangular and triangular microliths inserted along the inner curved edge of wooden handles or blades. Both Odell (1994) and Yerkes (1983, 1990) have used microscopic techniques of analysis to determine the function of bladelets. Independently, they determined that bladelets were used in a variety of activities that included cutting, graving, drilling, shaving, and use as projectiles. Additionally Odell suggested that when bladelets were used in a ceremonial context, they were only used to cut and scrape soft materials (1994). Clearly, these bladelets (or microblades or microliths) as a group cannot be associated necessarily with a single activity, but instead with a combination of activities such as hunting, or grass harvesting, or bone graving. The function of individual bladelets may vary depending upon the context, shape, size, and wear of the specimen.

Other morphologies of chipped stone tools

Unlike the numerous studies of hafted bifaces, endscrapers, and microliths, there have been few functional studies of other traditional forms of artifacts, specifically perforators, nonhafted bifaces, side scrapers, drills, burins, and spokeshaves. However, Lewenstein (1987) and Odell (1981) have examined some of these forms of artifacts. Lewenstein conducted a functional analysis on a sample of 1,449 chipped stone artifacts from Cerros in Belize. Her formal categories corresponded to many types recognized in several different parts of the world. She identified three different kinds of nonhafted bifaces: oval (n = 27), thin (n = 33), and nonstandard (n = 135). Her functional analysis revealed that chopping and pounding were the two most common functions for oval bifaces; other functions for oval bifaces included sawing, scraping, scraping/planing, abrading, and use as an adze. Thin bifaces were predominately used to cut and slice, but also for sawing, scraping, scraping/planing, and butchering. The nonstandardized bifaces were found to have had thirteen different functions; however, scraping was by far the most common function for nonstandard bifaces. Lewenstein's analysis provides some idea of the diverse uses of nonhafted bifaces.

Odell's analysis of chipped stone tools from the Netherlands (1980, 1981) also provides some indication of the diversity of functions for several different kinds of chipped stone artifacts. Although no bifaces were included in his sample, 109 side scrapers were analyzed. The two most common functions were the transverse motions of scraping and graving. Odell also found side scrapers were used in a cutting motion, chopping, as a projectile, and various combinations of these functions.

Lewenstein (1987) and Odell (1985) have also examined lithic tools that could be considered boring and perforating tools. Neither study determined what types of materials were being worked by these tools, but both studies have primarily identified these tools as performing the function of perforating. Functions such as scraping, graving, and cutting were also identified, but only as secondary functions.

Several studies primarily using retouched and nonretouched flakes in the analysis of artifact function demonstrated without exception that these artifacts, regardless of form, have multiple functions (Kamminga 1978; Semenov 1964). For example, Keeley's (1980) analysis of flake stone tools from the Golf Course site (Essex, England) revealed the functions of wood whittling, wood scraping, wood sawing, wood chopping, meat cutting, bone boring, and bone graving, among others. From Keeley's work alone it appears that flake tools were used for almost any function. This interpretation has been supported by ethnographic observation of flake tool use by aboriginal groups, as described in the examples below.

Ethnographic observations on tool form and function

Gould's (1968:119) ethnographic observations of the Ngatatjara of western Australia led him to the conclusion that stone tool functions were based upon the working edge of tools rather than the overall form of the artifact. Heider's observations of stone tool forms and functions among the Dani of New Guinea suggest that functional terms used by archaeologists for various forms of tools do not correlate with artifact function, and actually misrepresent the functional character of assemblages. He cautions (1967:56): "In many cases archaeologists prejudice their own attempts at reconstructing particular cultural behavior by building time-hallowed functional terms such as scraper or handaxe into their original typology. In the archaeological process, functional attributes should be end products, not opening assumptions."

Correlations of artifact form with artifact function are almost universally rejected by ethnographers and ethnoarchaeologists. White's (1967:409) observations in the Highlands of New Guinea conform to this position. He indicates that the New Guinea population does not regard a flaked stone as a functional whole in the archaeological sense; these people do not treat a stone tool as a type, but rather as a piece of stone that can be used to get the job done. White and Thomas (1972:278) make similar observations and they indicate that modern New Guinea Highlanders regard their stone tools as pieces of stone and do not recognize any series of formal or functional types. Hayden's work with Australian Aborigines also supports this lack of correlation between artifact form and artifact function. He remarked (1977:179): "There was no indication of any overall morphological ideal type, "classic" form, or "perfect" specimen, as collectors are wont to say, and as archaeologists often tacitly accept in conversation. Rather, the traditional attributes of importance in the Western Desert were: effective edges (which were surprisingly variable in morphological expression), and a suitable size for holding in the hand and exerting pressure."

Ethnographic and archaeological evidence casts some doubt upon the assertion that artifact morphology conforms to a particular function. Essentially, it can be said that various forms of stone tools may have several different functions, and that no artifact function can be ascribed to a particular form in all cases. It is also important to remember that when the function of a tool has been determined with a high degree of certainty, the mutifunctional character of the tool must then also be considered. Most stone tools were probably used for several different functions and the degree to which a tool was specialized or used for a single function or became generalized and multifunctional probably varied with individual tools. The multifunctional character of individual stone tools relates to aspects such as availability of raw materials for tool production, efficiency of tool design relative to task performance, and particular cultural or individual preferences for task performance. Additionally, many activities carried out by tool makers and users probably required different kinds of tools in different degrees so that any activity may have required various combinations of tools for variable amounts of work.

Site function models

Given the problems associated with the inferences of artifact function with artifact morphology, we must pose the question, "how can the function of sites be determined?" This is when the promise of stone tool microwear analysis is most enticing. Fortunately, microwear analysis is one avenue of assessing site functions, but only one. The macroscopic variability in stone tool form can also help determine site function, although not necessarily via the function of individual artifacts or artifact edges. Making inferences about the function of occupation areas from the analysis of individual artifacts may be perceived as going from individual components or parts to the larger whole. Another approach is to go from the whole to the individual components; in this case, site function constitutes the whole and artifacts and artifact assemblages are the components. This top-down approach, however, requires some initial knowledge about the nature of prehistoric site functions; then inferences can be made about the kinds of assemblages or artifacts that might be expected with various site functions.

Probably the one person who has contributed the most to this way of thinking is Lewis Binford. His work, first with the Nunuimut and later with more equatorial hunter-gatherers, was instrumental in bringing human organizational factors into prehistoric site analysis (1977, 1978, 1980). Binford's work characterized hunters-gatherers by the different types of strategies they used as they moved about in their resource exploitation range. Binford began by characterizing hunters and gatherers as either foragers or collectors. These strategies – foraging and collecting – were defined on the basis of the kind of mobility each practiced. Mobility was characterized as either residential or logistical. Residential mobility was defined as movement of the entire group from one location to another, and logistical mobility involved the movement of individuals or small groups from – and then back to – the residential location to perform a specific task. Foragers were defined by high residential mobility with logistical mobility playing a minor role. Figure 8.3 illustrates a hypothetical forager mobility strategy. Depending upon the resource parameters within the foraging range, groups would move their residences or base camps from one location and relocate collectively at another spot. Sometimes the residence move would require the group to disperse into smaller units best to exploit a certain resource. Collectors, on the other hand, make few residential moves with many logistical moves. Figure 8.4 illustrates a hypothetical collector mobility strategy. In this case the population remains in a single location for the duration of an annual cycle. Resources located away from the base camp are obtained by special task-oriented groups that leave and return to the base camp as resources become available. Depending upon the particular group being studied, collector base camps may be occupied for only part of

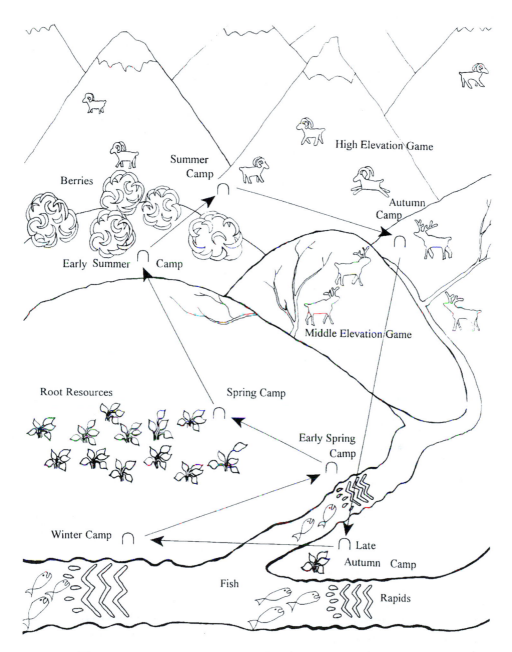

High Elevation Game

Summer
Camp

Berries

Autumn
Camp

Early Summer Camp

Middle Elevation Game

Root Resources

Spring Camp

Early Spring
Camp

Winter Camp

Late
Autumn Camp

Fish

Rapids

Figure 8.3   Schematic forager model showing seasonal movement of residence camps to exploit available resources. Based upon Binford's ideas of hunter-gatherers "mapping" on to locations (1980).

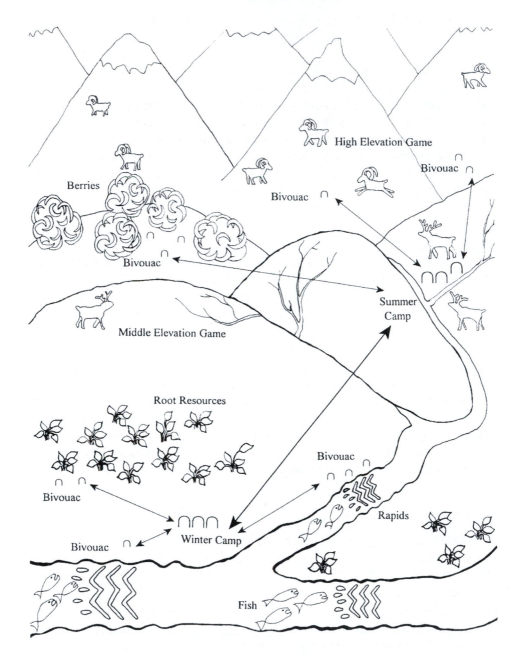

Figure 8.4   Schematic diagram illustrating a collector mobility strategy. Residence locations are more permanent and resources are obtained by special-task groups that return to residence camps with resources. Based upon Binford's ideas of hunter-gatherers using a "logistical" strategy for resource acquisition (1980).

an annual cycle, for an entire year, or for several years before they are abandoned for another location.

This forager/collector dichotomy is a convenient and simplified way to characterize a wide variety of hunter-gatherer residential patterns. Unfortunately, many archaeologists view prehistoric site types in a strict either/or manner, which was never Binford's intention (1980). The forager and collector strategies are expressed as a combination of different types of residences occupied for various amounts of time by different compositions of individuals. Each of the residences may be thought of as locations in geographic space where individual or sets of tasks or activities were performed. Such activities would vary depending upon the position of the residences within the larger structure of the foraging or collecting strategy. Essentially this amounts to the expectation that different locations or sites exist because of different residential strategies. Foragers, using residential mobility, would have base camps that were frequently moved to new locations to exploit seasonally available resources. Collectors, using logistical mobility, would have base camps that were not frequently moved, and would also utilize task-oriented camps to extract or procure resources located away from the base camp and bring those resources back to the base camp.

These strategies of hunter-gatherer residences have been adapted by archaeologists to particular regions of study and, in some cases, refined to predict the occurrence of artifact assemblages at various locations or sites. The locations or sites may be thought of as places where certain activities or functions take place. In this sense, the site functions have been anticipated and the artifacts or assemblages inferred. By working backwards in this manner archaeologists can then use morphological artifact types to assess site function based upon top-down hunter-gatherer residence models.

Assemblage diversity and site function

Chatters (1987) uses Binford's hunter-gatherer model to evaluate site types for excavated assemblages from the middle Columbia River in the Pacific Northwest. He uses several different artifact and feature signatures in his analysis. The stone tool analysis is described below to introduce how artifact assemblages may be used to assess site function through site type analysis. Using sources of data other than site assemblage data, Chatters (1987:356) recognizes three site types: winter base camps, winter hunt camps, and spring residence camps. The spring residence camps are equated to base camps in the Binfordian residential mobility strategy and the winter base camps are equated to logistical mobility base camps (1987:340). Chatters suggests that tool diversity should be high at base camps and residence camps when compared to field camps (winter hunt camps). Field camps are designed to process or acquire a narrow range of resources and should be reflected by a few specialized imple-

Table 8.1   *Similarity and evenness indices for three site types from the Pacific Northwest*

Site type	Component	Mean intrasite similarity score	Evenness index
Spring residence camp	45OK197 III	120	.82
Spring residence camp	45OK197 VI	123	.83
Spring residence camp	45OK197 VII	120	.84
Spring residence camp	45OK197 VIII	118	.81
Spring residence camp	45OK197 IX	118	.76
Winter hunt camp	45OK197 X	145	.90
Winter hunt camp	45OK197 XIV	150	.87
Winter hunt camp	45OK197 XV	139	.92
Winter base camp	45OK–2–2	176	–
Winter base camp	45OK–2	176	–
Winter base camp	45DO37211	N/A	–

Source: Data taken from Chatters (1987).

ments; therefore, tool diversity should be low. Base camps and residence camps, by definition, include a wide range of activities and do not focus upon a single task, and tool assemblages should be more diverse. Since residence camps are associated with the residential mobility strategy, the diverse tool assemblage on these site types should also reflect a multifunctional, generalized assemblage to reduce residential transportation costs. Base camps, on the other hand, may be dominated by specialized assemblages with various specialized tasks that are logistically organized and geared from the base camp.

Two of the measures used by Chatters to evaluate the amount of diversity in the lithic artifact assemblage were the mean intrasite similarity index and the evenness index (1987:363–6). Table 8.1 lists these index values with each of the site occupations used in his study. The mean intrasite similarity index measures the degree of variation within a class (site type) by obtaining a mean value between each site and all other members of the same site class. This index uses the Brainerd-Robinson coefficient (Brainerd 1951; Robinson 1951). In this case, nine different types were used in the analysis. The lowest similarity values were found for the spring residence camps and the highest values were found for the winter base camps, followed by the winter hunt camps. Chatters indicates that this is the expected pattern, given the discussion about artifact diversity presented for each site type. It might be expected that the winter hunt camps would have the lowest similarity indices and that the winter base camps and the spring residence camps would have values more closely spaced to each other relative to the hunt camp, since both are base camps in the Binfordian model.

The evenness index values listed in Table 8.1 were calculated only for winter hunt camps and spring residence camps owing to sampling differences in the original data. In addition, because sample sizes for morphological tool types were so disparate between sites, edge wear tool types were used in this calculation instead of general morphological types. The evenness index measures the frequency of artifacts found in each artifact type and gives a summary value for the spread of those artifacts over the entire site assemblage (see Odum 1971:144). This equation is calculated as:

$$E = \frac{\left(\dfrac{n_i}{n}\right)\left(\log\dfrac{n_i}{n}\right)}{\log_s}$$

where: n_i = the number of artifacts for each type
n = the number of artifacts for all types
s = the number of artifact types.

This index ranges from 1.0 to 0.0. The value of 1.0 means that all types are equally represented in the population, and the value of 0.0 means that only one type accounts for all specimens in the population. The values in Table 8.1 show that winter hunt camps have artifact assemblages more evenly spread than do spring residence camps.

The evenness index and the mean intrasite similarity index both show trends in the stone tool assemblages for the different site types. Unfortunately, it is difficult to determine what those trends mean with regard to assemblage diversity and site type. Given the discussions about artifact assemblages expected at these site types, should winter hunt camps or spring residence camps have the greater evenness values? Since the site type discussion predicted various degrees of artifact diversity, perhaps it would have been worthwhile calculating an artifact diversity measure? The stone tool artifact data in the Chatters study do not conform or fit well to the expectations presented in the discussion. However, he used several other different kinds of data sets, including faunal remains and features, and those data strengthened his arguments for discriminating site types (1987:359–61).

Unlike studies which attempt to determine site function from individual artifact functions, this study attempted to recognize site function as it relates to a settlement context from an assemblage of artifacts. Although the evenness index and similarity measure on stone tools did not show a strong association with site types, they did reveal some patterning to support the settlement model. Perhaps with a more refined stone tool classification scheme, the analytical results would have been stronger. This example suggests not only that assemblage composition might relate to site function, but that the number of artifact classes and the relative frequency of artifacts in each class may be an important clue to site function as well.

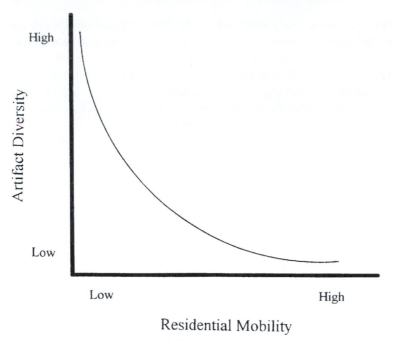

Figure 8.5   Theoretical relationship between artifact diversity and residential mobility. Adapted from Shott (1986:25).

Assemblage diversity and site types

Another way to view site types using the Binfordian model of residential and logistical mobility is to explore the relationship between artifact assemblages and relative amounts of mobility. Kelly's (1983, 1995) work with hunter-gatherer residential mobility parameters showed that mobility in human populations can be measured in many different ways. He noted that populations move their residences different distances and on several different occasions; the frequency with which populations move, the average distance of the move, and the total distance traveled can vary for any residentially mobile group.

The inverse relationship between assemblage diversity and mobility depicted in Figure 8.5 is based upon the number of artifact types and the frequency of moves during an annual cycle. Shott (1986) gathered artifact data and mobility information from over a dozen hunter-gatherer groups described in the ethnographic literature. Using Ammerman and Feldman's (1974) theory of site formation processes, he was able to predict the values of various dimensions of residential mobility. The primary artifact dimension he explored was assemblage diversity or the number of artifact types found in each assemblage. Artifact diversity was found to have an inverse relationship with residential

Table 8.2   *Artifact diversity compared with magnitude and frequency of move*

Group	Diversity	Magnitude	Frequency
Guayaki	2	295.0	50.0
Siriono	2	230.0	16.0
Montagnas	3	2700.0	50.0
Ona	3	–	60.0
Mbuti	3	73.9	17.0
Hadza	4	248.0	31.0
Paiute	4	–	35.0
G/wi	6	275.0	11.0
!Kung	6	262.5	17.0
Aranda	8	–	10.0
Chenchu	14	39.5	3.5
Twanda	16	–	3.5
Klamath	16	84.0	11.0

Source: Data taken from Shott (1986).

mobility – as mobility increases, artifact diversity decreases. Figure 8.5 shows this geometric relationship.

Shott found the same kind of relationship, although not as strong, with artifact diversity and magnitude, or the total distance traveled per year. Table 8.2 lists the hunter-gatherer groups and the values for artifact diversity, mean frequency of moves per year, and magnitude of the move used in his study. The total distance traveled per year, or the magnitude, does not correlate as well with tool diversity as does the frequency of moves per year. Nevertheless, an inverse relationship between magnitude and artifact diversity is apparent. A more refined calculation of technological diversity might make this relationship even stronger. As defined, technological diversity represents the number of tool classes used in the course of daily activities (Shott 1986:23). I would guess that the number of tool classes used during the day might change depending upon factors such as location of camps, season of the year, and particular adaptive strategies employed.

The forager-collector mobility model predicts different kinds of residences in various combinations. Both foragers and collectors use mobility in differing degrees. The artifact diversity values should vary with assemblages that are recovered from different site types situated in the different mobility strategies. Shott explores this relationship to some extent by examining the number of days the population stays in the wet season or winter season camps compared with the diversity of artifacts used at the camp. Wet season camps may be comparable to Binford's base camp designation. The greater amount of time various groups stay in the base camp, the greater the likelihood that they are practicing a logistical strategy. Shott's analysis shows that as residence stay

Table 8.3   *Artifact diversity compared with length of wet-season residence*

Group	Wet season residence (days)	Diversity
Andaman	120	8
Chenchu	180	14
Siriono	150	2
G/wi	30	6
!Kung	60	6
Paiute	45	4
Klamath	195	16
Montagnas	7	3
Ona	6	3

Source: Data taken from Shott (1986).

increases in wet season camps, so does artifact diversity. Table 8.3 shows this positive correlation between artifact diversity and length of stay in wet season camps for nine groups.

Although no ethnographic data on artifact diversity were available for special-task-oriented or field camps, it would be logical to assume that special-task-oriented camps, such as hunt camps, plant collecting stations, or butchering sites, would have a relatively low diversity of artifacts. In other words, if a narrow range of activities were performed at a particular location, one would expect to find a relatively low number of artifact types. Such a pattern is found in Price's study of Mesolithic settlement types in the Netherlands (1978). In this study sites were classified as either base camps or extraction camps. Price considered extraction camps to be special-purpose sites with a limited number of activities performed. His base camp designation was a location where general-purpose activities were conducted, such as food preparation and processing and the manufacture of tools and shelters. He used several different kinds of information, including artifact amounts, feature amounts, and site size in order to classify his site types. Table 8.4 lists site types by number of artifact types recovered and by artifact density per square meter. His base camp typology was stratified into small, medium, and large sizes. Table 8.4 has all base camps combined regardless of site size. His artifact analysis included only four kinds of tools: (1) points, (2) backed blades, (3) scrapers, and (4) cores. Even with a collapsed number of artifact types, the extraction camps contain consistently fewer chipped stone tool types than the base camps. Although base camps have a great range of artifact diversity, they are represented by greater densities of artifacts than the one extraction camp with density data. Even though these Mesolithic data are not conclusive, they certainly suggest, in general, that lithic artifact diversity would be greater at base camps than at special-purpose camps.

Table 8.4 *Number of artifact types and density for Mesolithic site types*

Site type	Component	Artifact Density (m²)	Artifact types
Extraction camp	18 Moerkilen I	–	3
Extraction camp	19 Moerkilen II	–	3
Extraction camp	20 Nijnsel I-5	8.5	3
Extraction camp	24 Waubach	–	3
Base camp	10 Havelte I:III	17.5	4
Base camp	15 Hazeputten II	16.6	4
Base camp	23 Siegerswoude	16.5	4
Base camp	1 Acht	34.0	4
Base camp	8 Havelte I:I	14.7	4
Base camp	9 Havelte I:II	13.7	4
Base camp	13 Havelte 3	12.4	4
Base camp	14 Hazeputten I	22.2	4
Base camp	21 Nijnsel II	16.7	4
Base camp	4 Duurswoude III	17.5	4
Base camp	11 Havelte 2:I	43.0	4
Base camp	12 Havelte 2:II	28.7	4

Source: Data taken from Price (1978:90).

Underlying the notion of artifact diversity and site function is the assumption of tool form equating to tool function at some level. If greater artifact diversity in the form of increased types is associated with greater numbers of activities it necessarily implies that variability in artifact types represents variability in artifact function. At first this may appear to contradict the previously cited microwear and ethnographic literature on artifact form and function, but the literature actually supports such an interpretation. Microwear analysis and ethnographic studies reveal that any one type of tool may not always conform to a particular function and that some tool types may be effective for multiple functions. Microwear and ethnographic studies have also shown that different tool types or tool edges are effective for different kinds of tasks. So although we may not be able to define the specific function(s) of particular tool types in all instances, it is not unreasonable to assume that increased numbers of tool types represent increased variability in activities in some or most instances.

In the Mesolithic example provided above, however, a more refined typological analysis of these stone tools might produce even stronger trends. For instance, if we assume that different kinds of backed blades (perhaps classified by size or edge angle) were used for different activities, it would not be unreasonable to expect the number of blade tool types to reflect numbers of functions. The same might also be said for "points" if the variability in the point assemblage was related to differential site activities. With such an increase in tool types, the compositional variability in assemblages between extraction camps and base camps might be more diagnostic.

From the above examples it is apparent that lithic assemblage composition – particularly assemblage diversity – may be an important determinant of relative mobility. Such a relationship can be tested if relative mobility can be determined independently of artifact assemblage diversity. One of the ways that some researchers have assessed relative mobility is by an analysis of lithic raw-material provenance studies (Dibble 1991; Marks *et al.* 1991; Montet-White 1988, 1991; Reher 1991; Rolland 1981; Seeman 1994; Tankersley and Morrow 1994). Barut's (1994) study of Upper Paleolithic sites in east Africa assessed the relative mobility of prehistoric populations by using measures of lithic raw material based upon distance from sources. This study analyzed two sites with multiple components that each contained Middle Stone Age (MSA) and Late Stone Age (LSA) occupations. The Lukenya Hill site in southern Kenya contained a single MSA occupation that was considered to have been inhabited by a relatively sedentary group. The site also had three LSA components, that were judged to have been occupied by more mobile groups (Barut 1994). The second site, Nasera, in northern Tanzania, was a rockshelter with seven discernible occupation components. Two components were LSA, three were MSA, and the remaining two were thought to be mixed components. Unlike the Lukenya Hill site, the relative mobility pattern of the Nasera rockshelter occupations was believed to have been reversed: the MSA was assessed as having had a highly mobile population and the LSA a more sedentary population (1994:66–7).

As with Price's (1978) Mesolithic study from the Netherlands, the East African stone tool analysis was not focused upon the detailed discrimination of artifact types with the result that differences in artifact diversity values were not great. However, from the data presented, there is a trend showing more artifact diversity in assemblages associated with relatively more mobile groups than more sedentary groups. Table 8.5 lists each site separately along with its rank based upon numbers of tool types and core types. In cases where rank is the same for more than one assemblage, the same number of artifact types were recovered. If the assumptions are made, first, that sites occupied by a relatively more mobile population were short term (perhaps special-task-oriented groups) and second, that more sedentary site occupants were living in base camps, then assemblage diversity would again be greater for base camps.

Summary of site functions

Site function can be approached from a number of different directions using the analysis of stone tools. I have cautioned against the use of morphological tool types as indicators of artifact function and then by extension as site

Table 8.5   *Lithic tool types compared with site types from East Africa*

Site type	Component	Period	Tool type count
Mobile	GVJM22e	LSA	8
Mobile	GVJM22f	LSA	9
Mobile	GVJM16b	LSA	11
Sedentary	GVJM16a	MSA	12
Mobile	MSA 2	MSA	11
Mobile	MSA 1	MSA	12
Mobile	MSA 3	MSA	12
?	Mixed 1	mixed	12
?	Mixed 2	mixed	12
Sedentary	LSA 2	LSA	12
Sedentary	LSA 1	LSA	13

Source: Data taken from Barut (1994:52).

functional indicators. However, if the function of individual artifacts can be determined with some degree of confidence, such information should be used to help infer site function. Artifact functional information can and should be used in conjunction with lithic assemblage analysis to support site function interpretations.

This section has emphasized the manner in which artifact assemblage diversity can help make site interpretations. One of the more critical aspects of this kind of analysis is the classification of lithic artifact types. If assemblage analysis is conducted to aid in the determination of site functions or site activities, then it is important to choose artifact classes or types that relate to activities or functions. For instance, if denticulates and side scrapers are used to perform the same kinds of tasks at a particular site, then it may not be useful to discriminate between these two morphological types when conducting an analysis attempting to recognize site function. Similarly, if different kinds of microlith forms (scalene triangles, rods, rhomboids, etc.) have been shown to be used for different kinds of activities in various contexts, it may be appropriate to include each microlith form as a separate tool type when conducting a site function analysis.

It should also be remembered that lithic tools undergo a uselife and that the individual artifact may acquire different functions as its morphology is adjusted through resharpening and usewear. It is also possible that the same individual specimen may have several different working edges for several different functions. In such cases it may be appropriate to count each edge or blade of the specimen as a separate tool. There is also the possibility that the same edge on an individual specimen was used for several different purposes or different activities. Depending upon the level of precision required in the analysis being conducted, such tools should perhaps be given more emphasis, or be recognized as something other than a single-function specimen.

In addition to the tools recovered from site areas, insight into site activities can be attained from recovered tool production debitage. In the course of performing subsistence and maintenance activities in living and working areas, stone tool users were also making their required tools. The various kinds of debitage analysis described in chapters 5 and 6 are very useful for characterizing the production efforts of stone tool makers. Such production activities were also a part of the site function, and probably linked very closely to the other activities performed in the site area. In some instances, and on some types of sites, it would be reasonable to assume that stone tool users incorporated tool production into the total process of task performance. This is in contrast to many modern tasks where, for example, the clippers are simply whipped off the garage hook and the shrubs trimmed. It is not inconceivable that for stone tool makers and users a similar task would include the additional duty of making the tool or tools required to complete the task. Hayden (1979b:214–20) observed Australian Aborigine stone tool makers who first found lithic raw material, made the stone tool(s), and then conducted the task – extracting a wooden plank from a tree to make a bowl, for instance. When such activities or tasks are intimately linked to the production of tools required to perform the task, the analysis of production debitage may be very important for interpreting site function.

It is apparent from hunter-gatherer organizational studies, both ethnographic and archaeological, that not all stone tools were expediently made as the need arose. Many tasks and activities were anticipated well in advance and the gear required for task performance was prepared well before the activity. In many instances, the tasks were performed in very different locations from where the tools were manufactured. This is one of the reasons why site functional analysis is best planned and conducted in a manner that depends upon local and regional site contexts. Researchers working with stone tool assemblages usually have so little information related directly to site function that it is necessary to structure and organize such analysis around the contexts of the data. Factors such as artifact preservation, attrition rate of tools, lithic raw-material abundance, quality, shape, prehistoric settlement configuration, and the site function itself will all be important influences on the kind of lithic analysis that can be performed on the individual specimens and the assemblage as a whole.

9

LITHIC ANALYSIS AND PREHISTORIC SEDENTISM

The formal design of stone tools is closely linked to the various tasks or functions for which tools are employed. The tasks may relate to the production and maintenance of houses, tools, and clothing, or food procurement, such as hunting and butchering. Traditionally archaeologists have focused upon these task-oriented activities when considering tool design constraints. However, the design of stone tools can be related to constraints that are in addition to specific-task-related activities and functions. It has been shown that stone tool design and production can be affected by the abundance, quality, and shape of raw materials (Andrefsky 1994b, 1995; Bamforth 1986, Flenniken 1981; Flenniken and Wilke 1989; Kuhn 1992; Lothrop 1989), by the relative mobility and sedentism of the people using the stone tools (Andrefsky 1991; Bamforth 1990, 1991; Kelly 1988; Parry and Kelly 1987; Shackley 1990; Shott 1986; Torrence 1983, 1989), and by artifact uselife (Goodyear 1974; Jelinek 1976; Marks 1988; Rolland and Dibble 1990). Still other constraints on tool design include stylistic factors (Close 1989; Sackett 1982, 1986; Wobst 1977), risk minimizing (Cashdan 1985; Wiessner 1982), and time optimization (Boydston 1989; Torrence 1983). The previous chapter discussed the relationship between artifact diversity and site functions within a context of prehistoric mobility. Related to the concept of prehistoric mobility is that of sedentism. This chapter explores the relationship between prehistoric sedentism and lithic artifact analysis. In so doing, special emphasis is placed upon the role of lithic raw materials as factors associated with tool design and production.

Sedentism and archaeology

The occurrence of sedentism in human populations is an important issue in the larger field of anthropological inquiry, partially owing to the fact that sedentism frequently occurs in conjunction with other kinds of socio-political and economic changes. Along with sedentism there is frequently a shift from egalitarian to nonegalitarian socio-political organization that may include hierarchical social organization, ascribed leadership, and differential access to wealth, and craft specialization. There is also usually a shift to food storage. It should also become clear that the analysis of stone artifacts may be one of the

211

best and only ways to determine when sedentism occurred in prehistoric populations.

As Kelly (1995:148–52) convincingly notes, sedentism is not easily defined: what may be considered residential sedentism for some may be residential mobility for others. Generally, sedentism refers to the location of residential units. Residential units are considered sedentary when populations remain at the same location year-round. However, this definition is complicated when considering issues such as the numbers of people living at a residence and the amount of time people actively live there. The question becomes, do we have a sedentary residence if only some of the people live at the location for the entire year? If not, then how many or what percentage of the entire population must live at the residence before it is considered sedentary? What if people are maintaining a residence at one location for the entire year, but leave for short intervals of time to conduct other tasks, such as hunting or warfare? How long are people required to be absent from their residence before they are considered nonsedentary? Residential sedentism, much like mobility, should not be viewed as an absolute state. Sedentary residential behavior appears in many different forms and can be measured on many different scales. Kelly demonstrates this point when he discusses the Batak (1995:149):

> Formerly nomadic, the Batak now maintain a central settlement at which someone is almost always present throughout the year (Eder 1984). They move this central settlement, however, every seven to ten years. An individual family spends only about 25 percent of the year in the central settlement. The rest of time is spent in field houses and forest camps. Moving among a limited number of locations, a Batak family changes location about ninety times a year, moving about 3 kilometers each time for a total yearly residential mobility of about 270 kilometers.

It is clear from the Batak example that sedentism and mobility can be evaluated at several different levels. The number of residential moves might be an important factor when trying to determine relative sedentism of a group. The distance – maximum or average – of residential moves might also be important for determining the relative sedentism of the population. Similarly, the frequency with which moves occur, and/or the duration of time between each move should perhaps be considered when determining relative sedentism. All of these factors make it relatively difficult to categorize any particular population as either mobile or sedentary.

The composition of the group moving its residence also complicates the pattern when trying to determine relative sedentism. Groups making and using stone tools may have as few as a single individual or as many as all individuals go out from the residence. In many hunter-gatherer populations only one or a few individuals will leave the residence and establish other living quarters to perform such tasks as root collecting, big game hunting, vision quests, and ritual warfare. This change in residence may be for very short or extended periods of time. However, group composition is very important when trying to determine relative sedentism or mobility.

This array of factors associated with sedentism of residential locations was introduced into the archaeological literature by Binford (1980). As discussed in the previous chapter, Binford characterized hunter-gatherer settlement types by the kind of mobility each group conducted during an annual cycle. To reiterate, residential mobility is defined as movement of the entire group from one location to another, and logistical mobility is defined as the movements of individuals or small groups to and from the residential location in order to perform specific tasks. However, as discussed above, mobility and sedentism may involve more than just residential and logistical movements; duration, frequency, and distance of moves are also important when characterizing relative sedentism.

Recent studies dealing with the way in which stone tool technology is organized in the broader pattern of hunter-gatherer adaptations have effectively linked residential sedentism to lithic technology (Andrefsky 1991; Henry 1989; Morrow and Jefferies 1989; Parry and Kelly 1987; Shott 1986). Most of these studies have established an association between the amount of effort expended in tool production and the settlement strategies used by tool makers and users. An important distinction has even been made between tools with little effort expended in their production (informal tools) and tools with more effort expended in their production (formal tools).

Formal tools have undergone a great amount of effort in production, whether the production has occurred over the course of several resharpening or hafting episodes or in one episode of manufacturing from raw material to finished product. These tools have the qualities of flexibility, can be easily rejuvenated, and have the potential for redesign for different functions (Goodyear 1979:4). Torrence (1983:11–13) attributes the characteristics of advance preparation, transportability, and anticipated use to these tools. Tools that meet these specifications include bifaces, some intentionally retouched flake tools, and formally prepared cores. Bifaces, as has been previously stated, can be used repeatedly, be resharpened (Bienenfeld and Andrefsky 1984; Sollberger 1971), be applied to many different tasks, such as cutting, sawing, and projectile use (Ahler 1971; Lewenstein 1987:160), and become sources of raw material as cores (Goodyear 1979:4–6; Kelly 1988).

In a continuum of production effort formal tools are at one end and informal tools are at the opposite end. Informal tools may be viewed as unstandardized or casual with regard to form. They include expediently manufactured tools that are made, used, and discarded over a relatively short period of time. Binford (1979) characterizes such tools as situational gear, or gear that is put to use in response to conditions rather than in anticipation of events or situations. This kind of technology is wasteful with regard to lithic raw materials: it tends to produce tools that are simpler and have less formal patterning, shape, or design.

Some of the studies that have linked stone tool technology to residential sedentism have, in general, associated formal tools with mobile hunter-gatherer populations and informal tools with more sedentary populations. The logic of this association is that mobile groups cannot risk being unprepared for a task while on the move. Unprepared in this sense means not having available tools to complete tasks, and thus mobile groups diminish the risk by transporting tools with them. These tools have the characteristics of being multifunctional, readily modifiable, and easily portable – the qualities of formal tools. Sedentary populations, on the other hand, do not have to expend extra effort in the production of flexible, transportable tools. The uncertainty of available resources for tool production is potentially not as serious a problem. Relatively more sedentary groups do not need to consolidate tools into multifunctional, light-weight configurations, but can safely manufacture, use, and discard tools according to the needs of the moment when raw materials are readily available.

If all of the above is assumed to be the case, lithic technological patterns can be explored and related to sedentism and its relative or variable states. The examples provided below illustrate such usages, but also draw attention to other factors that influence lithic technological variability, such as the abundance and availability of lithic raw materials and the processes by which raw materials are acquired. These are shown to be important constraints that affect individual lithic tool design as well as lithic assemblage composition.

Sedentism in North America

Parry and Kelly (1987) have convincingly demonstrated the general trend from formal tool use to expedient tool use relative to mobile and sedentary populations in four different areas of North America. Each of the four different areas (Mesoamerica, Plains, Southwest, and Eastern Woodlands) had undergone an evolution from residential mobility to relative sedentism over the course of several thousand years. In their study, many different classes of stone tools and debitage were examined through time for each area. Generally, they found that tools and tool technology changed according to the change in relative sedentism.

Core tools

Parry and Kelly used a battery of different analytical strategies to show that relatively more informal tools were used when populations became more sedentary. From those same areas populations used more formalized tools when they were less sedentary and more mobile. One of the first things Parry and Kelly did was establish the idea that bifaces need to be considered as very formalized cores. Since all areas that they studied also contained informal or expedient cores, a comparison of formal bifacial cores to informal cores over time should show significant trends. Table 9.1 lists each data set they examined

Table 9.1   *Ratio of Bifaces to Informal Cores*

	Plains data (North Dakota)		
	Early	Middle	Late
Ratio of bifaces to cores	3.52	2.92	1.34
	Southwest data (Chaco)		
	Early		Late
Ratio of bifaces to cores	0.80		0.13
	Southwest data (Black Mesa)			
	Early	Early/Middle	Late/Middle	Late
Ratio of bifaces to cores	5.75	2.38	0.45	0.04
	Southwest data (Dolores)				
	Early	Early/Middle	Middle	Late/Middle	Late
Ratio of bifaces to cores	5.75	2.83	0.71	0.95	0.75
	Mesoamerican data		
	Early		Late
Ratio of bifaces to cores	1.09		0.03

Source: Data taken from Parry and Kelly (1987).

by area, stratified from earliest period to latest period. The actual counts of bifaces and cores were not given but the ratios show consistent trends. In all cases sedentism gradually increased from earlier to later periods. In all cases the ratio of bifaces to informal cores decreases from earlier to later periods. This indicates that formal cores (bifacial cores) became less common as sedentism became more common, and it was the trend found in all five data sets. The only deviation in this pattern was between the Middle and Late/Middle period at Dolores (Colorado). The Middle period at Dolores, or the Basketmaker III period as defined by Parry and Kelly (1987:293), shows a marked decrease in use of bifacial cores. They suggest that this deviation from the overall pattern was relatively insignificant and that movement away from use of bifacial cores came between Basketmaker II (Early/Middle) and Basketmaker III (Middle). After Basketmaker III there was generally a low use of bifacial cores as compared to informal cores.

Bifaces and unifaces

The use of core data in this manner makes a very strong case for the correlation of stone tool technology with residential sedentism. To add more strength to

Table 9.2   *Percentage of Tools with Facial Retouch*

	Southwest Data (Chaco)			
	Early			Late
Percent of tools with facial retouch	22			6
	Southwest data (Black Mesa)			
	Early	Early/Middle	Late/Middle	Late
Percent of tools with facial retouch	29	14	14	2
	Southwest data (Dolores)				
	Early	Early/Middle	Middle	Late/Middle	Late
Percent of tools with facial retouch	22	17	13	12	9
	Mesoamerican data			
	Early			Late
Percent of tools with facial retouch	29			3

Note: Data taken from Parry and Kelly (1987).

their argument they looked at the tool data as a group irrespective of the tool function. They made the assumptions that tools with more effort expended in production would be more likely to be associated with mobile groups, and that tools with less effort expended in production would be associated with sedentary groups. Based on these assumptions they measured production effort on various tool types. Essentially, they considered tools with facial retouch more difficult and time consuming to make than tools with only marginal retouch or no retouch at all. Tools such as projectile points, bifaces, and unifaces were facially retouched and tools such as unmodified flakes that had usewear and were marginally retouched were nonfacially retouched tools. Only four of the five data sets they examined had data presented in this way. Table 9.2 lists the percentage of tools with facial retouch found during each time period for each assemblage. Again, no total counts were provided but the trends based upon percentages are consistent with the core data provided in Table 9.1: as relative sedentism increases the relative amount of formalized tools (those with facial retouch) decreases. For the example cited this necessarily means that informal tools increased in popularity as sedentism increased.

Debitage

Debitage types and/or debitage attributes reflect the kind of tool production and use in assemblages even if the tools themselves are not recovered from excavation. The Parry and Kelly study also examined debitage for evidence of formal tool production over time, although the Mesoamerican and Dolores data examined did not contain debitage information. Two aspects of the debitage were examined: (1) the percentage of proximal flakes and flake fragments identified as bifacial thinning flakes, and (2) the percentage of proximal flakes and flake fragments identified with faceted platforms. (Chapters 4 and 5 review the measurement techniques on debitage and also provide detailed illustrations of striking platform types and flake types.) The percentage of flakes associated with biface production relative to all other flakes in the assemblage should provide an indication of bifacial production and/or resharpening. Those assemblages with relatively more bifacial thinning flakes probably represent more formal tool production and/or use. Similarly, debitage with higher percentages of faceted platforms indicates more care and effort expended in tool production than debitage with nonfaceted platforms. In other words, faceted platforms suggest formal tool production and use, and nonfaceted platforms suggest informal tool production and use. Table 9.3 lists the change in relative frequencies of bifacial thinning flakes and striking platform facets over time. The bifacial thinning flake data for Black Mesa (Arizona) shows a slight increase from the Early (15%) to the Early/Middle (19%) period, but then an extremely large drop in the Late/Middle (2%) and Late (0%) periods. All other debitage data used by Parry and Kelly conform to the expectation that as sedentism increases so do debitage indicators of informal tool production and use.

An important characteristic of the lithic artifact data found in these western North American data sets is continuity of both formal and informal types. In no case did one technology get replaced by another technology (Parry and Kelly 1987:296). In all instances there was a shift in tool type preference only as settlement practices shifted. However, as discussed earlier, sedentism is not a unidimensional phenomenon, and can be scaled and measured in many different ways. All of the various configurations and differences in the concept of sedentism may have an effect upon the lithic technological system being used. A more detailed exploration of those differences is presented in some of the cases that follow.

Occupation duration and the Mousterian of west-central Italy

Kuhn examined a number of different stone tool factors related to lithic reduction in Mousterian assemblages from two sites in west-central Italy (Kuhn 1991). His analysis revealed that stone tool variability was related to a

Table 9.3   *Percent of Faceted Platforms and Biface Thinning Flakes Over Time*

	Plains data (North Dakota)		
	Early	Middle	Late
Percent of biface thinning flakes	27	15	9
	Southwest data (Chaco)		
	Early		Late
Percent of faceted platforms	7		3
	Southwest data (Black Mesa)			
	Early	Early/Middle	Late/Middle	Late
Percent of biface thinning flakes	15	19	2	0
Percent of faceted platforms	41	41	34	22

Source: Data taken from Parry and Kelly (1987).

variety of factors such as raw-material availability, differential transport of raw materials, and tool functions. He also noted that one of the sites, Grotta Guattari, was characterized by a relatively short period of occupation when compared to the second site, Grotta di Sant'Agostino, and that duration of occupation may also influence the character of lithic reduction found at each site (1991:97). Kuhn also points out that duration of occupation may not necessarily be equated to relative sedentism in the Binfordian sense (foragers versus collectors). As noted previously, duration of occupation is one of the factors that can define sedentism and is important for an understanding of it (Kelly 1995). So although Kuhn's research on the Mousterian of west-central Italy does not specifically address sedentism and stone tools his stone tool analysis is directly related to one of the most important components of sedentism – duration of occupation.

Stone tool retouch

According to Parry and Kelly (1987) relatively more sedentary populations will, in general, use an expedient technology and a more mobile population will use a formal technology. If this line of reasoning is followed, more sedentary tool makers would have lower amounts of retouched tools. Conversely, more mobile populations would have higher amounts of retouched

Table 9.4   *Frequencies of retouched and unretouched tools*

Site assemblage	Retouched tools	Unretouched flakes	Totals
Grotta Guattari	482 (66.9%)	239 (33.1%)	721
Grotta di Sant'Agostino	247 (33.6%)	488 (68.4%)	735

Source: Data taken from Kuhn (1991:84). $x^2 = 160.91$, $df = 1$, $p < 0.001$.

tools. If we also assume that sites with a longer duration of occupation represent a more sedentary population and sites with shorter durations of occupation are more mobile we may predict the relative amounts of retouched tools to be found at such sites. Following Parry and Kelly's (1987) line of reasoning with regard to relative sedentism and stone tool production we would expect that the Grotta di Sant'Agostino would have relatively fewer retouched tools than Grotta Guattari since the former site had a longer duration of occupation than the latter site. Table 9.4 lists the frequencies of retouched tools to unretouched flakes greater than 2 cm in length for both sites. The site with a short duration of occupation, Grotta Guattari, contains 66.9% retouched tools and 33.1% unretouched flakes. The site with a longer duration of occupation, Grotta di Sant'Agostino, contained only 33.6% retouched tools to 68.4% unretouched flakes. These are highly significant differences in lithic artifact assemblages for sites with different durations of occupation ($x^2 = 160.91$, $df = 1$, $p < 0.001$).

Another way to evaluate relative amounts of retouch on stone tools is to use the retouch index defined by Kuhn (1990). This index is used for retouched stone tools with only a single worked edge, and estimates the amount of the flake blank that has been removed by retouch. The index of retouch is a ratio between the maximum centerline thickness of a tool and its vertical thickness at the point where the retouch scars terminate (see Kuhn 1990). Unmodified flakes have a retouch index value of 0 and the most heavily modified tools have a retouch index of 1.0. Table 9.5 lists the reduction index values for all excavation levels from both sites. Again, the combined mean values for all excavation levels is significantly greater at Grotta Guattari than at Grotta di Sant'Agostino (K-W statistic comparing site medians = 13.17, $p < 0.001$). In addition to the greater retouch values for the site with a shorter duration of occupation there was a slightly higher proportion of tools with multiple retouched edges (17.75% versus 12.62%).

Raw material variability

Another line of evidence frequently examined when dealing with relative sedentism and lithic tool production is variability in raw materials. It is often assumed that lithic raw-material variability will be greater on sites with a

Table 9.5   *Reduction index values for single-edged tools*

Site assemblage	Mean	SD	N
Grotta Guattari			
Stratum 1	0.62	0.22	52
Stratum 2	0.57	0.23	91
Stratum 4	0.65	0.22	177
Stratum 5	0.64	0.24	85
All Strata	0.63	0.23	405
Grotta di Sant'Agostino			
Level 1	0.57	0.22	431
Level 2	0.58	0.24	120
Level 3	0.56	0.24	69
Level 4	0.56	0.19	34
All Levels	0.57	0.22	645

Source: Data taken from Kuhn (1991:85). K-W Statistic comparing site medians = 13.17, $p < 0.001$.

shorter duration of occupation and less on sites with greater durations of occupation (MacDonald 1991). Similarly some researchers believe that non-local raw materials are more likely to be found on shorter-duration sites than on longer duration sites. In some cases this makes a great deal of sense because groups occupying short-duration sites were believed to circulate over a greater range of territory more often than groups occupying sites for longer durations. It is important to remember that the increased frequency of visits within the total range occupied by the group is the key distinction here. Relatively sedentary groups who occupy sites for a longer duration may have as large a territorial range as groups who occupy sites for a shorter duration of time, but they may visit that range only once a year, once a decade, or less.

Returning to the Mousterian example with this scenario in mind we would expect that Grotta Guattari would have greater relative frequencies of exotic raw materials than would Grotta di Sant'Agostino since the former site is of shorter occupation duration than the latter. Unfortunately the exact location of lithic raw materials found in artifact form was not determined (Kuhn 1991:87). However, it is known that tool-quality raw materials occur in close proximity to each site and that these raw materials occur as small pebbles with cortex. One way to estimate the relative proportion of lithic artifacts that may have been derived from exotic sources is to determine the number of unusually large specimens and to determine the number of specimens with no cortex since most of the local raw materials were reduced by bipolar reduction. If unusually large flakes or flake tools are defined as longer or wider than the population mean by two standard deviations then there is a 95% probability that the specimen was drawn from a distinct population. In this case we might assume that unusually large specimens would be from exotic raw-material

Table 9.6 *Relative frequencies of unusually large lithic specimens*

Site assemblage	% of total assemblage	% with no cortex
Grotta Guattari		
Stratum 1	30	6.9
Stratum 2	33	7.4
Stratum 4	15	10.0
Stratum 5	9	0.0
Grotta di Sant'Agostino		
Level 1	9	1.6
Level 2	16	2.9
Level 3	15	0.0
Level 4	11	0.0

Source: Data taken from Kuhn (1991:89).

locations. It is also probable that flakes and flake tools with no cortex were drawn from an exotic population given the fact that small pebbles will tend to have relatively more cortical surface area to overall mass than larger cobbles with cortex. Table 9.6 lists the percentages of unusually large nonbipolar specimens (Levallois and centripetal) for each site by excavation level. Although the actual counts were not available the relative percentages show that greater amounts of unusually large specimens are found at Grotta Guattari then at Grotta di Sant'Agostino. This suggests that the latter site, having a longer occupation duration, contains fewer exotic raw materials. This pattern is reinforced when examining the percentage of unusually large specimens with no cortex. Again, Grotta Guattari is estimated to have greater amounts of exotic lithic raw materials.

Another simple way to evaluate relative sedentism using lithic raw materials is to count the relative frequencies of various kinds of raw materials and determine if two or more sites have significantly different raw-material variability. These data were not available for the Mousterian example above but the information that was available seems to suggest that duration of site occupation and, by extension, relative sedentism can be evaluated using lithic artifact data. However the study by Kuhn (1991) and several others suggest that availability of raw materials may complicate simple patterns of relative sedentism and lithic tool production (Andrefsky 1994b; Bamforth 1990; Bar-Yosef 1991; Jelinek 1991).

Raw-material qualities and relative sedentism

The importance of raw-material characteristics for the design and production of stone tools has been noted in ethnographic observations of stone tool makers and users. Gould (1980) explored the effects of raw-material abundance on stone tool production for the western Desert Aborigines of Australia and noted that when lithic raw materials were readily available near the habitation area, the Aborigines tended to use the available materials for production of all types of tools, both expedient and long uselife tools. This observation prompted Gould (1980:134) to generalize:

> Whenever random factors of geography place sources of usable stone, whether in the form of quarries or nonlocalized in nature, at or in close proximity to a water source where a habitation base-camp will occur, ease of procurement will outweigh other factors and unusually high percentages of artifacts of these locally available stones will be made, used, and discarded at such campsites.

O'Connell's (1977) work with the central Australian Aborigines shows that variation in the lithic assemblage is primarily due to the abundance of lithic raw materials. O'Connell concluded (1977:280):

> It seems fair to say that where such variation is recognized, it is generally seen either as functional, that is, as resulting from differences in the range of activities carried out at particular sites, or stylistic, reflecting certain traditional standards applied in the manufacture of artifacts. There is no doubt that such interpretations are often quite correct. Nevertheless, the data presented here indicate that a substantial amount of interassemblage variation may be the result of differences in access to material used in the manufacture of tools and of the particular characteristics of these materials as they affect the form of implements.

O'Connell's analysis of stone tools from a dozen sites shows that scrapers and adzes were primarily made from chert when the site was located near a chert source, and that these same tool types were primarily made from quartzite when the site was located near a quartzite source. This necessarily means there is a direct relationship between raw-material abundance and the production of stone tools.

Parry and Kelly (1987) did not evaluate lithic raw-material abundance in their study of tool production effort and relative sedentism, but their examples clearly show a relationship between the two. I emphasized the role of occupation duration in the Mousterian example from west-central Italy. However, Kuhn's study also emphasized the role of raw-material abundance and transportation (1991). Other studies from various regions of the world have shown that lithic raw-material abundance plays an important role in the production of stone tool forms (Dibble 1991; Dobosi 1991; Meltzer 1984; Wiant and Hassen 1985).

Tool frequencies and raw raterial

A study of raw material taken from archaeological survey information from southeastern Colorado (Andrefsky 1990) explores the relationship between relative sedentism, tool production effort, and raw-material abundance. In

Table 9.7   *Frequency of bifacial cores and informal cores by short-term and long-term occupations in southeastern Colorado*

	Core types		
Site duration	Bifacial	Informal	Total
Short-term	96 (32.2%)	169 (63.8%)	265
Long-term	31 (34.4%)	59 (65.6%)	90

Source: Data taken from Andrefsky (1994a:26). $x^2 = 0.092$, $df = 1$, $p > 0.75$.

southeastern Colorado relative sedentism was determined by the type of architectural remains found on sites. Short-duration occupation sites associated with mobile populations were assumed to be those sites characterized by spaced-stone circles or tipi rings. Sites characterized by aggregations of stone structures were assumed to be the locations of longer-duration occupations. Raw materials of highly chippable quality occur in great abundance throughout the survey area and were readily available to both mobile and sedentary populations of the area (Andrefsky 1994a).

Table 9.7 lists the frequencies and relative frequencies of cores that are either bifacial or informal for sites occupied by mobile groups and for those occupied by more sedentary groups. Bifacial cores in this case do not include hafted bifaces (projectile points) or bifacial drills. All other forms of bifaces, such as preforms and nondescript bifaces, are included in the bifacial core group. Informal cores represent all nonformalized shapes of cores. It is apparent that there is no significant difference between mobile and sedentary groups on the basis of the amount of effort expended in tool production ($X^2 = 0.092$, $df = 1$, $p > 0.750$). Given the observations of modern Australian Aborigines by O'Connell and Gould; it would appear that the southeastern Colorado data distribution can be attributed to the preference for locally available lithic raw materials – and not to relative sedentism.

This line of evidence can be extended to include artifact classes beyond core types. Table 9.8 separates artifact types into formal (projectile points, bifaces and specialized scrapers) and informal (flake knives and unmodified flake tools) tools. Locally available raw materials were preferred in the production of both types of tools. Not only were they preferred, but there is almost no difference in the relative frequencies of local raw material used for either tool type. Table 9.8 is also separated into two different site types based upon relative sedentism. There is, once again, no difference in raw material preference for tool forms for site assemblages of either sedentary or mobile groups when tested using raw materials from the known sources (all formal tools: $x^2 = 0.135$, $df = 1$, $p > 0.50$; all informal tools: $x^2 = 0.646$, $df = 1$, $p > 0.25$). These data support the belief that local availability of lithic raw materials is import-

Table 9.8   *Frequency of raw-material types and tool types by short-term and long-term occupations in southeastern Colorado*

Site	All formal tool types				All informal tool types			
Duration	Local	Nonlocal	Unknown	Total	Local	Nonlocal	Unknown	Total
Short-Term	463 (88.3%)	24 (4.6%)	37 (7.1%)	524	477 (92.8)	22 (4.3%)	15 (2.9%)	514
Long-term	116 (89.2%)	5 (3.9%)	9 (6.9%)	130	107 (93.0%)	3 (2.6%)	5 (4.4%)	115

Source: Data taken from Andrefsky (1994a:27). Local and nonlocal formal tools:$x^2 = 0.135$, $df = 1$, $p > .50$; local and nonlocal informal tools: $x^2 = 0.646$, $df = 1$, $p > 0.25$.

Table 9.9   *Frequency of formal and informal tool types by lithic raw-material type from eastern Washington*

Raw material	Informal tools	Formal tools	Totals
Local materials	34 (87.2%)	5 (12.8%)	39
Nonlocal materials	11 (4.6%)	229 (95.4%)	240
Unknown source	0 (0.0%)	19 (100%)	19

Source: Data taken from Andrefsky (1994b:281). x^2(for known sources) $= 169.16$, $df = 1$, $p < 0.001$.

ant regardless of the tool type or the relative sedentism of the group. The availability of raw materials plays a significant role in the stone tool production technology, at least in this data set, where raw materials were locally abundant and of good quality. What would the trend in stone tool production be in areas where highly chippable or good-quality raw materials did not exist in abundance?

Table 9.9 lists artifactual data from a site in eastern Washington in the United States where high-quality raw materials do not exist or exist in very small quantity, but very-poor quality lithic raw materials are locally available (Andrefsky 1994b). These data show a configuration for tool production different from the southeastern Colorado material. The eastern Washington data show that local raw materials dominate only the informal tool category, and that nonlocally available lithic raw materials dominate the formalized tool category. The raw materials of a known source are significantly discriminated by tool type ($x^2 = 169.16$, $df = 1$, $p = 0.001$). Another pattern in the data from Table 9.9 that differs from the southeastern Colorado assemblage is the much greater frequency of formal tools than informal tools. These data would suggest that availability of lithic raw materials plays an important role in the kind of assemblage produced (formal vs. informal), and also in the types of raw materials used to make these kinds of tools. It is also implied that a different strategy for stone tool procurement had to be implemented in the eastern Washington case than in the southeastern Colorado area.

Raw-material quality

The data from eastern Washington and southeastern Colorado may also be influenced by another factor important in the production of various stone tool forms. In addition to the abundance of lithic raw materials, the quality of raw materials undoubtedly plays a role in stone tool technology and affects how populations procure, produce, and discard stone tools.

The chipping quality of lithic raw materials has been shown to be an important characteristic in the selection of stone to be made into tools (Dibble 1991; Goodyear 1979; Hayden 1982). Some studies have shown that the quality of lithic raw materials is important for artifact function (Crabtree 1967; Flen-niken 1981:16–19). Other studies have suggested that raw-material quality may be important for the production of ritual artifacts or regalia (Winters 1984:20). If certain kinds of lithic raw materials are more, or less, effective for certain kinds of tasks it would be reasonable to suspect that prehistoric tool makers would take advantage of such variations in stone quality for the production of tools.

The differing uses of lithic raw-material types for different artifact types is evident from the hunter-gatherer assemblage recovered from Swift Bar on the lower Snake River in the Pacific Northwestern region of the United States (Andrefsky 1995). Relatively coarse-grained basalts and quartzites occur naturally within the site area and are ubiquitous for all parts of the lower Snake River. These materials occur in artifactual form and dominate the artifact assemblage. Cryptocrystalline raw materials have not been found in natural form at Swift Bar or within the gravels along the river edge; however, these raw materials do occur in artifactual form. Table 9.10 lists the frequency of various tool types and their raw-material composition. Basalt, metamorphosed basalt, and quartzite occur locally. Cherts are not found naturally at Swift Bar. The data show a strong correlation between raw-material type and artifact type ($x^2 = 151$; $df = 12$; $p < 0.001$). The tools that require less skill and craftsmanship for production (cobble and spall tools) tend to be made from locally available raw materials that are relatively coarse grained and do not chip as easily as chert. Cherts are used exclusively to make more refined kinds of tools, such as unifaces, bifaces, and projectile points. It is important to remember that there is a significant difference of textures between the very smooth cherts and the other relatively grainy raw materials. These data indicate that lithic raw material types are important for the production of different tool types.

Another interesting pattern in the Swift Bar data is the way basalt was used.

Table 9.10   *Frequency of artifact types by raw material from Swift Bar*

Raw material	Projectile points	Other bifaces	Unifaces	Cobble tools	Used spalls	Totals
Chert	15	23	11	0	0	49
	(30.6%)	(47.0%)	(22.4%)	(0%)	(0%)	
Basalt	15	40	10	147	46	258
	(5.8%)	(15.5%)	(3.9%)	(57%)	(17.8%)	
Metamorphic	0	1	1	32	15	49
	(0%)	(2.0%)	(2.0%)	(65.3%)	(30.7%)	
Quartzite	0	0	1	18	11	30
	(0%)	(0%)	(3.3%)	(60.0%)	(36.7%)	

Source: Data taken from Andrefsky (1995:104). $x^2 = 151$, $df = 12$, $p < 0.001$.

Basalt dominates all of the tool categories, as is to be expected since the basalts found in artifact form occur in a wide variety of textures. Almost all the basalt that occurs naturally in this part of the Snake River is fairly coarse-grained relative to other chippable-quality rock (such as chert). A survey for raw-material sources conducted on Swift Bar and in the surrounding area produced no very fine-grained basalts (Andrefsky 1994b). However, all projectile points and most other bifaces and unifaces made of basalt were from very fine-grained material. This suggests that these basalt artifacts, like the chert artifacts, were brought into the locality in finished or near finished form, a hypothesis supported by the discovery of a prehistoric basalt quarry approximately 150 km to the southeast where very high-quality basalts were manufactured into bifaces and points (Womack 1977). An analysis of debitage types also supports the premise that finished bifaces made from high-quality basalt were imported to the site; of 2,498 pieces of debitage recovered, only seven pieces (or less than 0.5%) were identified as biface thinning flakes (Sappington and Carley 1984:68, 104). This indicates an almost total absence of final-stage bifacial production on Swift Bar, and yet thirty projectile points and sixty-three bifaces were recovered. It is improbable that the basalt bifaces found on Swift Bar were made there and, in all probability, they were manufactured from materials not naturally occurring at Swift Bar.

These data support the notion that lithic raw-material quality plays a role in the production of various tool types. At Swift Bar at least, there is a significant trend in the use of fine-grained raw materials for certain tool types and more coarse-grained raw materials for other tool types. Additionally, however, raw-material size must be considered with regard to the Swift Bar data. The cobble tools and spall tools made from the coarse-grained raw materials are much larger than the points, unifaces, and bifaces, and may explain, in part, the distribution of tool types found on Swift Bar. Perhaps there was not necessarily a functional consideration in the preference for a certain type of raw material, but instead, the available shape and size of the raw material were the primary reasons that certain kinds of tools were made from certain kinds of raw materials.

Raw-material shape and size

Blank form and shape have been shown to be important factors in determining the final morphological configuration of flake stone unifaces (Bar-Yosef 1991; Kuhn 1992; Lothrop 1989) and bifaces (Flenniken and Wilke 1989). Different morphologies of blanks tend to determine the final morphology of tools. Large tools tend to be made from large blanks and small tools tend to be made from small blanks. It is not unreasonable to expect that the original form and size of raw materials also play a role in the final size and shape of stone tools produced, as well as the kind of production technology used to produce them.

Some archaeologists believe that bipolar technology is practiced by stone tool makers in order to maximize the use of lithic material. Bipolar technology is one of the ways that small-sized raw materials can be cracked and flaked to obtain usable cutting edges and blanks. Other archaeologists feel that bipolar technology is used when raw materials are not available in natural form, and in their stead existing stone tools are bipolarly flaked to obtain usable chips (MacDonald 1968). Bipolar technology is also used in places where lithic raw materials occur in small nodule form (Knudson 1978).

If bipolar technology is a technological reaction to the size of available lithic raw materials, then size and possibly shape have a great deal to do with prehistoric stone tool technology. Figure 9.1 illustrates the relative percentages of bipolar and freehand cores from sites in eastern Washington where only poor-quality lithic raw materials occur (Andrefsky 1994b). Core types are significantly discriminated by lithic raw-material availability ($x^2 = 21.54$, $df = 1$, $p < 0.001$). Bipolar cores tended to be manufactured primarily from the nonlocal lithic raw materials. Local raw materials were used primarily to produce the freehand cores. The locally occurring quartzite is coarse-grained and difficult to chip; all other stone types are nonlocal and of better chipping quality. There are a total of sixty-nine cores, and of that total, fifty-five are bipolar. This conforms to the expectation that bipolar cores would be used in a locality poor in raw material. That being the case, what accounts for the presence of fourteen freehand cores? The majority of freehand cores are manufactured from quartzite, and since quartzite is locally available, there is no need to maximize its use – an explanation for freehand core production. By contrast, with less than 4% of the total number of bipolar cores produced from locally available raw materials, the nonlocally available lithic raw materials are being maximized with bipolar technology. If bipolar technology is a raw-material maximizing strategy we would expect bipolar cores to be smaller

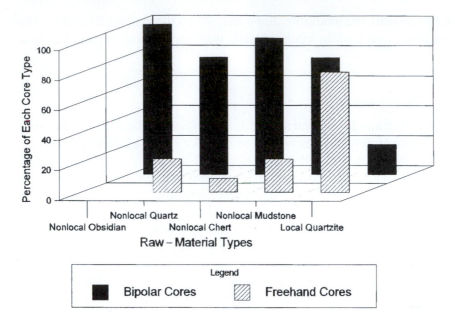

Figure 9.1 Relationship between core types and lithic raw-material availability. Bipolar cores tend to be manufactured from nonlocal materials and freehand cores tend to be made from local materials. (Bipolar core count: local = 2, nonlocal = 54; freehand cores: local = 7, nonlocal = 7; $x^2 = 21.5$, $df = 1$, $p < 0.001$). Adapted from Andrefsky (1994b:385).

or reduced in size when compared to other cores. Figure 9.2 lists the mean size of core types by site. Overall, bipolar cores are significantly smaller than freehand cores, and they are smaller than freehand cores on every site in which they occur. The sites with the two highest values for freehand cores have no bipolar cores represented. Once again it appears that the size of lithic raw materials may be an important consideration for the kind of production technology practiced by stone tool makers.

Summary

This discussion has illustrated several different methods used to recognize prehistoric sedentism by lithic assemblage analysis. The examples reveal that artifact variability is sensitive to relative sedentism in some cases. It is also shown that other factors related to lithic raw-material qualities can affect artifact variability regardless of relative sedentism. Raw-material characteristics such as size, shape, quality, and abundance are shown to be important influences upon the kind of lithic technology practiced by stone tool makers and users.

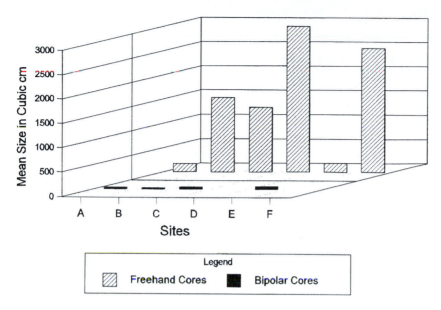

Figure 9.2 Size comparison of bipolar and freehand cores. Bipolar cores have a smaller mean size than freehand cores in all cases. (Bipolar core count: A = 26, B = 24, C = 3, D = 0, E = 2, F = 0; freehand core count: A = 4, B = 4, C = 2, D = 2, E = 1, F = 1). Adapted from Andrefsky (1994b:387).

Factors such as relative sedentism and raw-material characteristics are only two of the many that drive stone tool production decisions. Stone tool production technologies, like all other kinds of human technology, are dynamic processes connected on multiple levels to human cultural systems in many different locations. Relative sedentism may be linked to particular lithic technological characteristics in one culture, but those same technological characteristics may have nothing to do with sedentism in another cultural context. Ultimately, it is the tool maker who determines the kind of tool produced and the manner in which it is produced. In this regard, tool production strategies are culturally determined, and factors such as the qualities of lithic raw material and relative sedentism are part of the human decision-making process.

10

CONCLUSION

It should be obvious to the reader that prehistoric lithic artifacts were made, used, modified, and discarded in cultural contexts unlike any that exists today. Things that were intimately linked to prehistoric activities and tool uses, such as making the tool or searching for the lithic raw material, were probably common chores conducted before an activity was undertaken. Integrating the production of a tool into the process of its use, and then task completion, are all parts of a whole, and differ significantly from modern task accomplishment. The differences in the ideological perspectives of modern and prehistoric tool users is one of the most challenging areas for the interpreters of lithic artifacts and archaeologists in general.

Related to this concept of ideological differences is the fact that dynamic processes are associated with stone tool production and use. One of the most important considerations I have tried to stress in this book is the concept that stone tools change forms and shapes – as well as functions – during the period of time they are being used. That stone tool artifacts are the product of a dynamic process is, in some instances, incompatible with classification systems invented by archaeologists. This is further complicated by the common archaeological presumption that artifact shape reflects artifact function. Although stone tool shape often does indicate a function, I have tried to show that this is not always true and some stone tool shapes may be associated with more than one function. Archaeologists must move away from static typologies that pigeonhole an artifact into a single type with a single function. Any single artifact may be classified in a number of ways depending upon the criteria and rules for classification. Similarly, any artifact may have multiple functions or multiple meanings depending upon the context of classification. For example, a biface may be identified as a particular type of core in one instance, but it may be identified as representative of a particular type of cutting tool in another. In both cases the biface carries different kinds of interpretive information. However, such information is lost if we unwaveringly try to pigeonhole the biface as exclusively a core type or a knife type. All too often I have had long, fruitless discussions with archaeologists trying to explain to them that a particular biface is a core and at the same time is also a chopper or knife; the biface may in fact be all of these things. The problem often boils down to the fact that for many archaeologists an artifact name connotes a certain artifact shape and that shape connotes a certain function.

230

This is a problem for both classification and interpretation, as has been discussed fully in the book.

One of the ways that I have tried to overcome the problems of communication associated with lithic typologies is use of a morphological scheme like the one introduced in chapter 4. The classification chart (Figure 4.7) is a simple device to aid the recognition of lithic artifact morphologies. As discussed at length, this morphological typology is universal and general, and can therefore be used for all lithic artifacts. Importantly, no functional or temporal assumptions are attached to this classification scheme. The morphological typology is based upon recognition of standardized attributes that produce mutually exclusive types based upon shape. This generalized typology can be structured and modified for any particular region or area of the world.

One of the characteristics of lithic artifacts and lithic artifact analysis is the wide range of potential analytical approaches that can be conducted with lithic artifacts. For example, measurement of debitage size can be made by using its numerous characteristics, including length, width, thickness, weight, diameter of circle, sieve size, or various combinations of these, among others. One of the reasons why lithic analysis has so many potential analytical approaches is due to the lack of theoretical development associated with the data base of lithic analysis. Lithic artifact variability is extremely complex, and is linked not only to technological, cultural, and functional requirements, but also to aberrations in raw-material availability and other situational constraints. Because of this complexity it has been difficult to predict the kinds of lithic artifacts and/or artifact characteristics that may be associated with particular behavioral phenomena. There is no formula that tells a lithic analyst what number of flakes to expect as a result of biface production, or the amount of cortex to expect on debitage following microlith production. We are finding that this information varies with particular assemblages in particular contexts. However, experimental replication studies are one of the more promising areas of lithic analysis and seem to be helping fill this predictive void. As more replication studies are completed we are beginning to recognize redundancies in data characteristics that help eliminate some of the potential range of techniques employed. These studies also help researchers determine standardized procedures for data measurements.

Although standardizing measurement is important for the field of lithic analysis, the adequate description of measurement techniques is even more important at this time. The literature on lithic analysis is growing, and studies will too often appear without being replicable because the simple techniques of measurement have not been described. This happens because there are very few standardized ways to measure lithic artifacts. One of the most common examples of this failure is the listing of length, width, and thickness for cores; cores have great variability in shape and size, yet there is no standardized technique to measure length, width, or thickness. The same is true of any number of artifact types. Several chapters in this book have gone to great lengths to describe techniques for a standardized measurement of artifacts. Before theoretical development can occur in lithic analysis, replicable studies must be achieved in order to amass and synthesize large portions of the data base.

Because the field of lithic analysis is so open ended with regard to the number and kinds of manipulations that can be performed by an analyst, there are several ways to arrive at the same conclusions from lithic data. For example, a lithic researcher interested in identifying the adze production processes conducted at a particular site might analyze the adzes found in the assemblage. Alternatively, debitage could be analyzed and any number of possible debitage characteristics could be examined. For instance, dorsal cortex, flake size, striking platform shape, number of dorsal flake removals, or some other characteristic(s) could be measured to determine adze production. Similarly, any of these characteristics, such as flake size or striking platform shape can be evaluated using numerous techniques. In the face of this extensive range of analytical options I suggest that the best way to proceed with lithic analysis is to conduct multiple analytical passes. The most convincing behavioral interpretations in archaeology are those supported by multiple lines of evidence. If, for example, adze size analysis suggests that only initial production occurred at a particular site, then debitage size, cortical amount, and striking platform variability should also support that interpretation. The most convincing interpretations in lithic analysis are also those interpretations that have multiple lines of evidence for support.

During the past fifteen years that I have taught lithic analysis there have been many students who did not know how or where to begin an analysis of a lithic assemblage. In closing, the process that I have found successful in the analysis of a complex lithic assemblage is described. It is a general description because all analysis must be structured by the questions or objectives each researcher hopes to address.

In all cases I begin lithic analysis with gross identification and classification of artifacts. I simply determine which and how many of my artifacts are tools and debitage. If I have general classes of tools and debitage I sort them into those classes. The classification chart in Figure 4.7 is a good example of a gross identification chart that allows for sorting into replicable, mutually exclusive types.

Next I determine if certain kinds of tools dominate the assemblage. Is the assemblage dominated by flake tools or microliths? Are scrapers numerous? Any tool types with high representation might require a more refined classification to understand better the variability in the assemblage. It is important to remember that formal variability in stone tools is dependent upon dynamic processes of tool production and tool use. A review of chapter 2 (the background to these concepts) might be useful before a final tool typology is derived. Usually the regional literature will have "ready-made" classifications for an assemblage that are very useful. For instance, Mesolithic assemblages from Europe have a complex typology for microliths, and Archaic assemblages from North America have a typology for bifaces. Once the tool types are determined in an assemblage, it is important to get a sense of the overall distribution; tool type counts and relative percentages are important for distributions. With multicomponent assemblages, I examine such frequencies over time. I also stratify the assemblage by raw-material type. The review of lithic raw-material types in chapter 3 provides a good starting-point for those not familiar with geological variability in lithic assemblages.

The questions being addressed determine where the analysis goes from this point. Generally, I begin with the measurement of tool forms, followed by the measurement of debitage characteristics. I attempt to stage my analysis so that the results of tool analysis guide the kind of debitage analysis undertaken. For those researchers not familiar with lithic tool analysis, chapter 7 provides detailed descriptions of measurement techniques for cores, bifaces, and flake tools, along with how to proceed with the analysis. Chapter 8 provides examples of tool analysis that emphasize assemblage diversity. Chapter 9 characterizes formal and informal tool forms and the manner in which these forms relate to sedentism and raw-material availability.

The selection and measurement of debitage attributes should be done in a manner that clearly relates to the kind of tool types recovered in the assemblage. For instance, there is no need to use a striking platform typology for debitage that is based upon biface production models if the assemblage is composed of the remains of unidirectional cores. Practically all unidirectional core debitage specimens have flat platforms. A review of debitage striking platform characteristics and numerous other debitage attributes is found in chapter 5, as well as how to recognize and measure these attributes. Various techniques for the analysis of debitage are described in chapter 6. Chapters 8 and 9 combine debitage analysis with tool type analysis to understand patterning in assemblages.

As previously noted, I have deliberately tried to reduce the use of statistical and quantitative analysis in this book. However, the observant reader will notice references to various statistical tests throughout the book, particularly in the later chapters. This is primarily because many of the interpretations and generalizations about lithic assemblages are based upon population data. To say "most artifacts from a site are scrapers" or "flake shape varies with flake size" or "raw material is insignificant for determining artifact type" is to make a generalization based upon population quantification. In most cases unquantified generalizations are unsubstantiated generalizations, and the better-quantified generalizations are those that can be assessed with a probability value.

This book helps provide the reader with basic tools for turning lithic artifact assemblages into usable data. Serious students of lithic analysis should obtain the basic quantitative tools for turning data into generalizations.

When performing lithic analysis I attempt to bring together as much of the assemblage as possible to support an interpretation. We are beginning to understand that lithic assemblage variability is created as a result of many cultural, natural, and situational influences. It is therefore important to explore the relationships among the many assemblage variables in different archaeological contexts. In so doing, I suspect we will probably not develop or discover special formulas that match lithic artifacts with prehistoric behaviors. We may, however, find that the human condition was as variable during prehistoric times as it is today, and that lithic artifact variability reflects the manner in which humans have organized themselves in their cultural and natural contexts. In this regard, lithic artifact analysis has the potential to tell us a great deal more about prehistoric cultures and their behavior than we have yet been able to recognize.

REFERENCES

Ackerman, Robert E. 1992 Earliest Stone Industries on the North Pacific Coast of North America. *Arctic Anthropology* 29:18–27.

1994 Early Cultural Complexes in Southwestern Alaska. *Current Research in the Pleistocene* 11:109–11.

1996 Early Maritime Culture Complexes of the Northern Northwest Coast. In *Early Human Occupation in British Columbia*, ed. R. L. Carlson and L. Dalla Bona, pp. 123–37. University of British Columbia Press, Vancouver.

Adams, William Y., and Ernest W. Adams 1991 *Archaeological Typology and Practical Reality*. Cambridge University Press, Cambridge.

Ahler, Stanley A.1971 *Projectile Point Form and Function at Roger's Shelter, Missouri*. College of Arts and Science, University of Missouri-Columbia and the Missouri Archaeological Society, Columbia, Missouri.

1989 Mass Analysis of Flaking Debris: Studying the Forest Rather than the Trees. In *Alternative Approaches to Lithic Analysis*, ed. Donald O. Henry and George H. Odell, pp. 85–118. Archaeological Papers of the American Anthropological Association 1.

Ahler, Stanley A., and Julian VanNest 1985 Temporal Change in Knife River Flint Reduction Strategies. In *Lithic Resource Procurement*: *Proceedings from the Second Conference on Prehistoric Chert Exploitation*. ed. Susan C. Vehik, pp. 183–98. Center for Archaeological Investigations, Occasional Papers 4. Southern Illinois University, Carbondale.

Aigner, Jean S. 1970 The Unifacial, Core and Blade Site on Anangula Island, Aleutians. *Arctic Anthropology* 7:59–88.

Aikens, C. Melvin 1993 *Archaeology of Oregon*. US Department of Interior, Bureau of Land Management, Portland.

Amick, Daniel S., and Raymond P. Mauldin (eds.) 1989a *Experiments in Lithic Technology*. BAR International Series 528, Oxford.

1989b Comments on Sullivan and Rozen's "Debitage Analysis and Archaeological Interpretation." *American Antiquity* 54:166–8.

Amick, Daniel S., Raymond P. Mauldin, and Steven A. Tomka 1988 An Evaluation of Debitage Produced by Experimental Bifacial Core Reduction of a Georgetown Chert Nodule. *Lithic Technology* 17:26–36.

Ammerman, Albert J. 1979 A Study of Obsidian Exchange Networks in Calabria. *World Archaeology* 19:95–110.

Ammerman, Albert J., and William Andrefsky, Jr. 1982 Reduction Sequences and the Exchange of Obsidian in Neolithic Calabria. In *Contexts for Prehistoric Exchange*, ed. J. Ericson, and T. Earle, pp. 149–72. Academic Press, New York.

Ammerman. Albert J., and M.W. Feldman 1974 On the "Making" of an Assemblage of Stone Tools. *American Antiquity* 39:610–16.

1978 Replicated Collection of Site Surfaces. *American Antiquity* 43:734–40.

Anderson, D. D. 1970 Microblade Traditions in Northwest Alaska. *Arctic Anthropology* 7:2–16.

235

Anderson, P. C. 1980 A Testimony of Prehistoric Tasks: Diagnostic Residues on Stone Tool Working Edges. *World Archaeology* 12:181–94.

Anderson-Gerfaud, P. 1988 Using Prehistoric Stone Tools to Harvest Cultivated Wild Cereals: Preliminary Observations of Traces and Impact. In *Industrie lithiques: tracéologie et Technologie*, ed. S. Beyries, pp. 175–95. BAR International Series 411, Oxford.

Andrefsky, Jr., William 1983 Experimental Archaeology and Lithic Assemblage Analysis. In *Proceedings of the* 1983 *Middle Atlantic Archaeological Conference*, ed. J. Evans. Rehoboth Beach, Delaware.

1984 Late Archaic Prehistory in the Upper Delaware Valley: A Study of Classification, Chronology and Interaction. Ph.D. dissertation, State University of New York at Binghamton.

1986a A Consideration of Blade and Flake Curvature. *Lithic Technology* 15:48–54.

1986b Numerical Types and Inspectional Types: Evaluating Shape Characterization Procedures. *North American Archaeologist* 7:95–112.

1987 Diffusion and Innovation from the Perspective of Wedge Shaped Cores in Alaska and Japan. In *The Organization of Core Technology*, ed. J. K. Johnson and C. A. Morrow, pp. 13–44. Westview Press, Boulder, Colorado.

1991 Inferring Trends in Prehistoric Settlement Behavior From Lithic Production Technology in the Southern Plains. *North American Archaeologist* 12:129–44.

1993 Temporal Variability in Stone Tool Production from Cedar Falls. In *The Archaeology of Chester Morse Lake: Long Term Human Utilization of the Foothills in the Washington Cascade Range*, ed. S. Samuels, pp. 9.1–9.14. Center for Northwest Anthropology Project Report 21, Washington State University, Pullman.

1994a Raw Material Availability and the Organization of Technology. *American Antiquity* 59:21–35.

1994b The Geological Occurrence of Lithic Material and Stone Tool Production Strategies. *Geoarchaeology: An International Journal* 9:345–62.

1995 Cascade Phase Lithic Technology: An Example for the Lower Snake River. *North American Archaeologist* 16:95–115.

1997a Dynamic Morphological Processes and Stone Tool Typology in Americanist Archaeology. Paper presented at the 62nd Annual Meeting of the Society for American Archaeology, Nashville, Tennessee.

1997b Thoughts on Stone Tool Shape and Inferred Function. *Journal of Middle Atlantic Archaeology* 13:125–44.

Andrefsky, Jr., W. (ed.) 1990 *An Introduction to the Archaeology of Piñon Canyon, Southeastern Colorado*. Larson-Tibesar and Associates, Laramie, Wyoming. Submitted to National Park Service, Denver, Colorado, Contract No. CX 1200–7–B054. Copies available from NPS, Rocky Mountain Regional Office, Denver, Colorado.

Andrefsky, Jr., William, and Marilyn J. Bender (ed.) 1988 *The Piñon Canyon Maneuver Site Manual for the Conduct of Laboratory and Analytical Studies and Handling of Materials*. Prepared for NPS, Rocky Mountain Region and US Department of Army, Ft Carson.

Andrefsky, Jr., William, Elizabeth G. Wilmerding, and Steven R. Samuels 1994a *Archaeological Testing at Three Sites along the North Umpqua Drainage, Douglas County, Oregon*. Center for Northwest Anthropology, Project Report 23, Washington State University, Pullman.

1994b *Archaeological Testing at Three Sites along the South Umpqua Drainage, Douglas County, Oregon*. Center for Northwest Anthropology, Project Report 24, Washington State University, Pullman.

Annegarn, H. J., and S. Bauman 1990 Geological and Mineralogical Applications of PIXIE: A Review. *Nuclear Instruments and Methods in Physics Research* B49:264–70.

Bacon, W. S 1977 Projectile Point Typology: The Basic Base. *Archaeology of Eastern North*

America 5:107–21.

Bamforth, Douglas B. 1986 Technological Efficiency and Tool Curation. *American Antiquity* 51:38–50.

1988 Investigating Microwear Polishes with Blind Tests: The Institute Results in Context. *Journal of Archaeological Science* 15:11–23.

1990 Settlement, Raw Material, and Lithic Procurement in the Central Mojave Desert. *Journal of Anthropological Archaeology* 9:70–104.

1991 Technological Organization and Hunter-Gatherer Land Use: A California Example. *American Antiquity* 56:216–34.

Barut, Sibel 1994 Middle and Later Stone Age Lithic Technology and Land Use in East African Savannas. *The African Archaeological Review* 12:43–72.

Bar-Yosef, Ofer 1991 Raw Material Exploitation in the Levantine Epi-Paleolithic. In *Raw Material Economies Among Prehistoric Hunter-Gatherers*, ed. A. Montet-White and S. Holen, pp. 235–50. University of Kansas Publications in Anthropology 19, Lawrence.

Baumler, Mark F. 1988 Core Reduction, Flake Production, and the Middle Paleolithic Industry of Zobiste (Yugoslavia). In *Upper Pleistocene Prehistory of Western Eurasia*, ed. H. L. Dibble and A. Montet-White, pp. 255–74. University Museum Monograph 54, University of Pennsylvania, Philadelphia.

Baumler, Mark F., and Christian E. Downum 1989 Between Micro and Macro: A Study in the Interpretation of Small-Sized Lithic Debitage. In *Experiments in Lithic Technology*, ed. Daniel S. Amick and Raymond P. Mauldin, pp. 101–16. BAR International Series 528, Oxford.

Benfer, R. A. 1967 A Design for the Study of Archaeological Characteristics. *American Antiquity* 69:719–30.

Benfer, R. A., and A. N. Benfer 1981 Automatic Classification of Inspectional Categories: Multivariate Theories of Archaeological Data. *American Antiquity* 46:381–96.

Beyries, Sylvie 1988 Functional Variability of Lithic Sets in the Middle Paleolithic. In *Upper Pleistocene Prehistory of Western Eurasia*, ed. H. L. Dibble and A. Montet-White, pp. 213–24. University Museum Monograph 54, University of Pennsylvania, Philadelphia.

Bienenfeld, Paula 1995 Duplicating Archaeological Microwear Polishes with Epoxy Casts. *Lithic Technology* 20:29–39.

Bienenfeld, Paula, and William Andrefsky, Jr. 1984 Projectile Point Life Cycles and Use-Resharpening Analysis. Paper presented at the 49th Annual Meeting of the Society for American Archaeology, Portland.

Binford, Lewis R. 1963 A Proposed Attribute List for the Description and Classification of Projectile Points. In *Miscellaneous Studies in Typology and Classification*, ed. A. M. White *et al.*, pp. 193–221. Anthropological Papers 19, Museum of Anthropology, University of Michigan, Ann Arbor.

1972 Model-Building Paradigms, and the Current State of Paleolithic Research. In *An Archaeological Perspective*, ed. L. R. Binford, pp. 244–94. Seminar Press, New York.

1977 Forty-Seven Trips. In *Stone Tools as Cultural Markers*, ed. R. S. V. Wright, pp. 24–36. Australian Institute of Aboriginal Studies, Canberra.

1978 Dimensional Analysis of Behavior and Site Structure: Learning from an Eskimo Hunting Stand. *American Antiquity* 43:330–61.

1979 Organization and Formation Processes: Looking at Curated Technologies. *Journal of Anthropological Research* 35:255–73.

1980 Willow Smoke and Dogs' Tails: Hunter-Gatherer Settlement Systems and Archaeological Site Formation. *American Antiquity* 45:4–20.

Binford, Lewis R., and Sally R. Binford 1966 A Preliminary Analysis of Functional Variability in the Mousterian of Levallois Facies. *American Anthropologist* 68:238–95.

Binford, Lewis R., and George I. Quimby 1972 Indian Sites and Chipped Stone Materials in the Northern Lake Michigan Region. *Fieldiana: Anthropology* 36:277–307.

Blacking, John 1953 Edward Simpson, Alias "Flint Jack': A Victorian Craftsman. *Antiquity* 27:207–11.

Boeda, E. 1986 *Approche technolgique du concept levallois et évaluation de son champs d' Application: tude de trois gisements saaliens et weichseliens de la France septentrionale.* Doctoral dissertation, University of Paris X.

1988 Le Concept levallois et évaluation de son champ d'application. In *L'Homme de Néanderthal*, vol. 4: *La Technique*, ed. Marcel Otte, pp. 13–26. Etudes et recherches archéologiques de l'Université de Liège.

1993 Le Débitage discoide et le débitage levallois récurrente centripète. *Bulletin de la Société Préhistorique Française* 90:392–404.

Bordes, François 1961 *Typologie du paléolithique ancien et moyen.* Publications de l'Institut de Préhistoire de l'Université de Bordeaux, Mémoire 1, Bordeaux.

1968 *The Old Stone Age.* Weidenfeld and Nicolson, London.

1979 Comment. *Current Anthropology* 20:10–11.

1980 Le Débitage levallois et ses variantes. *Bulletin de la Société Préhistorique Française* 77:45–9.

Bordes, François, and Don E. Crabtree 1969 The Corbiac Blade Technique and Other Experiments. *Tebiwa* 12:1–21.

Bordes, F., and D. de Sonneville-Bordes 1970 The Significance of Variability in Paleolithic Assemblages. *World Archaeology* 2:61–73.

Bouey, P.D. 1991 Recognizing the Limits of Archaeological Applications of Non-Destructive Energy-Dispersive X-Ray Fluorescence Analysis of Obsidians. In *Materials Issues in Art and Archaeology II*, ed. P. B. Vandiver, J. Druzik, and G. S. Wheeler, pp. 309–20. Materials Research Society, Pittsburg.

Boydston, Roger A. 1989 A Cost Benefit Study of Functionally Similar Tools. In *Time, Energy and Stone Tools*, ed. Robin Torrence, pp. 67–77. Cambridge University Press, Cambridge.

Bradley, Bruce A. 1974 Comments on the Lithic Technology of the Casper Site Materials. In *The Casper Site*, ed. G. Frison, pp. 191–7. Academic Press, New York.

1977 Experimental Lithic Technology with Special Reference to the Middle Paleolithic. Ph.D. dissertation, University of Cambridge.

1978 Hard Hammer – Soft Hammer: An Alternative Explanation. *Flintknapper's Exchange* 1:8–10.

Bradley, Bruce A., and Yevgeny Giria 1996 Concepts of the Technological Analysis of Flaked Stone: A Case Study from the High Arctic. *Lithic Technology* 21:23–39.

Bradley, Bruce A., and C. Garth Sampson 1986 Analysis by Replication of Two Acheulian Artefact Assemblages from Caddington, England. In *Stone Age Prehistory: Studies in Memory of Charles McBurney*, ed. G. N. Bailey and P. Callow, pp. 29–45. Cambridge University Press, Cambridge.

Brainerd, George W. 1951 The Place of Chronological Ordering in Archaeological Analysis. *American Antiquity* 16:301–3.

Broyles, Bettye J. 1971 *Second Preliminary Report: The St. Albans Site, Kanawha County, West Virginia.* Report of Archaeological Investigations 3, West Virginia Geological and Economic Survey, Morgantown.

Burkitt, Miles C. 1925 *Prehistory: A Study of Early Cultures in Europe and the Mediterranean Basin.* Cambridge University Press, Cambridge.

Cahen, D., L. H. Keeley, and F. L. Van Noten 1979 Stone Tools, Toolkits, and Human Behavior in Prehistory. *Current Anthropology* 20:661–83.

Callahan, Errett (ed.) 1979 The Basics of Biface Knapping in the Eastern Fluted Point Tradition:

A Manual for Flintknappers and Lithic Analysts. *Archaeology of Eastern North America* 7:1–180.

1974 *Experimental Archaeology Papers, No.* 3. Department of Sociology and Anthropology, Virginia Commonwealth University, Richmond.

1976 *Experimental Archaeology Papers, No.* 4. Department of Sociology and Anthropology, Virginia Commonwealth University, Richmond.

Calvert, S. E. 1983 Sedimentary Geochemistry of Silicon. In *Silicon Geochemistry and Biogeochemistry*, ed. R. R. Aston, pp. 143–86. Academic Press, New York.

Carlson, Roy L. 1996 Introduction to Early Human Occupation in British Columbia. In *Early Human Occupation in British Columbia*, ed. R. L. Carlson and L. Dalla Bona, pp. 3–10. University of British Columbia Press, Vancouver.

Cashdan, E.A 1985 Coping with Risk Reciprocity among the Basara of Northern Botswana. *Man* 20:222–42.

Chang, K. C. 1967 *Rethinking Archaeology*. Random House, New York.

Chatters, James C. 1987 Hunter-Gatherer Adaptations and Assemblage Structure. *Journal of Anthropological Research* 6:336–75.

Childe, V. Gordon 1925 *The Dawn of European Civilization*. Kegan Paul, London.

Christenson, Andrew L. 1986 Projectile Point Size and Projectile Aerodynamics: An Exploratory Study. *Plains Anthropologist* 31:109–28.

Christenson, Andrew L., and Dwight D. Read 1977 Numerical Taxonomy, R-Mode Factor Analysis and Archaeological Classification. *American Antiquity* 42:163–79.

Chun, Chen, and Wang Xiang-Quian 1989 Upper Paleolithic Microblade Industries in North China and Their Relationships with Northeast Asia and North America. *Arctic Anthropology* 26:127–56.

Church, Tim 1994 *Lithic Resource Studies: A Sourcebook for Archaeologists*. Special Publication 3, Lithic Technology, Tulsa, Oklahoma.

Churchill, Steven E. 1993 Weapon Technology, Prey Size Selection, and Hunting Methods in Modern Hunter-Gatherers: Implications for Hunting in the Paleolithic and Mesolithic. In *Hunting and Animal Exploitation in the Later Paleolithic and Mesolithic of Eurasia*, ed. Gail Larson Peterkin, Harvey M. Bricker, and Paul Mellars, pp. 11–24. Archaeological Papers of the American Anthropological Association 4.

Clark, J., J. L. Phillips, and P. S. Staley 1974 Interpretations of Prehistoric Technology from Ancient Egyptian and Other Sources. Part 1: Ancient Egyptian Bows and Arrows and Their Relevance for African Prehistory. *Paléorient* 2:323–88.

Clark, J. D. 1958 Certain Industries of Notched and Strangulated Scrapers in Rhodesia, Their Time Range and Possible Use. *The South African Archaeological Bulletin*. 13:50.

Clark, John E. 1982 Manufacture of Mesoamerican Prismatic Blades, an Alternative Technique. *American Antiquity* 42:355–76.

1984 Counterflaking and the Manufacture of Mesoamerican Prismatic Blades. *Lithic Technology* 13:52–61.

1985 Platforms, Bits, Punches, and Vises: A Potpourri of Mesoamerican Blade Technology. *Lithic Technology* 14:1–15.

Clark, J. G. D. 1932 *The Mesolithic Age in Great Britain*. Cambridge University Press, Cambridge.

1969 *World Prehistory: A New Outline*. Cambridge University Press, Cambridge.

Clarke, David L. 1978 *Analytical Archaeology*. Columbia University Press, New York.

Close, Angela E. 1978 The Identification of Style in Lithic Artifacts. *World Archaeology* 10:223–37.

1989 Identifying Style in Stone Artefacts: A Case Study from the Nile Valley. In *Alternative Approaches to Lithic Analysis*, ed. Donald O. Henry and George H. Odell, pp. 3–26. Archaeological Papers of the American Anthropological Association 1.

Coe, Joffere L. 1964 *The Formative Culture of the Carolina Piedmont.* Transactions of the American Philosophical Society 54(5).

Coffey, Brian P. 1994 The Chemical Alteration of Microwear Polishes: An Evaluation of the Plisson and Mauger Findings through Replicative Experimentation. *Lithic Technology* 19:88–92.

Collins, Mary B., and William Andrefsky, Jr. 1995 *Archaeological Collections Inventory and Assessment of Marmes Rockshelter* (45FR50) *and Palus Sites* (45FR36A, B, C). Center for Northwest Anthropology Project Report 28, Washington State University, Pullman.

Conkey, Margaret W. 1978 Style and Information in Cultural Evolution: Toward a Predictive Model for the Paleolithic. In *Social Archaeology*, ed. C. L. Redman *et al.*, pp. 61–85. Academic Press, New York.

1980 The Identification of Prehistoric Hunter-Gatherer Aggregation Sites: The Case of Altamira. *Current Anthropology* 21:609–30.

Copeland, L. 1983 Levallois/Non-Levallois Determinations in the Early Levant Mousterian: Problems and Questions for 1983. *Paléorient* 14:95–105.

Corliss, D.W. 1972 *Neck Width of Projectile Points: An Index of Cultural Change and Continuity.* Occasional Papers of the Idaho State University Museum 29, Pocatello.

Cormack, R.M. 1971 A Review of Classification. *Journal of the Royal Statistical Society, Series A* 134:321–53.

Cotterell, Brian, and Johan Kamminga 1979 The Mechanics of Flaking. In *Lithic Usewear Analysis*, ed. B. Hayden, pp. 97–112. Academic Press, New York.

1986 Finials on Stone Flakes. *Journal of Archaeological Science* 13:451–61.

1987 The Formation of Flakes. *American Antiquity* 52:675–708.

1990 *Mechanics of Pre-Industrial Technology.* Cambridge University Press, Cambridge.

Cotterell, Brian, Johan Kamminga, and F. P. Dickson 1985 The Essential Mechanics of Conchoidal Flaking. *International Journal of Fracture* 20:205–21.

Cowgill, George L. 1982 Clusters of Objects and Associations between Variables: Two Approaches to Archaeological Classification. In *Essays in Archaeological Typology*, ed. R. Whallon and J. A. Brown, pp. 30–55. Center for American Archaeology Press, Evanston, Illinois.

Cox, S. L. 1986 A Re-Analysis of the Shoop Site. *Archaeology of Eastern North America* 14:101–70.

Crabtree, Don E. 1966 A Stoneworker's Approach to Analyzing and Replicating the Lindenmeier Folsom. *Tebiwa* 9:3–39

1967 Notes on Experiments in Flintknapping: 3, The Flintknapper's Raw Materials. *Tebiwa* 10:8–24.

1968 Mesoamerican Polyhedral Cores and Prismatic Blades. *American Antiquity* 33:446–78.

1970 Flaking Stone with Wooden Implements. *Science* 169:146–53.

1972 *An Introduction to Flintworking.* Occasional Papers of the Idaho State Museum 28, Pocatello.

Crabtree, Don E., and Earl H. Swanson 1968 Edge-Ground Cobbles and Blade-Making in the Northwest. *Tebiwa* 11:50–4.

Crawford, O. G. S. 1935 A Primitive Threshing Machine. *Antiquity* 9:335–9.

Curwin, Cecil 1930 Prehistoric Flint Sickles. *Antiquity* 4:179–86.

1935 Agriculture and the Flint Sickle in Palestine. *Antiquity* 9:62–6.

Cushing, Frank H. 1895 The Arrow. *American Anthropologist* 8:307–49.

Daugherty, Richard D., J. Jeffrey Flenniken, and Jeanne M. Welch 1987 *A Data Recovery Study of Judd Peak Rockshelter* (45–LE–222) *in Lewis County, Washington.* Studies in Cultural Resource Management 8, USDA Forest Service, Pacific Northwest Region, Portland, Oregon.

Deacon, J. 1984 Later Stone Age People and Their Descendants in Southern Africa. In *Southern African Prehistory and Paleoenvironments*, ed. Richard Klein, pp. 221–328. A. A. Balkema, Boston.

Dibble, Harold L. 1988 Typological Aspects of Reduction and Intensity of Utilization of Lithic Resources in the French Mousterian. In *Upper Pleistocene Prehistory of Western Eurasia*, ed. H. L. Dibble and A. Montet-White, pp. 181–97. University Museum Monograph 54, University of Pennsylvania, Philadelphia.

  1991 Local Raw Material Exploitation and Its Effects on Lower and Middle Paleolithic Assemblage Variability. In *Raw Material Economies among Prehistoric Hunter-Gatherers*, ed. A. Montet-White and S. Holen, pp. 33–48. University of Kansas Publications in Anthropology 19, Lawrence.

Dibble, Harold L., and John C. Whittaker 1981 New Experimental Evidence on the Relation between Percussion Flaking and Flake Variation. *Journal of Archaeological Science* 6:283–96.

Didier, Mary E. 1975 The Argillite Problem Revisited: An Archaeological and Geological Approach to a Classical Archaeological Problem. *Archaeology of Eastern North America* 3:90–101.

Dobosi, Viola T. 1991 Economy and Raw Material. A Case Study of Three Upper Paleolithic Sites in Hungary. In *Raw Material Economies among Prehistoric Hunter-Gatherers*, ed. A. Montet-White and S. Holen, pp. 197–204, University of Kansas Publications in Anthropology 19, Lawrence.

Doran, James E., and Roy F. Hodson 1975 *Mathematics and Computers in Archaeology*. Harvard University Press, Cambridge.

Draper, John A., and Gordon A. Lothson 1990 *Test Excavations at 10NP143 and 10NP292, Lower Clearwater River, West-Central Idaho*. Project Report 12, Center for Northwest Anthropology, Washington State University, Pullman.

Dumont, J. W. 1983 An Interim Report of the Star Carr Microwear Study. *Oxford Journal of Archaeology* 2:127–45.

Dunnell, Robert C. 1971 *Systematics in Prehistory*. Free Press, New York.

  1978 Style and Function: A Fundamental Dichotomy. *American Antiquity* 43:192–202.

Elder, J. 1984 The Impact of Subsistence Change on Mobility and Settlement Pattern in a Tropical Forest Foraging Economy: Some Implications for Archaeology. *American Anthropologist* 86:837–53.

Ellen, Roy F. 1979 Introductory Essay. In *Classifications and Their Social Contexts*, ed. R. F. Ellen and D. Reason, pp. 1–32. Academic Press, New York.

Ellis, H. Holmes 1939 *Flint-Working Techniques of the American Indians: An Experimental Study*. Ohio Historical Society, Columbus.

Ensor, H. Blaine, and Erwin Roemer, Jr. 1989 Comments on Sullivan and Rozen's Debitage Analysis and Archaeological Interpretation. *American Antiquity* 54:175–8.

Evans, John 1872 *The Ancient Stone Implements, Weapons, and Ornaments of Great Britain*. Longmans, Green, Reader and Dyer, London.

Faulkner, Aleric 1972 *Mechanical Principles of Flint Working*. Ph.D. dissertation, Washington State University. University Microfilms, Ann Arbor, Michigan.

Feder, Kenneth L. 1996 *The Past in Perspective*. Mayfield, Mountain View, California.

Fish, P. R. 1981 Beyond Tools: Middle Paleolithic Debitage Analysis and Cultural Inference. *Journal of Anthropological Research* 37:374–86.

Flenniken, J. Jeffery 1978 Reevaluation of the Lindenmeier Folsom: A Replication Experiment in Lithic Technology. *American Antiquity* 43:473–9.

  1981 *Replicative Systems Analysis: A Model Applied to the Vein Quartz Artifacts from the Hoko River Site*. Washington State University, Laboratory of Anthropology, Reports of Investigations 59, Pullman.

Flenniken, J. Jeffrey, and Anan W. Raymond 1986 Morphological Projectile Point Typology: Replication Experimentation and Technological Analysis. *American Antiquity* 51:603–14.

Flenniken, J. Jeffrey, and Philip J. Wilke 1989 Typology, Technology, and Chronology of Great Basin Dart Points. *American Anthropologist* 91:149–58.

Ford, James A. 1954 The Type Concept Revisited. *American Anthropologist* 56:42–53.

Frison, George C. 1968 A Functional Analysis of Certain Chipped Stone Tools. *American Antiquity* 33:149–55.

1989 Experimental Use of Clovis Weaponry and Tools on African Elephants. *American Antiquity* 54:766–83.

1991 *Prehistoric Hunters of the High Plains*. (2nd edition). Academic Press, New York.

Frison, George C., and Bruce Bradley 1980 *Folsom Tools and Technology of the Hanson Site, Wyoming*. University of New Mexico Press, Albuquerque.

1981 Fluting of Folsom Points: Archaeological Evidence. *Lithic Technology* 10:13–16.

Frison, George C., and Lawrence C. Todd 1987 *The Horner Site: The Type Site of the Cody Cultural Complex*. Academic Press, New York.

Gallagher, J. P. 1977 Contemporary Stone Tools in Ethiopia: Implications for Archaeology. *Journal of Field Archaeology* 4:407–14.

Garrod, D. A. E., and D. M. A. Bate 1937 *The Stone Age of Mount Carmel*, Vol.1. Clarendon Press, Oxford.

Gendel, Peter A. 1984 *Mesolithic Social Territories in Northwest Europe*. BAR International Series 218, Oxford.

Géneste, J.-M. 1985 *Analyse lithique d'industries moustériennes du Périgord: une approche technologique du comportement des groups humains au paléolithique moyen*. Doctoral dissertation, University of Bordeaux I.

Gero, Joan M. 1989 Assessing Social Information in Material Objects: How Well Do Lithics Measure Up? In *Time, Energy, and Stone Tools*, ed. Robin Torrence, pp. 92–105. Cambridge University Press, Cambridge.

Gilreath, Amy 1984 Stages of Bifacial Manufacture: Learning from Experiments. Paper presented at the 49th Annual Meeting of the Society for American Archaeology, Portland, Oregon.

Goodyear, Albert C. 1974 *The Brand Site: A Techno-Functional Study of a Dalton Site in Northeast Arkansas*. Arkansas Archaeological Survey Publications on Archaeology, Research Series 7.

1979 *A Hypothesis for the Use of Cryptocrystalline Raw Material among Paleo-Indian Groups of North America*. Research Manuscript Series 156, Institute of Archaeology and Anthropology, University of South Carolina, Columbia.

1993 Tool Kit Entropy and Bipolar Reduction: A Study of Interassemblage Lithic Variability among Paleo-Indian Sites in the Northeastern United States. *North American Archaeologist* 14:1–23.

Gould, Richard A. 1968 Living Archaeology: The Ngatatjara of Western Australia. *Southwestern Journal of Anthropology* 24:101–22.

1980 *Living Archaeology*. Cambridge University Press, Cambridge.

Gould, Richard A., Dorothy A. Koster, and Ann H. L. Sontz 1971 The Lithic Assemblage of the Western Desert Aborigines of Australia. *American Antiquity* 36:149–69.

Grace, Roger 1989 *Interpreting the Function of Stone Tools*. BAR International Series 474, Oxford.

Grace, R., K. Ataman, R. Fabregas, and C. M. B. Haggren 1988 A Multivariate Approach to the Functional Analysis of Stone Tools. In *Industries lithiques*, vol. 2: *Aspects méthodologiques*, ed. Sylvie Beyries, pp. 217–30, BAR International Series 411 (ii), Oxford.

Gramly, R. Michael 1980 Raw Material Source Areas and "Curated" Tool Assemblages.

American Antiquity 45:823–33.

Gramly, R. Michael, and Kerry Rutledge 1981 A New Paleo-Indian Site in the State of Maine. *American Antiquity* 46:354–61.

Greiser, Sally T. 1977 Micro-Analysis of Wear Patterns on Projectile Points and Knives from the Jurgens Site, Kersey, Colorado. *Plains Anthropologist* 22:107–16.

Griffin, James B. 1943 *The Fort Ancient Aspect: Its Cultural and Chronological Position in Mississippi Valley Archaeology.* University of Michigan Press, Ann Arbor.

Gunn, Joel 1981 Response to Benfer and Benfer. *American Antiquity* 46:397.

Gunn, Joel, and Elton R. Prewitt 1975 Automatic Classification: Projectile Points from West Texas. *Plains Anthropologist* 20:139–49.

Hamblin, W. K., and J. D. Howard 1971 *Physical Geology Laboratory Manual.* Burgess Publishing Company, Minneapolis.

Harold, Francis B. 1993 Variability and Function among Gravette Points from Southwestern France. In Hunting and Animal Exploitation in the Later Paleolithic and Mesolithic of Eurasia, ed. Gail Larson Peterkin, Harvey M. Bricker, and Paul Mellars, pp. 69–82. Archaeological Papers of the American Anthropological Association 4.

Hayden, Brian 1977 Stone Tool Functions in the Western Desert. In *Stone Tools as Cultural Markers: Change, Evolution, and Complexity*, ed. R. V. S. Wright, pp. 178–88. Australian Institute of Aboriginal Studies, Canberra.

1979a Snap, Shatter, and Superfractures: Usewear of Stone Skin Scrapers. In *Lithic Usewear Analysis*, ed. B. Hayden, pp. 207–30. Academic Press, New York.

1979b *Paleolithic Reflections: Lithic Technology and Ethnographic Excavation among Australian Aborigines.* Australian Institute of Aboriginal Studies, Canberra. Humanities Press, New Jersey.

1980 Confusion in the Bipolar World: Bashed Pebbles and Splintered Pieces. *Lithic Technology* 9:2–7.

1982 Interaction Parameters and the Demise of Paleo-Indian Craftsmanship. *Plains Anthropologist* 27:109–23.

1986 Use and Misuse: The Analysis of Endscrapers. *Lithic Technology* 15:65–70.

Hayden, Brian (ed.) 1979c *Lithic Usewear Analysis.* Academic Press, New York.

Hayden, Brian, Nora Franco, and Jim Spafford 1996 Evaluating Lithic Strategies and Design Criteria. In *Stone Tools: Theoretical Insights into Human Prehistory*, ed. G. H. Odell, pp. 9–50. Plenum Press, New York.

Hayden, Brian, and W. Karl Hutchings 1989 Whither the Billet Flake. In *Experiments in Lithic Technology*, ed. D. S. Amick and R. P. Mauldin, pp. 235–58. BAR International Series 528, Oxford.

Hayden, Brian, and Johan Kamminga 1973 Gould, Koster, and Sontz on "Microwear": A Critical Review. *Newsletter of Lithic Technology* 2:3–14.

Heider, Karl G. 1967 Archaeological Assumptions and Ethnographic Facts: A Cautionary Tale from New Guinea. *Southwestern Journal of Anthropology* 23:52–64.

Henry, Donald O. 1989 Correlations between Reduction Strategies and Settlement Patterns. In *Alternative Approaches to Lithic Analysis*, ed. D. O. Henry and G. H. Odell, pp. 139–212. Westview Press, Boulder, Colorado.

Henry, D. O., C. V. Haynes, and B. Bradley 1976 Quantitative Variations in Flaked Stone Debitage. *Plains Anthropologist* 21:57–61.

Hester, Thomas R. 1993 Lithic Typology: Background, Goals, and a Personal Perspective. *Lithic Technology* 18:36–45.

Hill, J., and R. Evans 1972 A Model for Classification and Typology. In *Models in Archaeology*, ed. D. L. Clarke, pp. 231–73. Methuen, London.

Hiraguchi, Tetsuo 1992 Catching Dolphins at Mawaki Site, Central Japan, and Its Contribution to Jomon Society. In *Pacific Northwest Asia in Prehistory: Hunter-Fisher-Farmers, and Sociopolitical Elites*, ed. C. M. Aikens and S. N. Rhee, pp. 35–46. Washington State University Press, Pullman.

Hodson, Roy F. 1982 Some Aspects of Archaeological Classification. in *Essays on Archaeological Classification*, ed. R. Whallon and J. A. Brown, pp. 21–9. Center for American Archaeology Press, Evanston, Illinois.

Hofman, Jack L. 1981 The Refitting of Chipped-Stone Artifacts as an Analytical and Interpretive Tool. *Current Anthropology* 22:35–50.

Holmes, William H. 1891 Manufacture of Stone Arrow-Points. *American Anthropologist* 4:49–58.

1894 Natural History of Flaked Stone Implements. In *Memoirs of the International Congress of Anthropology*, ed. C. S. Wake, pp. 120–39. Schulte, Chicago.

Honea, Kenneth H. 1965 The Bipolar Flaking Technique in Texas and New Mexico. *Texas Archaeological Society Bulletin* 36:259–67.

Hurcombe, L. 1988 Some Criticisms and Suggestions in Response to Newcomer *et al.* (1986). *Journal of Archaeological Science* 15:1–10.

Jacobi, R. M. 1976 Britain Inside and Outside Mesolithic Europe. *Proceedings of the Prehistoric Society* 42:67–84.

1978 Northern England in the Eighth Millennium BC: An Essay. In *The Early Postglacial Settlement of Northern Europe*, ed. Paul Mellars, pp. 295–332. Duckworth, London.

1980 The Early Holocene Settlement of Wales. In *Culture and Environment in Prehistoric Wales*, ed. J. A. Taylor and R. Bowens, pp. 131–206. BAR British Series 76, Oxford.

Jarvis, K. E. 1988 Inductively Coupled Plasma Mass Spectrometry: A New Technique for the Rapid or Ultra-Trace Level Determination of the Rare-Earth Elements in Geological Materials. *Chemical Geology* 68:31–9.

Jelinek, Arthur J. 1965 Lithic Technology Conference, Les Eyzies, France. *American Antiquity* 31:277–8.

1976 Form, Function, and Style in Lithic Artifacts. In *Culture Change and Continuity*, ed. C. E. Cleland, pp. 19–33. Academic Press, New York.

1991 Observations on Reduction Patterns and Raw Materials in Some Middle Paleolithic Industries in the Perigord. In *Raw Material Economies Among Prehistoric Hunter-Gatherers*, ed. A. Montet-White and S. Holen, pp. 7–32. University of Kansas Publications in Anthropology 19, Lawrence.

Jeske, Robert J. 1992 Energy Efficiency and Lithic Technology: An Upper Mississippi Example. *American Antiquity* 57:467–81.

Johnson, Jay K. 1987 Cahokia Core Technology in Mississippi: The View from the South. In *The Organization of Core Technology*, ed. Jay K. Johnson and Carrol A. Morrow, pp. 187–206. Westview Press, Boulder, Colorado.

1989 The Utility of Production Trajectory Modeling as a Framework for Regional Analysis. In *Alternative Approaches to Lithic Analysis*, ed. Donald O. Henry and George H. Odell, pp. 119–38. Archaeological Papers of the American Anthropological Association 1.

Juel Jensen, H. 1989 Plant Harvesting and Processing with Flint Implements in the Danish Stone Age. *Acta Archaeologica* 59:131–42.

Kalin, Jeffrey 1981 Stem Point Manufacture and Debitage Recovery. *Archaeology of Eastern North America* 9:134–75.

Kamminga, Johan 1978 Journey into the Microcosms: A Functional Analysis of Certain Australian Prehistoric Stone Tools. Ph.D. dissertation, University of Sydney.

1979 The Nature of Use Polish and Abrasive Smoothing on Stone Tools. In *Lithic Usewear Analysis*, ed. B. Hayden, pp. 143–58. Academic Press, New York.

1982 *Over the Edge: Functional Analysis of Australian Stone Tools*. Occasional Papers in

Anthropology 12, Anthropology Museum, Queensland University, Brisbane.

Katz, Paul R. 1976 A Technological Analysis of the Kansas City Hopewell Chipped Stone Industry. Ph.D. dissertation, University of Kansas. University Microfilms, Ann Arbor, Michigan.

Keeley, Lawrence H. 1974 Technique and Methodology in Microwear Studies: A Critical Review. *World Archaeology* 5:323–36.

1977 An Experimental Study of Microwear Traces on Selected British Paleolithic Implements. Ph.D. dissertation, University of Oxford.

1980 *Experimental Determination of Stone Tool Uses: A Microwear Analysis.* University of Chicago Press, Chicago.

1982 Hafting and Retooling: Effects on the Archaeological Record. *American Antiquity* 47:798–809.

Keeley, Lawrence H., and M. H. Newcomer 1977 Microwear Analysis of Experimental Flint Tools: A Test Case. *Journal of Archaeological Science* 4:29–62.

Kelly, Robert L. 1983 Hunter-Gatherer Mobility Strategies. *Journal of Anthropological Research* 39:277–306.

1988 The Three Sides of a Biface. *American Antiquity* 53:717–34.

1995 *The Foraging Spectrum.* Smithsonian Institution Press, Washington, D.C.

Kempe, D. R. C., and J. A. Templeman 1983 Techniques. In *The Petrology of Archaeological Artefacts,* ed. D. R. C. Kempe and Anthony P. Harvey, pp. 26–53. Clarendon Press, Oxford.

Kendall, M. G., and A. Stuart 1969 *The Advanced Theory of Statistics,* vol. 1, *Distribution Theory.* Griffin, London.

Kidder, Alfred V. 1924 *An Introduction to the Study of Southwestern Archaeology.* Papers of the Southwestern Expedition, Philips Academy, 1, New Haven, Connecticut.

Kinsey, W. Fred 1972 *Archaeology of the Upper Delaware Valley.* Anthropological Series 2, The Pennsylvania Historical and Museum Commission, Harrisburg.

Knudson, Ruthann, 1978 Experimental Lithocology: Method and Theory. *Lithic Technology* 5:44–6.

1979 Inference and Imposition in Lithic Analysis. In *Lithic Usewear Analysis,* ed. B. Hayden, pp. 269–82. Academic Press, New York.

Knutsson, Kjel 1988 *Patterns of Tool Use.* Societas Archaeologica Uppsaliensis, Uppsala.

Kobayashi, T. 1970 Microblade Industries in the Japanese Archipelago. *Arctic Anthropology* 7:38–58.

Kraft, Herbert C. 1970 *The Miller Field Site, Warren County, N.J.* Seton Hall University Press, South Orange, New Jersey.

1975 *The Archaeology of Tocks Island Area.* Archaeological Research Center, Seton Hall University, South Orange, New Jersey.

Kuhn, Steven L. 1990 A Geometric Index of Reduction for Unifacial Stone Tools. *Journal of Archaeological Science* 17:585–93.

1991 "Unpacking" Reduction: Lithic Raw Material Economy in the Mousterian of West-Central Italy. *Journal of Anthropological Archaeology* 10:76–106.

1992 Blank Form and Reduction as Determinants of Mousterian Scraper Morphology. *American Antiquity* 57:115–28

1995 *Mousterian Lithic Technology.* Princeton University Press, Princeton, New Jersey.

Larson, Thomas K., Dori Penny, Ross G. Hilman, and Paul H. Sanders 1988 *A Data Recovery Program for Sites within the Dome Unit, Santa Fe National Forest.* Report Prepared by Larson-Tibesar Associates, Laramie, Wyoming for USDA, Forest Service, Santa Fe National Forest, Santa Fe, New Mexico.

Latham, T. S., P. A. Sutton, and K. L. Verosub 1992 Non-Destructive XRF Characterization of Basaltic Artifacts from Trukee, California. *Geoarchaeology* 7:81–101.

Lawrence, Robert A. 1979 Experimental Evidence for the Significance of Attributes Used in Edge-Damage Analysis. In *Lithic Usewear Analysis*, ed. Brian Hayden, pp. 113–21. Academic Press, New York.

Leakey, L. S. B. 1954 Working Stone, Bone, and Wood. In *A History of Technology*, vol. 1, ed. C. Singer, E. J. Holmyard, and A. R. Hall, pp. 128–43. Clarendon Press, Oxford.

Leonard, Robert D., and George T. Jones 1989 *Quantifying Diversity in Archaeology*. Cambridge University Press, Cambridge.

Leroi-Gourhan, A. 1964 *Le Geste et la parole*, vol. 1: *Technique et langage*. Albin Michel, Paris.

Lévi-Sala, I. 1986 Usewear and Post-Depositional Surface Modification: A Note of Caution. *Journal of Archaeological Science* 13:229–44.

Levitt, Jeff 1979 A Review of Experimental Traceological Research in the USSR. In *Lithic Usewear Analysis*, ed. Brian Hayden, pp. 27–38. Academic Press, New York.

Lewenstein, S. M. 1987 *Stone Tool Use at Cerros*: *The Ethnoarchaeological and Use-Wear Evidence*. University of Texas Press, Austin.

Lothrop, Jonathan C. 1989 The Organization of Paleoindian Lithic Technology at the Potts Site. In *Eastern Paleoindian Lithic Resource Use*, ed. C. J. Ellis and J. C. Lothrop, pp. 99–138. Westview Press, Boulder, Colorado.

Lothrop, Jonathan C., and R. Michael Gramly 1982 Pièces Esquillées from the Vail Site. *Archaeology of Eastern North America*. 10:1–22.

Luedtke, Barbara E. 1992 *An Archaeologist's Guide to Chert and Flint*. Archaeological Research Tools 7, Institute of Archaeology, University of California, Los Angeles.

Lyons, William H. 1994 *Lithic Technology at the Hall Creek Site* (*35GR420B*), *Silvies Valley, Grant County, Oregon*. M.A. thesis, Washington State University, Pullman.

MacDonald, Douglas H. 1994 Lithic Technological Organization at the Hunting Camp Spring Site (35WA96), Blue Mountains, Oregon. M.A. thesis, Washington State University, Pullman.

MacDonald, G. F. 1968 *Debert*: *A Paleo-Indian Site in Central Nova Scotia*. National Museum of Man, Anthropological Papers 16.

MacDonald, G. F., and D. Sanger 1968 Some Aspects of Microscope Analysis and Photomicrography of Lithic Artifacts. *American Antiquity* 33:237–40.

MacDonald, Kevin, and P. Allsworth-Jones 1994 A Reconsideration of the West African Macrolithic Conundrum: New Factory Sites and an Associated Settlement in the Vallée du Serpent, Mali. *The African Archaeological Review* 12:73–104.

MacDonald, Mary M. A. 1991 Technological Organization and Sedentism in the Epipalaeolithic of Dakhleh Oasis, Egypt. *The African Archaeological Review* 9:81–109.

McKern, W. C. 1939 The Midwest Taxonomic Method as an Aid to Archaeological Culture Study. *American Antiquity* 4:301–13.

McLaughlin, R. J. W. 1977 Atomic Absorption Spectroscopy. In *Physical Methods in Determinative Mineralogy*, ed. J. Zussman, pp. 371–89. Academic Press, London.

McNerney, Michael J. 1987 Crab Orchard Core Technology at the Consol Site, Jackson County, Illinois. In *The Organization of Core Technology*, ed. J. K. Johnson and C. A. Morrow, pp. 63–86. Westview Press, Boulder, Colorado.

Magne, Martin P. 1985 *Lithics and Livelihood*: *Stone Tool Technologies of Central and Southern Interior British Columbia*. Archaeological Survey of Canada Paper No. 133, Ottawa; National Museum of Man Mercury Series, Ottawa.

1989 Lithic Reduction Stages and Assemblage Formation Processes. In *Experiments in Lithic Technology*, ed. D. S. Amick and R. P. Mauldin, pp. 15–31. BAR International Series 528, Oxford.

1996 Comparative Analysis of Microblade Cores from Haida Gwaii. In *Early Human Occupa-*

tion in British Columbia, ed. R. L. Carlson and L. D. Bona, pp. 151–8. University of British Columbia Press, Vancouver.

Magne, Martin P., and David Pokotylo 1981 A Pilot Study in Bifacial Lithic Reduction Sequences. *Lithic Technology* 10:34–47.

Mansur-Franchomme, M. E. 1983 Scanning Electron Microscopy of Dry Hide Working Tool: The Role of Abrasives and Humidity in Microwear Polish Formation. *Journal of Archaeological Science* 10:223–30.

Marks, Anthony E. 1988 The Curation of Stone Tools during the Upper Pleistocene: A View from the Central Negev, Israel. In *Upper Pleistocene Prehistory of Western Eurasia*, ed. H. L. Dibble and A. Montet-White, pp. 275–86. University Museum Monograph 54, University of Pennsylvania, Philadelphia.

Marks, Anthony E., J. Shokler, and João Zilhão 1991 Raw Material Usage in the Paleolithic. The Effects of Local Availability on Selection and Economy. In *Raw Material Economies among Prehistoric Hunter-Gatherers*, ed. A. Montet-White and S. Holen, pp. 127–40, University of Kansas Publications in Anthropology 19, Lawrence.

Mauldin, Raymond P., and Daniel S. Amick 1989 Investigating Patterning in Debitage from Experimental Bifacial Core Reduction. In *Experiments in Lithic Technology*, ed. D. S. Amick and R. P. Mauldin, pp. 67–88. BAR International Series 528, Oxford.

Meeks, N. D., G. de Sieveking, M. S. Tite, and J. Cook 1982 Gloss and Usewear Traces on Flint Sickles and Similar Phenomena. *Journal of Archaeological Science* 9:317–40.

Mellars, Paul 1974 The Paleolithic and Mesolithic. In *British Prehistory: A New Outline*, ed. C. Renfrew, pp. 41–99. Duckworth, London.

1976 Settlement Patterns and Industrial Variability in the British Mesolithic. In *Problems in Economic and Social Archaeology*, ed. G.de G. Sieveking, I. H. Longworth, and K. E. Wilson, pp. 375–99. Duckworth, London.

1996 *The Neanderthal Legacy*. Princeton University Press, Princeton, New Jersey.

Mellars, Paul, and S. C. Reinhardt 1978 Patterns of Mesolithic Land-Use in Southern England: A Geological Perspective. In *The Early Postglacial Settlement of Northern Europe*, ed. Paul Mellars, pp. 243–94. Duckworth, London.

Meltzer, David J. 1981 A Study of Style and Function in a Class of Tools. *Journal of Field Archaeology* 8:313–26.

1984 On Stone Procurement and Settlement Mobility in Eastern Fluted Point Groups. *North American Archaeologist* 6:1–24.

Meltzer, David J., Robert D. Leonard, and Susan K. Stratton 1992 The Relationship between Sample Size and Diversity in Archaeological Assemblages. *Journal of Archaeological Science* 19:375–88.

Meschel, S. V. 1978 Chemistry and Archaeology: A Creative Bond. In *Archaeological Chemistry*, Vol. II, ed. G. F. Carter. *Advances in Chemistry Series* 171:3–24.

Mierendorf, Robert R., and Sheila J. Bobalik 1983 Lithic Analysis. In *Cultural Resources of the Rocky Reach of the Columbia River*, Vol. II, ed. Randall F. Schalk and Robert R. Mierendorf. Center for Northwest Anthropology, Project Report 1, Washington State University, Pullman.

Mobley, Charles E. 1984 A Report to the Alaska Historical Commission for the Campus Site Restudy Project. MS on file, University of Alaska Museum, Fairbanks.

1991 *The Campus Site: A Prehistoric Camp at Fairbanks, Alaska*. University of Alaska Press, Fairbanks.

Montet-White, Anta 1988 Raw Material Economy among Medium-Sized Late Paleolithic Campsites of Central Europe. In *Upper Pleistocene Prehistory of Western Eurasia*, ed. H. L. Dibble and A. Montet-White, pp. 361–74. University Museum Monograph 54, University of Pennsylvania, Philadelphia.

1991 Lithic Acquisition, Settlements and Territory in the Epigravettian of Central Europe. In *Raw Material Economies among Prehistoric Hunter-Gatherers*, ed. A. Montet-White and S. Holen, pp. 205–20. University of Kansas Publications in Anthropology 19, Lawrence.

Morlan, Richard E. 1970 Wedge-Shaped Core Technology in Northern North America. *Arctic Anthropology* 7:17–37.

Morrow, Carol A. 1984 A Biface Production Model for Gravel-Based Chipped Stone Industries. *Lithic Technology* 13:20–8.

Morrow, Carol A., and Richard W. Jefferies 1989 Trade or Embedded Procurement? A Test Case from Southern Illinois. In *Time, Energy and Stone Tools*, ed. R. Torrence, pp. 27–33. Cambridge University Press, Cambridge.

Moss., E. H. 1987 A Review of "Investigating Microwear Polishes with Blind Tests". *Journal of Archaeological Science* 14:473–81.

Moss, E. H., and M. H. Newcomer 1982 Reconstruction of Tool Use at Pincevent: Microwear and Experiments. Tailler! Pourquoi faire: préhistoire et technologie lithique 2. Recent Progress in Microwear Studies. *Studia Prehistorica Belgica* 2, ed. D. Cahen, pp. 289–312. Musée Royale de l'Afrique Central, Tervenuren.

Murata, K. J., I. Friedman, and J. D. Gleason 1977 Oxygen Isotope Relations between Diagenetic Silica Minerals in Monterey Shale, Temblor Range, California. *American Journal of Science* 277:259–72.

Murdoch, J. 1892 Ethnological Results of the Point Barrow Expedition. *U.S. Bureau of American Ethnology, Ninth Annual Report*.

Muto, Guy R. 1971 A Technological Analysis of the Early Stages in the Manufacture of Chipped Stone Implements. M.A. thesis, Idaho State University.

Myers, Andrew 1989 Reliable and Maintainable Technological Strategies in the Mesolithic of Mainland Britain. In *Time, Energy and Stone Tools*, ed. R. Torrence, pp. 78–91. Cambridge University Press, Cambridge.

Nance, Jack D. 1971 Functional Interpretations from Microscopic Analysis. *American Antiquity* 36:361–6.

1977 Numerical Taxonomy Studies of Microwear on the Los Tapiales Artifacts. *Proceedings of the American Philosophical Society* 121:264–73.

Nelson, E. W. 1899 The Eskimo about Bering Strait. *U.S. Bureau of American Ethnology, Eighteenth Annual Report*.

Nelson, Nels C. 1916 Chronology of the Tano Ruins, New Mexico. *American Anthropologist* 18:159–180.

Neumann, T. M., and E. Johnson 1979 Patrow Site Lithic Analysis. *Midcontinental Journal of Archaeology* 4:79–111.

Newcomer, M. H., R. Grace, and R. Unger-Hamilton 1986 Investigating Microwear Polishes with Blind Tests. *Journal of Archaeological Science* 13:203–17.

Newcomer, M. H. and C. Karlin 1987 Flint Chips from Pincevent. In *The Human Uses of Flint and Chert*, ed. M. H. Newcomer and G. de G. Sieveking, pp. 33–6. Proceedings of the Fourth International Flint Symposium held at Brighton Polytechnic.

Nissen, Karen, and Margaret Dittemore 1974 Ethnographic Data and Wear Pattern Analysis: A Study of Socketed Eskimo Scrapers. *Tebiwa* 17:67–88.

Oakley, Kenneth, P. 1949 *Man the Tool Maker*. British Museum, London.

1957 *Man the Tool Maker*. University of Chicago Press, Chicago.

O'Connell, James F. 1977 Aspects of Variation in Central Australian Lithic Assemblages. In *Stone Tools as Cultural Markers: Change, Evolution and Complexity*, ed. R. V. S. Wright, pp. 269–81. Australian Institute of Aboriginal Studies, Canberra.

Odell, George H. 1975 Micro-Wear in Perspective: A Sympathetic Response to Lawrence H. Keeley. *World Archaeology* 7:226–40.

1977 The Application of Micro-Wear Analysis to the Lithic Component of an Entire Prehistoric Settlement: Methods, Problems, and Functional Reconstructions. Ph.D. dissertation, Harvard University. University Microfilms, Ann Arbor, Michigan.

1980 Toward a More Behavioral Approach to Lithic Concentrations. *American Antiquity* 45:404–31.

1981 The Morphological Express at Function Junction: Searching for Meaning in Lithic Tool Types. *Journal of Anthropological Research* 37:319–42.

1985 Microwear Analysis of Middle Woodland Lithics. In *Smiling Dan: Structure and Function at a Middle Woodland Settlement in the Illinois Valley*, ed. B. Stafford and M. B. Sant, pp. 298–326. Center for American Archaeology, Research Series 2., Kampsville, Illinois.

1989 Experiments in Lithic Reduction. In *Experiments in Lithic Technology*, ed. D. S. Amick and R. P. Mauldin, pp. 163–98. BAR International Series 528, Oxford.

1994 The Role of Stone Bladelets in Middle Woodland Society. *American Antiquity*. 59:102–20.

Odell, George H., and F. Odell-Vereecken 1980 Verifying the Reliability of Lithic Usewear Assessments by "Blind Tests": The Low-Power Approach. *Journal of Field Archaeology* 7:87–120.

Odum, Eugene P. 1971 *Fundamentals of Ecology*. Harper and Row, New York.

Olszewski, Deborah I. 1993 Zarian Microliths from Warwasi Rockshelter, Iran: Scalene Triangles as Arrow Compenents. In *Hunting and Animal Exploitation in the Later Paleolithic and Mesolithic of Eurasia*, ed. Gail Larson Peterkin, Harvey M. Bricker, and Paul Mellars, pp. 199–206. Archaeological Papers of the American Anthropological Association 4.

Parkes, P. A. 1986 *Current Scientific Techniques in Archaeology*. Croom Helm, London.

Parry, William J. 1987 Technological Change: Temporal and Functional Variability in Chipped Stone Debitage. In *Prehistoric Stone Technology on Northern Black Mesa, Arizona*. ed. William J. Parry and Andrew L. Christenson, pp. 199–256. Center for Archaeological Investigations, Occasional Paper 12, Southern Illinois University, Carbondale.

Parry, William J., and Robert L. Kelly 1987 Expedient Core Technology and Sedentism. In *The Organization of Core Technology*, ed. J. K. Johnson and C. A. Morrow, pp. 285–304. Westview Press, Boulder, Colorado.

Patterson, Leland W. 1979 Quantitative Characteristics of Debitage from Heat Treated Chert. *Plains Anthropologist* 24:255–60.

1982 Replication and Classification of Large Size Lithic Debitage. *Lithic Technology* 11:50–8.

1985 Distinguishing between Arrow and Spear Points on the Upper Texas Coast. *Lithic Technology* 14:81–9.

1990 Characteristics of Bifacial-Reduction Flake-Size Distribution. *American Antiquity* 55:550–8.

Patterson, Leland W., and J. B. Sollberger 1978 Replication and Classification of Small Size Lithic Debitage. *Plains Anthropologist* 23:103–12.

Peterkin, Gail Larson 1993 Lithic and Organic Hunting Technology in the French Upper Paleolithic. In *Hunting and Animal Exploitation in the Later Paleolithic and Mesolithic of Eurasia*, ed. Gail Larson Peterkin, Harvey M. Bricker, and Paul Mellars, pp. 49–68. Archaeological Papers of the American Anthropological Association 4.

Pettijohn, F. J. 1975 *Sedimentary Rocks*. Harper and Row, New York.

Plastino, Brooke 1994 Prehistoric Artifacts. In *Data Recovery Excavations from Site 45PC101 Pacific County, Washington*, ed. Raymond DePuydt, pp. 75–118. Eastern Washington University Reports in Archaeology and History 100–79, Cheney, Washington.

Pokotylo, David 1978 Lithic Technology and Settlement Patterns in Upper Hat Creek Valley, B.C. Ph.D. dissertation, University of British Columbia.

Pond, Alonzo W. 1930 Primitive Methods of Working Stone: Based on Experiments of Halvor L. Skavlem. *Logan Museum Bulletin* 2:1–143.

Pope, Melody K. 1994 Mississippian Microtools and Uruk Blades: A Comparative Study of Chipped Stone Production, Use, and Economic Organization. *Lithic Technology* 19:128–45.

Prentiss, William C., and Eugene J. Romanski 1989 Experimental Evaluation of Sullivan and Rozen's Debitage Typology. In *Experiments in Lithic Technology*, ed. D. S. Amick and R. P. Mauldin, pp. 89–100. BAR International Series 528, Oxford.

Price, T. Douglas 1978 Mesolithic Settlement Systems in the Netherlands. In *The Early Postglacial Settlement of Northern Europe*, ed. Paul Mellars, pp. 81–114. Duckworth, London.

Raab, L. Mark, R. F. Cande, and D. W. Stahle 1979 Debitage Graphs and Archaic Settlement Patterns in the Arkansas Ozarks. *Midcontinential Journal of Archaeology* 4:167–82.

Radley, J., V. R. Switsur, and J. H. Tallis 1974 The Excavation of Three "Narrow Blade" Mesolithic Sites in the Southern Pennines, England. *Proceedings of the Prehistoric Society* 40:1–19.

Rau, C. 1869 A Deposit of Agricultural Flint Implements in Southern Illinois. *Annual Report of the Smithsonian Institution*, 1868, pp. 401–7, Washington, D.C.

Read, Dwight D. 1974 Some Comments on the Use of Mathematical Models in Archaeology. *American Antiquity* 39:3–15.

Reeves, R. D., and R. R. Brooks 1978 *Trace Element Analysis of Geological Materials*. Interscience Publishers, Wiley, New York.

Reher, Charles A. 1991 Large Scale Quarries and Regional Transport Systems on the High Plains of Eastern Wyoming. Spanish Diggings Revisited. In *Raw Material Economies Among Prehistoric Hunter-Gatherers*, ed. A. Montet-White and S. Holen, pp. 251–84, University of Kansas Publications in Anthropology 19, Lawrence.

Reher, Charles A., and George C. Frison 1991 Rarity, Clarity, Symmetry: Quartz Crystal Utilization in Hunter-Gatherer Stone Tool Assemblages. In *Raw Material Economies among Prehistoric Hunter-Gatherers*, ed. A. Montet-White and S. Holen, pp. 375–98. University of Kansas Publications in Anthropology 19. Lawrence.

Rhode, David 1988 Measurement of Archaeological Diversity and the Sample-Size effect. *American Antiquity* 53:708–16.

Ritchie, William A. 1944 *The Pre-Iroquoian Occupation of New York State*. Rochester Museum of Arts and Sciences, Memoir 1. Rochester, New York.

1965 *The Archaeology of New York State*. Natural History Press, Garden City, New Jersey.

Robinson, W. S. 1951 A Method of Chronologically Ordering Archaeological Deposits. *American Antiquity* 40:22–38.

Rogers, Richard A. 1986 Spurred End Scrapers as Diagnostic Paleoindian Artifacts: A Distributional Analysis on Stream Terraces. *American Antiquity* 51:338–41.

Rolland, Nicolas 1981 The Interpretation of Middle Paleolithic Variability. *Man* 16:15–42.

1988 Observations on Some Middle Paleolithic Time Series in Southern France. In *Upper Pleistocene Prehistory of Western Eurasia*, ed. H. L. Dibble and A. Montet-White, pp. 161–79. University Museum Monograph 54, University of Pennsylvania, Philadelphia.

Rolland, Nicolas, and Harold L. Dibble 1990 A New Synthesis of Middle Paleolithic Variability. *American Antiquity* 55:480–99.

Rondeau, Michael F. 1996 When Is an Elko? In *Stone Tools: Theoretical Insights Into Human Prehistory*, ed. G. H. Odell, pp. 229–44. Plenum Press, New York.

Root, Matthew J. 1992 The Knife River Flint Quarries: The Organization of Stone Tool Production. Ph.D. dissertation, Washington State University. University Microfilms, Ann Arbor, Michigan.

Rule P., and J. Evans 1985 The Relationship of Morphological Variation to Hafting Techniques among Paleoindian Endscrapers at the Shawnee Minisink Site. In *Shawnee Minisink: A*

Stratified Paleoindian-Archaic Site in the Upper Delaware Valley of Pennsylvania, ed. C. McNett, pp. 211–20. Academic Press, New York.

Sackett, James R. 1977 The Meaning of Style in Archaeology. *American Antiquity* 42:369–80.

1982 Approaches to Style in Lithic Archaeology. *Journal of Anthropological Archaeology* 1:59–112.

1986 Isochrestism and Style: A Clarification. *Journal of Anthropological Archaeology* 5:266–77.

1990 Style and Ethnicity in Archaeology: The Case for Isochrestism. In *The Uses of Style in Archaeology*, ed. M. W. Conkey and C. A. Hastorf, pp. 105–12. Cambridge University Press, Cambridge.

Sanders, Paul H. 1992 *Archaeological Investigations along the Pend Oreille River: Site 45PO149.* Center for Northwest Anthropology, Project Report 18, Washington State University, Pullman.

Sappington, Robert L. 1991 *Archaeological Investigations at the Clearwater Fish Hatchery Site (10CW4), North Fork of the Clearwater River, North Central Idaho.* University of Idaho Anthropological Reports 91, Moscow.

Sappington, Robert Lee and Caroline Carley 1984 *Archaeological Test Excavation and Evaluation of Three Prehistoric Sites at Swift Bar, on the Lower Snake River, Southeastern Washington.* University of Idaho Anthropological Research Manuscript Series 81, Moscow.

Sassaman, Kenneth E. 1994 Changing Strategies of Biface Production in the South Carolina Coastal Plain. In *The Organization of North American Prehistoric Chipped Stone Tool Technologies*, ed. P. J. Carr, pp. 99–117. International Monographs in Prehistory: Archaeological Series 7, Ann Arbor, Michigan.

Seeman, Mark F. 1994 Intercluster Lithic Patterning at Nobles Pond: A Case for "Disembedded" Procurement among Early Paleoindian Societies. *American Antiquity* 59:273–87.

Sellet, Frederic 1993 Chaîne opératoire: The Concept and Its Applications. *Lithic Technology* 18:106–12.

Semenov, Sergei A. 1964 *Prehistoric Technology*, trans. M. W. Thompson. Cory, Adams and MacKay, London.

Serizawa, Chosuki 1976 The Stone Age of Japan. *Asian Perspectives* 19:1–14.

Shackley, M. Steven. 1990 Early Hunter-Gatherer Procurement Ranges and Mobility in the American Southwest: Evidence from Obsidian Geochemistry and Lithic Technology. Ph.D. dissertation, Arizona State University, Tempe.

Shackley, Myra L. 1974 Stream Abrasion of Flint Implements. *Nature* 248:501–2.

Sharrock, F. W. 1966 *Prehistoric Occupation Patterns in S.W. Wyoming and Cultural Relationships with the Great Basin and Plains Areas.* University of Utah, Department of Anthropology, Anthropology Papers 77.

Shea, John J. 1988 Spear Points from the Middle Paleolithic of the Levant. *Journal of Field Archaeology* 15:441–50.

1993 Lithic Usewear Evidence for Hunting by Neanderthals and Early Modern Humans form the Levantine Mousterian. In *Hunting and Animal Exploitation in the Later Paleolithic and Mesolithic of Eurasia*, ed. Gail Larson Peterkin, Harvey M. Bricker, and Paul Mellars, pp. 189–98. Archaeological Papers of the American Anthropological Association 4.

Shott, Michael J. 1986 Settlement Mobility and Technological Organization: An Ethnographic Examination. *Journal of Anthropological Research* 42:15–51.

1989 Bipolar Industries: Ethnographic Evidence and Archaeological Implications. *North American Archaeologist* 10:1–24.

1993 *The Leavitt Site: A Parkhill Phase Paleo-Indian Occupation in Central Michigan.* University of Michigan Museum of Anthropology, Memoirs 25, Ann Arbor.

1994 Size and Form in the Analysis of Flake Debris: Review and Recent Approaches. *Journal of Archaeological Method and Theory* 1:69–110.

1995 How Much is a Scraper? Curation, Use Rates, and the Formation of Scraper Assemblages. *Lithic Technology* 20:53–72.

1996 Innovation and Selection in Prehistory: A Case Study from the American Bottom. In *Stone Tools: Theoretical Insights into Human Prehistory*, ed. G. H. Odell, pp. 279–314. Plenum Press, New York.

Siegel, Peter E. 1984 Functional Variability within an Assemblage of Endscrapers. *Lithic Technology* 13:35–51.

Sieveking, A. 1958 The Paleolithic Industry of Kota Tampan, Perak, Northwest Malaya. *Asian Perspectives* 2:91–102.

Siever, R., K. C. Beck, and R. A. Berner 1965 Composition of Interstitial Waters of Modern Sediments. *Journal of Geology* 73:39–73.

Sievert, April K. 1992 *Maya Ceremonial Specialization: Lithic Tools from the Sacred Cenote at Chichen Itza, Yucatan.* Prehistory Press, Madison, Wisconsin.

Singer, C. A. 1984 The 63–Kilometer Fit. In *Prehistoric Quarries and Lithic Production*, ed. J. E. Ericson and B. A. Purdy, pp. 35–48. Cambridge University Press, Cambridge.

Skertchly, Sydney B. J. 1879 *On the Manufacture of Gun-Flints, the Methods of Excavating for Flint, the Age of Paleolithic Man, and the Connection between Neolithic Art and Gun-Flint Trade.* Memoirs of the Geological Survey of England and Wales, London.

Sneath, P. H. A., and Robert R. Sokal 1973 *Numerical Taxonomy.* W. H. Freeman and Co., San Franciso.

Sollberger, J. B. 1971 A Technological Study of Beveled Knives. *Plains Anthropologist* 16:209–18.

Sonnenfeld, J. 1962 Interpreting the Function of Primitive Implements. *American Antiquity* 28:56–65.

Spaulding, Albert C. 1953 Statistical Techniques for the Discovery of Artifact Types. *American Antiquity* 18:305–13.

Speth, John D. 1972 Mechanical Basis of Percussion Flaking. *American Antiquity* 37:34–60.

1974 Experimental Investigations of Hard-Hammer Percussion Flaking. *Tebiwa* 17:7–36.

1975 Miscellaneous Studies in Hard-Hammer Percussion Flaking: The Effects of Oblique Impact. *American Antiquity* 40:203–7.

1981 The Role of Platform Angle and Core Size in Hard-Hammer Percussion Flaking. *Lithic Technology* 10:16–21.

Spurrell, R. C. J. 1892 Notes on Early Sickles. *Archaeological Journal* 49:53–9.

Stafford, Barbara 1980 Prehistoric Manufacture and Utilization of Lithics from Corduroy Creek. In *Studies in the Prehistory of the Forestdale Region, Arizona*, ed. C. Russell Stafford and Glen E. Rice, pp. 251–97. Anthropological Field Studies 1, Arizona State University, Tempe.

Stahle, David W., and James E. Dunn 1982 An Analysis and Application of the Size Distribution of Waste Flakes from the Manufacture of Bifacial Tools. *World Archaeology* 14:84–97.

Stanford, Dennis J. 1973 The Origins of Thule Culture. Ph.D. dissertation, Univeristy of New Mexico.

Steel, Robert G. D., and James H. Torrie 1960 *Principles and Procedures of Statistics.* McGraw-Hill, New York.

Stiner, Mary C., and Steven L. Kuhn 1992 Subsistence, Technology, and Adaptive Variation in Middle Paleolithic Italy. *American Anthropologist* 94:306–39.

Straus, Lawrence G., and Geoffery A. Clark 1986 *Stone Age Hunter-Gatherer Adaptations in Northern Spain.* Anthropological Research Papers 36. Arizona State University, Tempe.

Sullivan III, Alan P., and Kenneth C. Rozen 1985 Debitage Analysis and Archaeological Interpretation. *American Antiquity* 50:755–79.

Sussman, C. 1988 *A Microscopic Analysis of Usewear and Polish Formation on Experimental Quartz Tools*. BAR International Series 398, Oxford.

Tankersley, Kenneth B., and Juliet E. Morrow 1994 Clovis Procurement and Land Use Patterns in the Confluence Region of the Mississippi, Missouri, and Illinois Rivers. In *Highways to the Past: Essays in Honor of C. J. Bareis*, ed. T. Emerson, A. Fortier, and D. McElrath, pp. 119–29. Illinois Archaeological Survey, Champaign.

Thacker, Paul T. 1996 Hunter-Gatherer Lithic Economy and Settlement Systems: Understanding Regional Assemblage Variability in the Upper Paleolithic of Portuguese Estremadura. In *Stone Tools*, ed. G. H. Odell, pp. 101–24. Plenum Press, New York.

Thomas, David H. 1976 *Figuring Anthropology: First Principles of Probability and Statistics*. Holt, Rinehart, and Winston, New York.

1986 Points on Points: A Reply to Flenniken and Raymond. *American Antiquity* 51:619–27.

1989 *Archaeology*. Holt, Rinehart, and Winston, Ft Worth.

Thompson, M., P. R. Bush, and J. Ferguson 1986 The Analysis of Flint by Inductively Coupled Plasma Atomic Emission Spectrometry, as a Method of Source Determination. In *The Scientific Study of Flint and Chert*, ed. G. de G. Sieveking and M. B. Hart, pp. 243–8. Cambridge University Press, Cambridge.

Titmus, Gene 1985 Some Aspects of Stone Tool Notching. In *Stone Tool Analysis: Essays in Honor of Don E. Crabtree*, ed. Marc G. Plew and Max G. Pavesic, pp. 243–64. University of New Mexico Press, Albuquerque.

Titmus, Gene, and James C. Woods 1986 An Experimental Study of Projectile Point Fracture Patterns. *Journal of California and Great Basin Anthropology* 8:37–49.

Tixier, Jacques 1963 Typologie de l'épipaléolithique du Maghreb. *Mémoires du Centre de Recherches Anthropologiques, Préhistoriques et Ethnographiques* 2. Paris: Arts et Métiers Graphiques.

1974 *Glossary for the Description of Stone Tools*. Newsletter of Lithic Technology: Special Publication 1. Washington State University, Pullman.

Tomka, Steven A. 1989 Differentiating Lithic Reduction Techniques: An Experimental Approach. In *Experiments in Lithic Technology*, ed. D. S. Amick and R. P. Mauldin, pp. 137–62. BAR International Series 528, Oxford.

Torrence, Robin 1983 Time Budgeting and Hunter-Gatherer Technology. In *Hunter-Gatherer Economy in Prehistory*, ed. G. Bailey, pp. 11–22. Cambridge University Press, Cambridge.

1984 Monopoly or Direct Access? Industrial Organization at the Melos Obsidian Quarries. In *Prehistoric Quarries and Lithic Production*, ed. Jonathon E. Ericson and Barbara A. Purdy, pp. 49–64. Cambridge University Press, Cambridge.

1989 *Time, Energy and Stone Tools*. Cambridge University Press, Cambridge.

Towner, Ronald H., and Miranda Warburton 1990 Projectile Point Rejuvenation: A Technological Analysis. *Journal of Field Archaeology* 17:311–21.

Tringham, R., G. Cooper, G. Odell, R. Voytek, and A. Whitman 1974 Experimentation in the Formation of Edge Damage: A New Approach to Lithic Analysis. *Journal of Field Archaeology* 1:171–96.

Truncer, James J. 1990 Perkiomen Points: A Study in Variability. In *Experiments and Observations on the Terminal Archaic of the Middle Atlantic Region*, ed. R. W. Moeller, pp. 1–62. Archaeological Services, Bethlehem, Connecticut.

Tsirk, Are 1979 Regarding Fracture Initiations. In *Lithic Usewear Analysis*, ed. Brian Hayden, pp. 83–96. Academic Press, New York.

Unger-Hamilton, R. 1985 Microscopic Striations on Flint Sickle-Blades as an Indication of Plant Cultivation: Preliminary Results. *World Archaeology* 17:121–6.

Unrath, G., R. L. Owen, A. van Gijn, E. H. Moss, H. Plisson, and P. Vaughan 1986 An Evaluation of Usewear Studies: A Multi-Analysis Approach. In *Technical Aspects of*

Microwear Studies on Stone Tools. Early Man News 9/10/11, ed. L. R. Owen and G. Unrath, pp. 117–76. Archaeologica Venatoria, Tubingen.

Van Peer, Philip 1991 Interassemblage Variability and Levallois Styles: The Case of the Northern African Middle Paleolithic. *Journal of Anthropological Archaeology* 10:107–51

1992 *The Levallois Reduction Strategy.* Prehistory Press, Madison, Wisconsin.

Vaughan, Patrick C. 1985 *Usewear Analysis of Flaked Stone Tools.* University of Arizona Press, Tucson.

Vayson de Pradenne, André 1920 La Plus Ancienne Industrie de Saint-Acheul. *L'Anthropologie* 32:1–38.

Villa, Paola 1982 Conjoinable Pieces and Site Formation Processes. *American Antiquity* 47:276–90.

Voorrips, A. 1982 Manbrino's Helmet: A Framework for Structuring Archaeological Data. In *Essays in Archaeological Typology*, ed. R. Whallon and J. A. Brown, pp. 93–126. Center for American Archaeology Press, Evanston, Illinois.

Walker, Danny N., and Lawrence C. Todd 1984 *Archaeological Salvage at 48FR1398: Castle Gardens Access Road Site, Fremont County, Wyoming.* Occasional Papers on Wyoming Archaeology 2, Laramie.

Warashina, T. 1992 Allocation of Jasper Archaeological Implements by Means of ESR and XRF. *Journal of Archaeological Science* 19:357–73.

Warren, S. H. 1914 The Experimental Investigation of Flint Fracture and Its Application to Problems of Human Implements. *Journal of the Royal Anthropological Institute* 44:412–50.

Werner, David J. 1972 The Zimmerman Site, 36–Pi–14. In *Archaeology in the Upper Delaware Valley*, ed. W. F. Kinsey III, pp. 55–130, Anthropological Series 2, The Pennsylvania Historical and Museum Commission, Harrisburg.

West, Frederick H. 1981 *The Archaeology of Beringia.* Columbia University Press, New York.

Whallon, Robert, and James A. Brown 1982 *Essays in Archaeological Typology.* Center for American Archaeology Press, Evanston, Illinois.

White, J. Peter 1967 Ethno-Archaeology in New Guinea: Two Examples. *Mankind* 6:409–14.

1968 Fabricators, Outils Ecaillés, or Scalar Cores? *Mankind* 6:658–66.

White, J. Peter, and David H. Thomas 1972 What Mean These Stones? Ethno-Taxonomic Models and Archaeological Interpretations in the New Guinea Highlands. In *Models in Archaeology*, ed. D. L. Clarke, pp. 275–308. Methuen, London.

Whittaker, John C. 1994 *Flintknapping: Making and Understanding Stone Tools.* University of Texas Press, Austin.

Wiant, Michael, and Harold Hassen 1985 The Role of Lithic Resource Availability and Accessibility in the Organization of Technology. In *Lithic Resource Procurement: Proceedings from the Second Conference on Prehistoric Chert Exploitation*, ed. Susan C. Vehik, pp. 101–14. Center for Archaeological Investigations, Occasional Paper 4, Carbondale, Illinois.

Widemann, F. 1980 Neutron Activation Analysis for Provenance Studies of Archaeological Artefacts. *Journal of Radioanalytical Chemistry* 55:271–81.

Wiessner, Polly 1982 Risk, Reciprocity and Social Influences on !Kung San Economies. In *Politics and History in Band Societies*, ed. E. Leacock and R. Lee, pp. 61–84. Cambridge University Press, Cambridge.

1983 Style and Social Information in Kalahari San Projectile Points. *American Antiquity* 48:253–76.

Williams, L. A., and D. A. Crerar 1985 Silica Diagenesis, II: General Mechanisms. *Journal of Sedimentary Petrology* 55:312–21.

Wilmsen, Edwin S. 1968 Lithic Analysis in Paleoanthropology. *Science* 161:982–7.

Wilmsen, Edwin S., and F. H. H. Roberts 1978 *Lindenmeier: Concluding Report on Investigations.* Smithsonian Contributions to Anthropology 24, Washington, D.C.

Winters, Howard D. 1969 *The Riverton Culture*. Published jointly by the Illinois State Museum Reports of Investigations, 13 and the Illinois Archaeological Survey, Springfield.

1984 The Significance of Chert Procurement and Exchange in the Middle Woodland Traditions of the Illinois Area. In *Prehistoric Chert Exploitation: Studies from the Midcontinent*, ed. B. M. Butler and E. E. May, pp. 3 22. Occasional Paper 2, Center for Archaeological Investigations, Carbondale, Illinois.

Witthoft, John 1955 Worn Stone Tools from Southeastern Pennsylvania. *Pennsylvania Archaeologist* 25:16–31.

1967 Glazed Polish on Flint Tools. *American Antiquity* 32:383–8.

1971 A Paleo-Indian Site in Eastern Pennsylvania. In *Foundations of Pennsylvania Prehistory*, ed. Barry C. Kent, Ira F. Smith III, and Catherine McCann, pp. 13–64. Anthropological Series of the Pennsylvania Historical and Museum Commission 1, Harrisburg.

Wobst, H. Martin 1977 Stylistic Behavior and Information Exchange. In *Papers for the Director: Research Essays in Honor of James B. Griffin*, ed. C. E. Cleland, pp. 317–42. University of Michigan Anthropological Papers 61, Ann Arbor.

Womack, Bruce 1977 An Archaeological Investigation and Technological Analysis of the Stockhoff Basalt Quarry, Northeastern Region. M.A. thesis, Washington State University, Pullman.

Woodman, Peter 1978 The Chronology and Economy of the Irish Mesolithic: Some Working Hypotheses. In *The Early Postglacial Settlement of Northern Europe*, ed. Paul Mellars, pp. 333–70. Duckworth, London.

Wylie, Henry G. 1975 Tool Microwear and Functional Types from Hogup Cave, Utah. *Tebiwa* 17(2):1–31.

Yerkes, Richard W. 1983 Microwear, Microdrills, and Mississippian Craft Specialization. *American Antiquity* 48:499–518.

1987 *Prehistoric Life on the Mississippi Floodplain*. University of Chicago Press, Chicago.

1990 Using Microwear Analysis to Investigate Domestic Activities and Craft Specialization at the Murphy Site, a Small Hopewell Settlement in Licking County, Ohio. In *The Interpretive Possibilities of Microwear Studies*, ed. B. Graslund, H. Knutsson, K. Knutsson, and J. Taffinder, pp. 167–76. AUN 14, Societas Archaeologica Uppsaliensis, Uppsala, Sweden.

1994 A Consideration of the Function of Hopewell Bladelets. *Lithic Technology* 19:109–27.

Yerkes, Richard W., and P. Nick Kardulias 1993 Recent Developments in the Analysis of Lithic Artifacts. *Journal of Archaeological Research* 1:89–119.

Yoshizaki, M. 1961 Shirataki Iseki to Hokkaido no Mudoki Bunka. (The Shirataki Site and the Preceramic Culture in Hokkaido.) *Minzokugaku Kenkyu* 26:13–23.

Zier, Christian J., Stephen M. Kalasz, Anne H. Peebles, Margaret A. Van Ness, and Elaine Anderson 1988 *Archaeological Excavation of the Avery Ranch Site (5PE56) on the Fort Carson Military Reservation, Pueblo County, Colorado*. Centennial Archaeology, Inc., Fort Collins, Colorado. Submitted to USDI National Park Service, Rocky Mountain Regional

INDEX